THE
IMPROBABLE
RISE OF
REDNECK ROCK

THE IMPROBABLE RISE OF REDNECK ROCK

by
jan reid
photographs by
melinda wickman

A DA CAPO PAPERBACK

Library of Congress Cataloging in Publication Data

Reid, Jan.
The improbable rise of redneck rock.

(A Da Capo paperback)
Reprint of the ed. published by Heidelberg Publishers,
Austin, Tex.
1. Rock music—Texas—History and criticism.
I. Title.
[ML3561.R62R4   1977]   784   76-30434
ISBN 0-306-80065-9

ML
3561
.R62
.R4
1977

ISBN 0-306-80065-9

First Paperback Printing 1977

This Da Capo Press paperback edition of *The Improbable Rise of Redneck Rock* is an unabridged republication of the first edition published in Austin, Texas, in 1974. It is reprinted by arrangement with Heidelberg Publishers, Inc.

The Prologue quote is from *In a Narrow Grave,* by Larry McMurtry and published by the Encino Press, 1968.

Published by Da Capo Press, Inc.
A Subsidiary of Plenum Publishing Corporation
227 West 17th Street
New York, N.Y. 10011

In hopes they're still singing, this book is dedicated to a half-pint, off-key chorus: Henry and Earl, Jason and Johnny, soprano jive; Mercy and Ruthie, alto soul; Donnie at bullfrog; and Debbie and Freddie Ray, sheer rock & roll.

contents

prologue

If this book had any beginning, it was probably in a little building with brown asbestos siding at the corner of 23rd and Grace Streets in Wichita Falls, a small city on the Texas side of the Red River whose hymn was enduringly sung by novelist Larry McMurtry:

> *I once had a character say it was the ugliest place on earth, but since that time extensive readings in the literature of Patagonia, Siberia and Central Asia have convinced me that while dramatically apt, the statement should not be pressed as literally true. Ulan-Bator, Omsk, Semipalatinsk, Tashkent and some of the villages in the district of the Lob Nor, these are all at least as ugly, and doubtless the list will grow even longer as I read on.*

McMurtry was a native son, practically. He grew up on a nearby ranch, which possibly accounted for some of his antipathy toward the old hometown. Of course, some people wouldn't live anywhere else. It was a quiet, clean town, they argued, a good place to raise a family. Why, it was known as the City That Faith Built. Maybe so, the counter argument ran, but faith picked a hell of a place to set up shop.

The little structure at 23rd and Grace was an unpretentious manifestation of that faith. It housed blond, uncushioned pews which rarely seated more than 300 people, a modest pulpit, a stark baptistry, a two-story classroom addition. Over the years it had its problems—a fire that traveled through the heating ducts and left the place stinking for months, ministers forever on the lookout for greener pastures, the disfellowship of a popular deacon gone wrong. And it served an aging neighborhood, which meant there was never much money in the church coffers, and when the old died off, they were increasingly replaced by Catholic Mexicans, not members. But the congregation at 23rd and Grace persisted; it socialized together, planned for the future together, cared for its impoverished, aged and retarded together. It was a workingman's neighborhood, a workingman's church. On the building's front were letters cut from aluminum by a member's metal shears: Church of Christ.

An Irish Presbyterian and immigrant named Thomas Campbell unintentionally founded that sect in Washington, Pennsylvania in 1807. However, the gospel was spread by his son Alexander, who once debated the subject of infant baptism with a Presbyterian for sixteen days while Henry Clay moderated, and a score of transient evangelists like Raccoon John Smith, an Alabaman who one day disrupted a Methodist service by quaffing down the infant baptismal water and telling the stunned minister, "Brother, I drank your Jordan dry." But those of us who grew up in the church at 23rd and Grace knew nothing of that; all we knew was that it was *the* Church, the one built in the first century on the rock of the apostle Peter's faith, not his person. It was the one in accordance with Scriptures, the one on guard against frills and misdirection, the one that stayed alive in attics and catacombs during the deviancy of the Middle Ages and the Protestant Reformation. Which was the reason we didn't have a piano like our Baptist brethren down the street.

The Campbells' movement fractured in 1906, primarily over the means of making a joyful noise unto the Lord, as commanded in Psalms. One faction reasoned that since the Scriptures weren't explicit on the precise mode of the joyful noise-making, surely the Lord wouldn't mind if the music which reached his ears was concordant. The other said it was taking no chances. The former became the First Christian Churches of most towns in the Midwest and South, the more affluent Disciples of Christ. The latter became the bedrock Churches of Christ.

As a result the members of the church at 23rd and Grace lifted their voices without the assistance of a piano or organ or even a trained chorus of leaders. There was just a brother in the pulpit who could tell one pitch from another, who waved a hand in the air and tried to get the lumbering vocal flight off the ground. Roughly half the members tried to discipline their voices in soprano, alto, tenor and bass ranges. The others sang to the best of their ability. If the a cappella gathering at 23rd and Grace had ever gathered in the Mormon Tabernacle, they probably would have set off harmonic vibrations that would have brought the house down, but if there was any beauty in that determined sect, it was in its music.

Some of the songs in the hymnal were cumbersome and plodding, as if written by some aging, alchemistic monk, but others took off in simple soaring flights of emotion. Songs written by lyricists with evocative Southern names like Jessie Brown Pounds and Fannie J. Crosby. Songs of a loving God who nevertheless had stated a law and meant to keep his word, sorrowful yet exultant songs about Jesus at Calvary, imagistic songs about the Gentile Zion, songs of sweet, sweet assurance that the next life wouldn't be as hard on faithful Christians as this one had been. And most important, songs of invitation.

Though the sermon occasionally began with a quip or anecdote, the message was dead serious. Those were utopian Christians who hoped against long odds that the world would adhere to the example of the first-century church, and like most utopians, they reserved scant sympathy for those outside the enlightened inner circle. The road to the promised land was in fact so straight and narrow that it could only accommodate faithful members of the Church of Christ, and by mid-sermon the address usually boiled over into virtual attack, upon rival sects, upon members who failed to live up to their commitment, upon those truculent members of the audience who had not taken the first step.

Those words resounded in the ears of adolescents reminded daily that we were now accountable for our actions, but the sermon alone was more likely to leave us petrified in our pews than at the front professing our faith in Jesus. However, toward the end the minister's rhetoric softened, and with a final plea he relinquished the microphone to the song director, who led the congregation in a hymn that was soft, lilting and sad:

Softly and tenderly Jesus is calling . . .

The contrast between the two appeals was jarring. While the sermon instilled guilt and dread, the invitation hymn provided emotion and hope. For most adolescents the combined appeal eventually worked. We bolted down the aisle on the verge of tears, confessed our faith and endured our dunking in the baptistry while our mothers cried. They would have cried a great deal more had they known that, for far too many of us, it was simply an emotional moment, lacking in either comprehension or conviction. We had just succumbed to the pressure.

After that signal moment was past, we of course continued to grow up. Some of our legs outgrew the space between the pews, and all of us had friends outside the church. We were missing out on a lot of things, and we knew it. We chalked up considerable mileage responding to subsequent invitations and renewing our wavering faiths, but the seeds of backsliding were being sown on those very pews. Sermons became drones of sound of uncomfortable length. The pews tacitly reserved for "the young people" became a playground of covert social gamesmanship. Coy notes were passed back and forth, the seating arrangement became the indicator of dating trends, sly elbows nudged brassiered ribs every time the congregation stood to sing "Let Him Have His Way with Thee." After the nighttime services we piled in old Mercurys and Fords and circled the town for hours, copping feels and engaging in the prevalent titillation, profanity.

As time progressed many of us abandoned that faith altogether, though we would carry the stamp of those years as long as we lived. There was the Sunday morning in 1960 the preacher urged the membership to vote for Richard Nixon, thereby avoiding a papal takeover. There was the afternoon we watched a filmstrip that set creation in the year 4004 B.C., a chronology advanced by an English archbishop named James Ussher in 1650 and debunked ever since. But those were reasons in retrospect. A likelier cause of our disaffection was the realization that while there was security in the knowledge that one held the keys to the kingdom of heaven, there was also loneliness in the proposition that one's friends, even one's father, didn't have a prayer. Soon all that was left of our faith was our love for the music. We never dreamed those melodies would visit us again one day in the form of popular music.

The break was rarely abrupt; we drifted back and forth on the social tides. But the farther we got from shore, the more probable it became that we would set sight on some fascinating territory . . . in my case, next door. In 1951 a kind old woman named Cochran sold one of her lots on Keeler Street to her son Lee and his growing family, and sold the adjoining lot to a stable family of four named the Reids. An unlikelier match of neighbors could not have been arranged. My parents were earnest depression-scarred people who worked hard in the daytime and slept at night, except when my father had to work the graveyard shift at the refinery. Lee Cochran played country-swing trumpet for the Miller Brothers Band, and his wife kept right up. My father spent half his time clipping hedges and pushing a lawn mower; once in a while you'd kick up a crumpled beer can in the Cochrans' yard. Saturday night was the quietest night of the week around the Reid household, but it was something the Cochrans recuperated from. As for the children, there were two Reids, four Cochrans. But as the older Reid moved into adolescence, she came to regard even her brother with cheerful disdain, which left me to deal alone with four rival males. I considered the Cochrans pugnacious, cantankerous, yet somehow sissified. They dismissed me as one of the breed that spat on sidewalks, took baseball seriously, and asked his mother for permission before he went somewhere. The only thing we really had in common was that we were kids from the other side of the tracks. Our FHA houses faced a railroad right-of-way, and by accident of school boundary lines we crossed those tracks daily to consort with well-groomed children whose grandfathers struck it very rich in the oil boom, which left us with something of the outlook of a Cockney thrown into the company of Princess Anne. I'd have to say, though, that the Cochran offspring handled that better than I. My face burned red when my father dropped me off at Ben Franklin School in a 1948 Chevrolet, but one day in 1952 Corky Cochran swaggered past the I Like Ike buttons sporting a lapel pin which indicated *his* parents were faithful Democrats. I had to give him credit for that. But I was tougher and smarter than Corky Cochran and was thinking about being a preacher when I grew up. All he did was play with his mean Chow dog and talk about his daddy's band. The Cochrans watched when I departed for Wednesday night Bible study. I watched when they loaded the Pontiac for another Saturday night on the town. We viewed each other with high suspicion.

One day a school chum asked me what the Cochrans' old man did for a living, and I pantomimed a horn lick and snorted, ''A trumpet player.'' My mother boxed my jaws for the remark, and after that I kept my snobbery to myself. But the snobbery was half-hearted anyway. I didn't hold the adults' lifestyle against them. There was even an element of pride in being able to turn on our new television and see my next-door neighbor, dressed in western suit and hat, step up on cue and play his trumpet for the Wichita Falls audience. In terms of longevity and reputation, the Miller Brothers were a qualified success. You could pretty well assess a band by its means of travel. The successful ones flew, the aspiring ones owned a personal Greyhound bus, the struggling ones drove 200 miles for gigs in NCO clubs. The Miller Brothers owned a 1955 Chevrolet stretched like an accordion into a bizarre twelve-passenger limousine.

The band formed in Wichita Falls in 1941, and after the war regrouped and landed a five-year date at the local Labor Temple. But in 1952 they joined up with a music entrepreneur and built their own forum, a dance hall replete with plaid table cloths where you could set your bourbon beside a bucket of ice, dance the night away, and fistfight to your heart's content, at least until a bouncer wandered by. Naturally enough, they called their joint the MB Corral. Why they were called the Miller Brothers, incidentally, was anybody's guess. Most of them were named Gibbs. There were eight members of the band, but the ones I remember most clearly were Lee on trumpet, Brylcreem Bill on steel guitar, Sister Marge on piano, Sam on stand-up bass and Leon, the band leader and lead singer who had a disconcerting way of grinning up into the television camera when he played his fiddle. The only time I saw them perform, in fact, was on television, but I saw them nurse their hangovers, and I saw the racy snapshots of their motel rooms and I was intrigued.

The Miller Brothers were great travelers. They toured twenty-three states, Canada, Greenland and according to a retired member, were the first country-swing band ever booked in Bermuda and Puerto Rico, a booking that must have set off waves of cultural shock. They even cut several records for Four-Star and made some money off their sales. But for me they were strictly a local phenomenon. They were Wichita Falls' claim to fame in the fifties.

Unfortunately, the theater outlived the act. After nearly two decades, the Miller Brothers went their separate ways in 1959, and all too soon people were wondering why the local saloon was called the MB

Corral. The MB on country-western nights was a raucous, rowdy place where, as legend had it, a roughneck one night stomped the bejesus out of a sideburned singer named Elvis Presley. Simply defending her honor, and his pride.

It was a nice place to be on Saturday night, as long as your number wasn't up. A bland but noxious breed of petroleum *nouveau riche* held the economic reins of the city, but their Cadillacs weren't the ones parked outside the MB. The Cadillacs outside the MB had dents in the doors. The sure-enough rich drank their weekend bourbon in Dallas or at the country club, while the MB patrons mixed their own and drank the same stuff cheaper. Though most of the patrons had lived inside the city limits more years than they cared to remember, they donned boots and stetsons and high-heeled shoes and descended on the MB for a wild old Saturday night. They courted, kissed and damn near committed adultery on the dance floor, and entertained themselves during band breaks by tossing quarters at a trio of jukebox dancers remembered by one patron as ''those jive-ass shufflin' tap-dance niggers.''

Now the fact that the older Cochrans hung out at the MB was one thing, but allowing their kids to tag along was another. The Cochran boys were great name-droppers, though most of the country-western names didn't mean anything to me at the time, and they liked to taunt me with their mastery of the latest dance steps. The Church of Christ deemed heterosexual dancing a wanton, sinful activity, but the dance issue was a lost cause. Every kid in town watched *American Bandstand* when he wasn't out chasing some ball, and briefly there was even a locally televised sock hop, run by a disc jockey and eventual record producer of Los Angeles repute named Snuff Garrett. But regardless of which dance I mastered, the Cochrans were always one step ahead, primarily because they had access to the people who usually set the dance trends, the blacks.

Wichita Falls was effectively segregated then. There were segregated drinking fountains downtown and a rest room for unisexual coloreds at the bus station. I encountered black faces occasionally at the Kid Baseball World Series and on city buses headed toward domestic jobs in the mansions of the country club, but their world was a city away from mine. The dual system even applied to music. The country bands trooped through the South and played for white audiences in honky-tonks like the MB, while the black rhythm & blues bands traveled the same highways and played in the same dance halls, but those Thursday or Sunday-night affairs were generally off-limits to whites. Yet because of their father's connections, the Cochrans went to those coloreds-only dances at the MB Corral. They fairly babbled with excitement the mornings after. More niggers than you could count but they left you alone, even treated you friendly, and lord how they danced, danced to the finest music imaginable. Bo Diddly and Jimmy Reed and B.B. King, Chuck Berry and Bobby Blue Bland and Ike and Tina Turner.

Those were the stories that tipped the balance. The dances sounded primitive and wild, yet somehow niggers with razors didn't sound any more dangerous than cowboys with bottles. Besides, any fruit that forbidden just had to taste sweet. The afternoon before one of those dances the Cochrans extended a rare, mocking invitation for me to join them, and I went home to sulk, wrestle with temptation, consider the consequences, and surrender.

"Mother, can I go out to the MB tonight?"

"No," she said, startled, then she looked at me, a foreknowledge of defeat welling in her eyes.

Several years later, I sat by myself in a Wichita Falls bar while the sun went down outside. Behind me were five years on the campus of a college nicknamed Hometown Harvard. Half a decade, spent not in the pursuit of knowledge but in the pursuit of the surface camaraderie of a fraternity, of that elusive, understanding woman, of whatever it was we sought in the narcotic glow of a blacklight with Ravi Shankar on the stereo.

It was just a bar. The only other occupants were the broad-hipped matron of the place, who stood by her cash register counting receipts, a waitress who nibbled Fritos and swiveled on her stool, offering periodic glimpses of her panty girdle, and a large young man who practiced the same pool shot over and over, missing most of the time. He was a high school football hero who a few years earlier had bounced a basketball off my chest, called me a hot-shot college punk, and invited me to do something about it. Now he had been cut by his Canadian Football League team and didn't recognize me.

The waitress slid off the stool, smoothed her mini-skirt, and flounced my way. "You got some jukebox change, *honey?*" I begrudged her a quarter, and she flounced over to the jukebox, which lit up and started clicking when she dropped the coin.

Music hadn't played much of a part in my life in recent years. Jazz struck me as tedious, classical music was an incomprehensible bore, and folk had gone the way of Johnny Rivers and the Whisky á Go Go. The Kingston Trio got ploughed under with the New Frontier, and Bob Dylan stopped singing protest songs when he was most needed. And my interest in rock music was half-hearted. Most of the groups I listened to had been copying the Beatles so long they just seemed tired, and try as I might, I could not get into acid-rock. My aspiring hippie friends tried to drag me along when Cream or Country Joe and the Fish came to Dallas, but I steadfastly refused, for a couple of reasons: I knew if they got me down there they'd stuff some substance down my gullet that would paralyze my medulla and drive me to suicide or worse, and I wasn't sure I wanted my hearing permanently damaged by some amplified shrieking guitar.

I had never been to a rock concert. The closest I had come was when my fraternity brought the first of the American Liverpool groups, the Sir Douglas Quintet, to the MB Corral, a project that had our heads swimming with dollar signs at its inception and left us with a net profit of fifteen dollars and seventy-five cents. Our teeny-bopper patrons conducted themselves pretty much in the manner of their MB parents, but that night policemen descended like a swarm of mosquitoes. The consumption of alcohol was forbidden inside the premises, and the leader of the quint, a San Antonian in mod dress named Doug Sahm, seemed generally aghast at the youthful glue-sniffing going on around him.

As for my ties with country music, they were practically severed. God knows what had happened to all the Miller Brothers. Leon was still playing around, but his brother Sam was running a booking agency, and one member was reduced to playing with makeshift bands, disciplining a stoned drummer whose attention seemed to wander with a glare and a stern, *"Two* four, *two* four." Lee Cochran opened an ice cream parlor after the band broke up; his children had grown up furtive and shy. I watched the Porter Wagoner Show on television occasionally, with the same morbid fascination I would have felt had I been allowed to watch medical students perform surgery on a cadaver. Country music was worse than soap opera television. Divorce and alcoholism and struggling to get rich for nothing, country music dealt with the standard derangements all right, but it turned them into sentimentalized virtues. It was the music of a despairing status quo. Hence my apprenhension when the barmaid plugged my quarter into the jukebox.

Yet her first choice was one that pleased me. A new country singer named Willie Nelson had come along and I found myself liking him, though I didn't discuss the matter with my acid-rock peers. Like too many Nashville recordings, his songs were sugared by violin arrangements and his lyrics offered no more solutions than the average hillbilly wail of mourning, but at least he sang like they were genuine problems. There was an element of suffering in Willie Nelson's songs, a rasp of Panhandle dust in his craw. He sounded like he'd done some time in a Texas town himself.

The barmaid walked away from the jukebox, and left me alone with Willie Nelson. It was a song about social inertia, and it seemed aimed directly at me. When Larry McMurtry wrote about the ugliness of Wichita Falls, he wasn't talking about the surrounding countryside. If millions of Americans could find beauty in a televised moonscape, surely something could be said for a winter thicket of mesquites. Rather it was the dreadful sameness of towns like Wichita Falls, and what it did to you. It was a spiritual ugliness, a sense of one's youth leading nowhere.

> *Turn out the light   the party's over*
> *It seems that all   good things must end*
> *Let's call it a night   the party's over*
> *And tomorrow starts the same old thing again*

If anything in my life was a certainty, it was the realization that it was time to get out of that town.

PART I

Hell, I don't live in Texas.
I live in Austin.

Jerry Jeff Walker

the gay place

Most descriptions of Austin started with its terrain — a blackland prairie broken by ancient upheaval into tiers of wooded ridges where the legendary ghosts of Comanches dance at night — and ended with the bacchanalian circus of Texas politics, with perhaps an ambivalent dart or two thrown at that shaft of higher learning, the University of Texas tower. Austin was of course more than that. It was a growing city of 250,000 with its own Air Force base, ethnic ghettos, neon strips and suburban sprawl. But for decades Austin's image derived from the central, adjoining regions of the capitol and campus. Students, journalists, lobbyists and legislators were by nature a transient lot, and their social antics gave Austin a reputation as a night-life playground for those bright irresponsibles who passed through. An LBJ aide named Bill Brammer turned Austin's sheets back in 1962 with a political novel called *The Gay Place,* and a decade later the real-life identities of his unfaithful wives were still as much a topic of speculation as the models for his fictional politicians. Austin was still that kind of town. Love affairs, or at least flings, were still relatively easy to come by.

In outward appearance, Austin had changed somewhat. Few legislators wore LBJ stetsons anymore, and turquoise vendors, Hare Krishnas, drug dealers and panhandlers crowded the University sidewalks once strafed by Charles Whitman. But those were manifestations of social trends hardly indigenous to Texas. Socially, Austin hadn't changed much since Brammer wrote his novel, but its image was changing, and there was a new center of attention. University football

1

games were no longer the nationalistic events they once were; the storied political hangout, Scholz Beer Garten, was no longer the place to be on Saturday night.

In the late sixties popular music was no more than a dab of rouge on Austin's social cheek. Interest in music was healthy enough—record shops flourished by the score—but there were few reasons to believe Austin would ever be nationally known for its music. The state capital was often by-passed by major touring performers in those days, for the chances for packed houses were greater in the larger cities of Dallas, Houston and San Antonio. When major acts came to town, they repeated the show they had played in Little Rock the night before, conceded to an encore or two after a sufficient period of clapping and foot-stomping, then caught the next plane out for Tucson. In the interval between those concerts, Austinites contented themselves with what was available locally. Folksingers strummed their guitars for nickels and dimes in the university area. Rock & rollers lived communally, tried to imitate their psychedelic heroes' best licks in free concerts in the park and paid for their new amplifiers by playing rubber-stamp dance music for the fraternities and sororities. Rhythm & blues bands played wherever they could, which was usually limited to the black east side. Country bands played in dimly-lit beer taverns as waitresses circled the room with tambourines in their hands, soliciting donations for the musicians. Any of those musicians might attract spirited local followings, but they knew, and their followers knew, that if they were going to make any sort of national impression, one day they would have to try their luck in the major music centers — New York, Los Angeles, Nashville.

In 1970 two developments changed all that. A number of musicians who were already battered and bruised by the major music centers began to settle in Austin. They were songwriters and singers of varied experience and potential, but they were good enough to land recording contracts with major companies. Many had backgrounds in folk and rock music that was not native to Texas, but the music they spawned in Austin was rooted in the forms young Texans had grown up with: fundamentalist gospel, black blues and most important, country-western. That same year, a small group of young men and women launched a music-business enterprise with the unlikely name, Armadillo World Headquarters. It was a counter-cultural concert hall

2

with adequate floor space but almost no furnishings. That first year the south Austin enterprise appeared particularly ill-fated, but it survived through the tenacity of its founders, who were goaded by a dream of a community center for artistic expression. Armadillo World Headquarters grew in community acceptance, if not profitability, and it became known as the forum for the unique music offered by the immigrant musicians. As the musicians grew in popularity they created an audience famous for its exuberant response to music, and performers from other parts of the country began to covet appearances at Armadillo World Headquarters. The success of the recorded Austin artists encouraged other local performers to return to the roots of their musical heritage, and the success of the Armadillo prompted other aspiring entrepreneurs to bid for a piece of the action. Soon Austin was swarming with talented young musicians, and the most popular public spectacle was no longer football or political chicanery, but live music. Through the interest of a curious national press and word-of-mouth communication by touring musicians, Austin gained almost overnight a reputation as one of the most exciting centers of musical activity in the country.

A mild chill hung in the air one April night in 1973, a faint reminder of the harshest winter Austin had seen in years. But there was also a flowering smell of spring, a dance of light on the Colorado River. Trusting hitchhikers lined the curbs. Armadillo World Headquarters, an abandoned armory with a skating rink for a next-door neighbor, and the adjoining buildings were flanked by a parking lot riddled with chugholes. A muffled, metallic hum came from inside the skating rink. Leaning against the wall outside were a trio of young blacks whose leader watched the movement of loosely-clad white girls with long slow sweeps of his hat brim, turned a quarter over in his palm, and addressed every other male, "Hey brother, you got a dime?" On the other end of the parking lot, a German shepherd watchdog impounded for the night in an auto repair shop yard reacted to the stream of intruders with alternating bluff and bewilderment.

Inspiration had apparently visited the Armadillo staff artist again. He had started off on an outdoor wall with a mural that portrayed Ravi Shankar and band at ethereal work while in the background a nine-banded armadillo devoured the moon, but the mural on the new building housing additional toilets was more complex. It was a hazy

3

landscape of the blue Texas Hill Country, enlivened by slices of watermelon, an ice cream bar, an old Chevrolet pickup parked near a stand of shade trees, an apple half with the Alamo for a core.

The interior sensation of the Armadillo was one of dark, airy space, at least until the cloud of smoke began to build. No one was onstage yet except a black cat which slept with one paw hanging off the piano, and elsewhere in the hall the look was barren. There were concrete walls, sparrows fluttered around the heaters and scraps of carpet suspended from the ceiling, a concrete floor partially covered with more patches of used carpet, a few tables and folding metal chairs. Nothing of visual interest except another mural, this one depicting Freddie King in agonized guitar play while an armadillo burst from his chest, splattering blood. Freddie King recorded an album at the Armadillo once.

A group of young boys played touch football with a pillow on the carpeted section of the floor, hurdled toddlers in diapers and taunted their young sisters. But then their football field began to shrink as the growing crowd ran out of tables and chairs and staked claims on the floor. The first band onstage was Whistler, a group that introduced Austin to country-rock in an east side barbecue dive in 1969 but disbanded shortly afterward because of nagging creditors. Whistler was together again for the first time in several months and the set was somewhat ragged, but the singer and piano player sounded a little like Linda Ronstadt, and they got a nostalgic reception.

Next onstage were Man Mountain & the Green Slime Boys, one of the more hopeful bands in town at the time. Man Mountain wasn't all that obese, but he sat down with a steel and dobro while his fellow San Antonians—individualized by a straw cowboy hat, a railroad cap and Jesus-length blonde hair—parodied Buck Owens, praised the legendary Chicken Ranch whorehouse in LaGrange, and brought the house down with a colored barbershop revival of the old Cadillacs' hit, "Speedo." The crowd got off to Man Mountain and brought them back for an encore, which left the boys a little abashed, considering who was waiting in the wings.

The next band began to drift out of the darkness after a short break: a woman with waist-length hair and a Barbara Streisand nose who walked over and sat down at the piano with her back to the audience, a long-haired young man who flapped his elbows as he tuned his bass, an older man in a Honolulu shirt with long blonde hair and a harrowed face who slouched over a pedal steel, and the drummer, costumed in a Machiavellian beard, Dracula cape and Pancho Villa cartridge belt. Finally he started a drum roll, and a white spotlight inspected each of the band members then settled on a short man in boots, beard, cowboy hat and gold earring who walked to the microphone.

Willie Nelson and his band looked different, but except for the addition of some rock licks and lyrical references to Rita Coolidge's cleavage, it was the same time-worn music—the thumping bass, the rinky-tonk piano, the vocal steel, the same flat, sorrowful baritone. A Willie Nelson performance consisted of a tight, virtual medley of the songs he had written, but for those familiar with country top forty the list was astonishingly long: "Hello Walls," "The Party's Over," "Night Life," "Funny How Time Slips Away," "Me and Paul," "Yesterday's Wine." Nelson didn't record all those songs in hit-single form, but he sang most of them better than the artists who borrowed them. Yet the contagion of his performance derived more from the singer than the songs. Disembodied on record, Nelson was a good country artist, but in person he was a magician.

The guitar-and-song performance became the great American ritual well before Willie Nelson made his debut, but he was a master of the art. Young girls didn't scream when he walked onstage, and it was hard to imagine Nelson whanging his guitar against an amplifier, aborted voltage sparking all around him. He stood considerably less than six feet tall, his torso was beginning to belly out a little with age, and he cocked his hip and dipped his shoulder as he played his guitar and seemed forever in want of a comfortable stance. But he was always seeking eye contact with the people in front of him, nodding and grinning once it was established. Women flushed with pleasure when the skin around Nelson's eyes wrinkled in their behalf, but his look was just as direct and genuine when it fell on another male. He involved the audience with himself, his music, and they felt better for it. His songs might be sad, but he had the look of a happy man, a rare animal indeed, in these times.

As remarkable as Nelson's act that night was his audience. While freaks in gingham gowns and cowboy boots sashayed like they invented country music, remnants of Nelson's old audience had themselves a time too. A prim little grandmother from Taylor sat at a table beaming with excitement. "Oh lord, hon," she said. "I got ever one of

5

Willie's records, but I never got to see him before.'' A booted, western-dressed beauty from Waxahachie drove 150 miles for the show, and she said, ''I just love Willie Nelson and I'd drive anywhere to see him . . . but you know, he's sure been doin' some changin' lately.'' She looked around. ''I have never seen so many hippies in my life.'' Be that as it may, she abandoned her date to dance a good part of the night away with one of them, a brawny thirty-year-old named Sunshine who used to ride broncs and play football for Texas Tech before he underwent some changes of his own.

The crowd pressed toward the stage, resulting in a bobbing, visually bizarre mix of beehive hairdos, naked midriffs and bare hippie feet. An aging man in a turtleneck stubbed out his cigar and dragged his wife into the mayhem, where she received a jolt she probably did not deserve: a marijuana cigarette passed in front of her face. She had heard about it, she had seen it on television, and she probably considered herself fairly enlightened on the subject, but that was clearly asking too much of her. A young girl observed the woman frantically fanning the air in front of her face, smiled, looked the woman in the eye and took another hit.

But Nelson relieved any tension that developed beneath him. He played straight through for nearly two hours, singing all his recorded songs then starting over. They handed him pitchers of beer, threw bluebonnets onstage, yelled, ''We love you, Willie''—a sentiment he returned when he finally called it quits: ''I love you all. Good night.'' A night which for many had been a sort of hillbilly heaven, though Tex Ritter would have undoubtedly taken issue with the form.

Willie Nelson had not always been the object of such adulation. For more than ten years he had been an extraordinarily successful country songwriter but he had never really come into his own as a performer, and he had begun to feel like he was wearing a strait-jacket weighted with Nashville lead. The hobo funk of Jimmy Rodgers was gone from country music. It was polished, packaged and sold like any other form of commercial music, and behind it all, one suspected, were men with graying sideburns, Brooks Brothers suits and television advertising mentalities who wanted to make damn sure all those folks in the hinterlands had some little ditty to tap their toes to, thereby assuring the flow of dimes and dollars. And the sad thing about it was, even the best country artists were eventually corrupted by that kind of condescending dishonesty.

6

A generation of new country musicians who surfaced in Austin, Texas in 1970 altered the image of a city known for its politicians and party-goers, its woods and water.

The style-setters of the Austin music community were a hip boogie joint named Armadillo World Headquarters and a nucleus of frustrated recording artists on the run from the major music centers. Foremost among them was Willie Nelson, the battle-scarred Nashville veteran who brought a pleasant, personal dimension to the live concert ritual and started people wondering why country and rock audiences always had to be at odds.

They were coaxed and wheedled by the country-music oligarchy, and most of all, they were made very rich. Johnny Cash rose from the humblest of circumstances to sing about World War II heroes who died unnoticed in the gutter, and to entertain inmates behind prison walls. He was asked to entertain at the White House and later accepted the host's role on a bland television variety show, only to die a slow death at the hands of the Nielson Ratings, no longer in touch with the people his voice represented so long. Merle Haggard came out of prison with a working-class chip on his shoulder and a caustic view of those who thought education or wealth or youth made one man better than another. But then those songs of working-class resentment made Merle Haggard a superstar, and while he continued to sing unconvincingly about getting laid off down at the factory, he spent much of his time squandering his excess money in the casinos of Nevada. Kris Kristofferson was a former Rhodes Scholar who took a job pushing a broom in Nashville before he bowled that town over with songs that fashioned poetry from the idiom of truck drivers, hitchhikers, and dirt-poor country musicians. He broadened the perspective of country music by courting the favor of the rock audience and going to bat for new artists like Steve Goodman and John Prine, who sang like they came out of Chattanooga rather than their hometown of Chicago but introduced left-wing political sentiment to the traditionally conservative country form. However, Kristofferson became a star too. He sang the praise of official Nashville because it had been kind to him, moved to Los Angeles and started writing songs about the love affairs of showbusiness celebrities, and became more interested in making movies than making music.

All along, the real Nashville rebel was Willie Nelson. He made enough money to sit back and be grateful, but he never toed the Nashville line. He flew in the face of country-music racism by going to bat for Charley Pride, whose success in turn created the need for the *chicano* superstar, Johnny Rodriguez. Nelson encouraged an old member of Buddy Holly's Crickets, Waylon Jennings, who added "Midnight Rider" and "MacArthur Park" to his country repertoire and in turn lent a helping hand to another broke Texas songwriter, Billy Joe Shaver, who credited Nelson with starting it all: "Willie laid down such a heavy track record that nobody could ignore him. He's the one that busted it wide open." Nelson did not grovel in the presence of

Chet Atkins, and he was the first to say to hell with what Nashville thought, he was going to take his recording business to New York and go home to Texas and run around with Leon Russell if he wanted to. Young Austinites loved him for that, and they had drawn closer because of Nelson and his younger running mates.

Nelson was different from the younger recorded Austinites because he was a country musician from start to finish and did not aspire to be more than that. As the oldest and most established, as the man who might have scaled the heights of Nashville but pulled out because he didn't like what he saw . . . and still kept his career alive, he was inevitably their leader. The younger performers had also skinned their noses on the pavement of the major music centers, and like Nelson, they came to Austin to rescue their self-respect and sanity. Michael Murphey was a factory songwriter for Screen Gems before he returned to Texas. Jerry Jeff Walker was a jail-bent drifter who took a beating in New York. Steve Fromholz was the unfortunate victim of a transcontinental shift of his recording company's offices. B. W. Stevenson stalked the sidewalks of Los Angeles in search of a music businessman who would listen. Willis Alan Ramsey was turned down by James Taylor's producer. Bobby Bridger was manipulated by his Nashville recording company. Rusty Wier auditioned for recording talent scouts but made his living in the bars of Fayetteville and East Lansing. Kinky Friedman achieved a measure of success by resorting to hard-sell hype. The styles of those performers were highly individualized, but together they distilled a blend of music that reflected the background, outlook and needs of a unique Austin audience.

For decades a small class of social hangers-on had refused to leave the city simply because the legislative session or college semester was over and economic opportunity lay elsewhere, but now there were more of them, and many never set foot on the capitol grounds or university campus. In the main they were middle-class youths who hailed from Texas' cities, but as such, they were rarely more than two or three generations removed from more rural times, and they came to Austin because the ease of those times lingered there. Relatively free of hassle, in Austin they could smoke their dope, sail their Frisbees, walk their dogs without a leash and in a few secluded coves outside the city limits, sunburn their posteriors swimming naked. Most worked at some task or another, but somehow it didn't cost as much to live in

Austin, and many would just as soon quit as report to work on Monday. Politically, they constituted a new breed of conservative, one which despaired over big-city hype and twentieth-century progress and romanticized "getting back to the land."

(Which, incidentally, was just dandy with the ruling establishment. At least they weren't painting Walt Rostow Go Home on university buildings anymore, and they weren't out in the streets 10,000 strong, like they were the Friday after Kent State.)

Whether American youth would prove as passive in the seventies as it was in the fifties was an intriguing question that would be easy to answer in another ten years, but without doubt the pace had slowed considerably, and that slowdown was reflected in the popular music of the early seventies. The stasis of rock music might be no more than a temporary lull before another storm, but it was as if the musicians and audience burned themselves out in their psychedelic search, or like Jimi Hendrix, Jim Morrison and Janis Joplin, found that reality was worse than they originally thought. You could throw a rock through a window if all you had to worry about was the Vietnam War, but what could you do when the Houston ship channel was threatening to ignite, University of Texas students were locked out of their dormitories because there was no natural gas to heat them, and Richard Nixon was the choice of sixty-four percent of the American people? Take another tab of acid? The craze for nostalgia, to get away from it all, engulfed almost all popular forms of American expression, and in Austin, the musical retreat to the fifities led naturally enough to country-western. Aspiring vocalists began to sound exactly like Ernest Tubb, and a scuffed pair of cowboy boots became an essential ingredient of a hip wardrobe.

At many levels Austin music was little more than a glorified strain of nostalgia rock, but the young performers near the top of the pyramid accomplished considerably more than that. None were country purists. Most paid their dues in rock or folk music. Moreover, they were not the first to adapt their styles to country-western. Everybody from Ringo Starr to Judy Collins to Mick Jagger to B.J. Thomas had turned to it occasionally to disrupt the monotony of pop music, and the classic country-rock album remained *Sweetheart of the Rodeo* by the ex-perimentalist Byrds, who also pioneered folk-rock and Jesus-rock. The most popular country-rock artists still lived on the West Coast. Indeed,

11

one of the Austin lyricists wrote, "Them city-slicker pickers got a lot of slicker licks than you and me." But Los Angeles country-rock suffered from its slickness; most of its practicioners were basically mimicking a form, and were generally too citified to play country without a trace of put-down. But in Austin the roots were real, and the music rang true.

Instrumentally, the best Austin musicians wove blues reflection, rock energy and gospel hope into the fabric of country, but lyrically they voiced the same old suspicion that maybe moving to the city wasn't such a good idea after all. But while mainstream country contented itself with self-pitying accounts of the state of suburban captivity, Austin music suggested an active disengagement, a quest for a freer way of life. The best place to stand on one's two feet, it seemed to say, was at home, and that implied coming to terms with one's heritage and making the most of it. By giving it positive direction, Austin's musicians transformed country from a music of middle-class misery to one of down-home delight.

Because of its music, some people predicted Austin would emerge as America's next cultural subcapital. But popular music was a changeable, faddish art, and if a new messiah strapped on his guitar and stepped out of the wilds of Hoboken or Walla Walla, the country-rock boom could go the way of sitars and moogs quickly. Also, many musicians weren't sure they wanted Austin to become a full-fledged music center. It was an era of alleged cocaine payola in the music industry, and the extant music centers often destroyed as much as they created. The musicians came to Austin to get away from that. What lay in store for Austin music was anybody's guess, and nobody's insurance policy. But for the moment, Austin was a social oasis in the middle of a Texas desert, and music was its cultural spring.

mister
threadgill

Ghostly in its desertion, the birthplace of Austin music was the decaying husk of a service station that hadn't pumped gasoline in forty years. A fallen television antenna resided on its overhang, a restroom door flapped in the wind. A sign staked near the curb offered the place for sale. Dust prevailed.

A bespectacled man with an ever-broadening belly grew old inside those walls, serving beer and supervising the enjoyment of young people whose fashionable attire evolved from pleated trousers and watch chains to bleeding Madras shirts and penny-loafers to farmer's overalls and headbands. But it was more than a college tavern. For more than two decades the little bar was a practice field and proving ground for aspiring musicians who were so unsure of themselves they could barely stand to perform in public. Hootenanny, holler, jam session, stomp—all the labels for spontaneous amateur music applied to the gatherings where the music was free and no customer was an intruder. Most of the bar's patrons were amateurs themselves, their lives still before them, and few would pursue their futures in Austin. But of their times in Austin, one of their favorite memories would be the little bar with the outmanned overhead fan and the barkeep who greeted them all like his favorite niece or nephew. (Personally, when I thought of Threadgill's I would remember a grizzled, 180-pound off-duty carhop who nudged my knee with hers one night and demanded, "Come on you long-haired thang. Dance with me." I recalled the shuffling country-tonk steps somehow, and the crowd made a little room for us, but as we whirled I caught the eye of an old Little League chum who was now a law student. He turned toward his pretty wife, pretending he didn't know me.) Soon memories were all that we would have. The proprietor of the bar was falling prey to the infirmities of old age, and the deserted bar was an architectural relic standing in the way of progress. Community leaders called it an eyesore and urged the city council to condemn it. There's nothing of value in a deserted bar.

Kenneth Threadgill was born the son of a Nazarene minister in 1909, but when Travis County voted wet in 1933 he purchased Austin's first beer license and opened his bar in the abandoned filling station on the northern edge of the city. Threadgill was also the first of Austin's tavern operators to realize there was gold in those nearby university hills. He catered to the students, and for four decades—until city fire marshalls issued an ultimatum in 1973 to either expand the premises or turn away customers at the door—Threadgill's was the favorite college hangout in Austin.

In addition to being a shrewd bartender, Threadgill was also a country singer of the old cut and an appreciative student of music. After the war, first on Fridays and then on Wednesdays, his cramped little bar swelled with musicians. Threadgill would briefly entertain the crowd with his Jimmy Rodgers yodeling and a shuffling little jig he called "a modified Charleston two-step," but then he would return to his bartending duties and listen. Anyone with enough nerve to stand up and sing was welcome to the microphone.

Musically, the most exciting days at Threadgill's were the early sixties, when the little bar became a haven for folk purists, and a young regular named Julie Paul first brought Janis Joplin to meet Mr. Threadgill, as almost everybody called him. Janis was a fallen Church of Christ girl, a homely, overweight victim of the cosmetic fifties and a coastal Texas town called Port Arthur. By the time she reached Austin she was already neurotic with rejection. She cursed like a sailor, drank anything she could get her hands on, wore no makeup, wore no bra. She apparently wanted just one person, damn it, to notice her. That person was Kenneth Threadgill.

When Threadgill first saw her she was traveling in the company of a banjo player named Lanny Wiggins and a harmonica player, Powell

16

St. John, who later went on to play with a nationally respected rhythm & blues band, Mother Earth. Threadgill thought St. John was the best musician of the three at the time, but he got a kick out of Janis's screeching version of "Silver Threads and Golden Needles." Janis stayed around Austin for several months, performing at a number of low-paying clubs and the student union, and her singing continued to improve, but she was still most comfortable at Threadgill's. There were no hecklers, and he treated her like a daughter. But her university peers were not so benevolent. It was still an era of button-down collars and crewcuts at the university, and she was flying in the face of conservative tradition. The fraternity interests tolerated her presence for a while, but then struck back with cruel smugness, voting her the ugliest male on campus. According to biographer Myra Friedman, that hurt was more than Janis could bear, and she fled bitterly to California.

Meanwhile, the modest fame of Kenneth Threadgill was growing, though if it weren't for some smart investments along the way, he wouldn't have had much of an old-age income. He was a folksinger of the true definition, for his reputation spread by word-of-mouth. Threadgill found just how far his fame had spread—and how many people once attended the University of Texas—when he and his band, the Hootenanny Hoots, were booked to perform for an artists' convention at the Walker Art Center in Minneapolis, Minnesota. The organizers of the convention ran a newspaper ad announcing only that Kenneth Threadgill from Texas would provide the entertainment, but when Threadgill checked into his hotel room the phone rang all night long. "Are you the Threadgill that used to run that beer joint in Austin?" the callers wanted to know. Yes, Threadgill said, he was.

Bolstering the audience the next night were doctors, lawyers and farmers who had all gone to the University at one time or another, but it was a homogeneous crowd. "It was a huge stage," Threadgill remembered, "like a theater—up, up, up, you know what I mean? Seats. And when they got in there that night, the whole left side was just people in tuxedos and gowns—sculptors, artists of all kinds, that high muckety-muck bunch of people from Europe—but over on the other side was young people, hippies."

Threadgill was a hillbilly warbler; he rolled the words out of the side of his mouth and threw his head back to yodel. Accompany that with the hoedown fiddle of his old sidekick, Cotton Collins, and it became a music that set a crowd in motion. The young members of the audience that night were soon jumping and clapping in the aisles, but there was no room for them to dance, so when Threadgill took his break he told the organizer of the concert he'd play the last hour free if she'd allow them to come onstage with him.

"My god," she said, "will they keep order?"

"Don't worry about them," Threadgill said. "I know 'em all." Before the night was over the stage resembled a pagan ritual: young persons arm in arm danced in a circle around Threadgill and his band.

However, national fame does not always translate into national recognition. Threadgill received no real national exposure until 1968, when an Austin promoter named Rod Kennedy introduced him to Pete Seeger and the promoter of the Newport Jazz and Folk Festivals, who recognized an authentic folksinger when they saw one. Threadgill sang and danced his jig before 21,000 people at the Rhode Island festival, but his real commercial opportunity was two more years in coming.

Ridicule and rejection had driven Texas' brightest native talent to the pinnacle of rock & roll stardom, but Janis Joplin never forgot her kindly benefactor in Austin. At the height of her career, in the summer of 1970, Janis canceled a $15,000 date in Hawaii to fly back to Austin to celebrate Threadgill's birthday. It was an outdoor affair west of town, beer and barbecue for a dollar, and several local bands signed on to play for a crowd of maybe 800. But word got around that a Joplin appearance was a possibility, and 5,000 showed up. Threadgill knew he wasn't about to cancel any $15,000 engagement for a birthday party, and he was as surprised as anybody when she walked onstage drunk on Southern Comfort and rasped, "Now, Kenneth, I just want you to know I brought you a Hawaiian leigh."

Threadgill chuckled and retorted, "Honey, that's one thing I don't know what I'd do with."

Janis concluded she was too drunk to tune the guitar someone handed her, sang a couple of songs, then her admirers descended. Threadgill talked with her just briefly, long enough to say she'd been staying away too long, and she told him, "Don't you worry, Daddy. You and I are going to see lots of each other." But then the autograph-seekers surrounded her, she flew out the next morning, and 88 days later, Janis Joplin was dead.

Stan Alexander, a University graduate student who had played his guitar while Janis waited her turn during those days at Threadgill's bar, was there when she returned to celebrate her old mentor's birthday. Alexander wrote on the back of a mimeographed assignment sheet after he heard the news, "I wasn't surprised to hear of Janis Joplin's death; I'm not sure why I wasn't. Maybe since as early as James Dean none of us has been capable of the shock that sudden dying once brought. But one reason for this numbness of mine was the death only two weeks ago of Hendrix. I was more shocked by that, and I didn't even know him."

Recalling her unexpected appearance at Threadgill's birthday party, Alexander wrote, "I was surprised and a little put off when I saw her. She was wearing the feathers and other regalia of her act, and I suppose I'd wanted to see her in casual clothes or business suit, anything to indicate she was herself something apart, separate from the act. Nothing I saw that evening indicated any division at all. Everything, including the slight show of recognition as she breathed on my cheek, indicated that she was no longer Janis Joplin but JANIS, of this time but of no particular place."

Threadgill took Janis Joplin's death harder than that, and for months afterward he wondered about her promise that they would see more of each other. "It always went through my mind," he said. "What did she mean, what did she have in mind?"

He found out a year later when a disc jockey at KOKE, a country-western station in Austin, called and said he had a recording of Janis singing "Me and Bobby McGee" that his hillbilly audience wasn't quite ready for. Did Threadgill want the thing?

"I'll be right on down," Threadgill said. When he reached the studio the disc jockey asked, "How well do you know Kris Kristofferson?"

"I never met him in my life. I saw him once on TV."

The disc jockey said Kristofferson knew Threadgill. It had something to do with Janis Joplin, something about an interview Kristofferson promised. Threadgill and his band crowded into a phone booth that night and contacted the hottest songwriter in the country at his hotel in New York, but Kristofferson said he was on his way to California, he'd keep in touch. So much for that, or so it appeared at the time. Threadgill was rapidly becoming a legend, but commercially, he was still undiscovered. He might have remained that way had it not been for an abortive country Woodstock, and the social intervention of the football coach at the University of Texas.

In the spring of 1972 an ambitious group of moneymakers convinced a man that a canyon on his ranch near Dripping Springs, a small town twenty miles west of Austin, was a perfect site for a three-day, country-music festival. Roads were graded, a large stage was erected, portable privies soon lined one ridge and an impressive list of Nashville performers signed on. Unfortunately, the Dripping Springs Reunion was insufficiently publicized, and the promoters forgot that March winds were no idle term in Central Texas. Blowing dust from a late norther kept many would-be customers away the first two days, and better weather and a larger crowd on Sunday weren't enough to stave off financial disaster.

Standing in the wings during all that was Darrell Royal, the Longhorn football coach who had befriended Willie Nelson and was rapidly becoming Austin's number-one country-music groupie. Nelson was Royal's house guest during the festival, and after the last performance Royal hosted a party which lasted until six-thirty the next morning and featured Nelson, Charlie Rich, Waylon Jennings, Kris Kristofferson and Rita Coolidge. The first to play at the party, however, was Kenneth Threadgill, and less than a month later Kristofferson, Jennings and their studio partner, Jack Clement, had Threadgill and his guitar player in Nashville recording an album with the assistance of some of the best studio sidemen in town.

Unfortunately, the album went unreleased. Kristofferson departed for Mexico with Bob Dylan and James Coburn to play the role of a highly romanticized Billy the Kid for the *machismo* film-maker, Sam Peckinpah. Jennings came down with mononucleosis, and Clement said he couldn't proceed until he got his two stars together. The friendship of Kristofferson and Jennings cooled off. Two years after the album was recorded, Jennings told Austin columnist Townsend Miller that Kristofferson and Clement had abandoned the project altogether, which left the weight on Jennings' shoulders. Pledges of trust were taken lightly in the music business.

Threadgill shrugged it all off and proceeded. He closed his bar because he couldn't afford to remodel it, yet couldn't bear to tell young customers there was no room inside for them. But the Austin estab-

Kenneth Threadgill was perhaps Austin's first music businessman. He was also a country singer of the Jimmy Rodgers cut, and for more than two decades weekly jam sessions in his little bar became the proving ground for Austin music. For sentimental reasons, Threadgill refused even to empty the ashtrays after he was forced to close his place in 1973.

Threadgill's most notable pupil was moody Janis Joplin, driven from Austin by ridicule and rejection to the heights, and depths, of rock & roll stardom. Threadgill's photograph collection illustrated the contrast between her Austin days and her last ones.

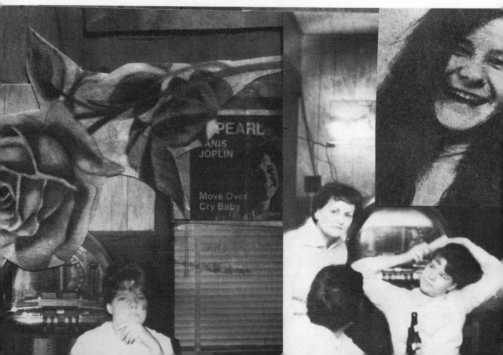

Remembered and loved by generations of university students, honored at a concert by Earl Scruggs and University of Texas football coach Darrell Royal, Threadgill in time gained a reputation of his own. He performed at the Newport Folk Festival, signed a belated record contract, and when his old colleagues fell by the wayside, formed a new band with Air Force sergeants and a legal secretary.

Youth seemed to revisit Threadgill when the new generation of musicians arrived. He welcomed interviewers, refused to file an unlisted number with the telephone company, treated strangers to his photographs, and became the grand old man of the Austin music community.

lishment kept after him. when condemnation petitions began to circulate toward the city council in early 1974, cynics observed that his property was extremely valuable commercially and a public auctioneer would sell it considerably cheaper than Threadgill's realtors, but there was no rush of historical society members to his rescue. Threadgill attended the city council meeting where the petition was discussed and told a newspaper reporter afterward that he couldn't stand to order the building torn down, yet it would be folly to modernize the structure, for it probably wouldn't fit the needs of a new owner. Finally he agreed to restore it just to save it.

Threadgill's old band, the Hootenanny Hoots, dissolved with a measure of pain. Two of the mainstays of the band decided that divorce was the solution to their marital problems, and the fiddler, Cotton Collins, had to abandon the life because of emphysema, an alcoholic liver, and an ulcerated stomach. However, Threadgill hardly sat back twiddling his thumbs. He couldn't travel as far as he once did because of the employment duties of the legal secretary and Air Force sergeants who led his new band, and he rarely danced his jig anymore because of his arthritis. He reserved each afternoon for a long nap, but he remained one of the hottest acts in Austin, even when the gifted newcomers arrived. A pizza restaurant dramatically increased its profits when the management abandoned a gay nineties atmosphere in favor of Threadgill, and he solidified his position as the grand old man of the Austin music community, the lovable bridge across the generation gap.

But Threadgill's young manager was more critical of the treatment Threadgill received in Nashville. "Hell, Threadgill's sixty-five years old," he said. "One of these days he's gonna die, and everybody's gonna be real sorry, and they're gonna release that album and make a fortune."

The oral historian for the Austin public library awoke with a normal weekday hangover, and as soon as she remembered what lay in store for her that day, her stomach began to churn. Most mornings she contented herself with menial tasks in the Austin-Travis County Collection, or if possible, a leisurely reading of the new *Rolling Stone* or *Texas Observer*. But when it came to oral history, she took an active interest in her job. For one thing, it got her out of the office. She had broadened the scope of the program, interviewing *chicano* politicians and old ladies with liberationist leanings, and lately she had begun to build a file on Austin music. This morning she had an interview with Kenneth Threadgill, and that was the source of her digestive concern. Interviewing made her extremely nervous. She seemed to think if she asked foolish questions, posterity would remember the interviewer as a fool.

In addition to all that, she had overslept again. She leaped out of bed, her head whirling, stumbled over her deaf dog, dressed hurriedly, surveyed her apartment for the rodentary remains often left as a gift by her cats and rushed into the traffic, trying to organize the questions she wanted to ask. Threadgill's discovery of Janis Joplin was ground already heavily trodden by rock journalists, and she was more interested in his life before that. She wanted to ask him about the white hair that curled down over his collar, the road trips in his Winnebago, his practice of buying whiskey by the gallon. Most of all, she was curious how a man that old could be that much alive.

When she reached the flagstone house in northwest Austin that morning, Threadgill offered her a glass of breakfast wine. Threadgill's wife was in another room watching television, and he ushered his interviewer into a room adorned with photographic mementos of his singing career. She said she had read that he was first inspired by church music.

"Well, you see when I was born Daddy was already preaching," Threadgill said, "and we were traveling a lot, same way as today. I don't recall, I guess my earliest remembrance was singing in church. I always loved to sing, and I had some brothers and sisters older than me that were singers, soloists. My oldest sister is still living; she's a great church worker, lives in California. I have another sister that lives in Kilgore and the next sister died. I have a brother who lives right here in town."

"Does he come to hear you?"

"He comes to sing with me, every once in a while. He's, I think, seventy-eight or seventy-nine now."

"Can he yodel too?"

"He's not a yodeler but he's a good tenor singer," Threadgill said. "We sing quite a few songs together."

She asked if there had ever been a conflict between Threadgill's religious ties and his livelihood.

"Well, see," Threadgill said, "my church affiliations were like this. My daddy was a preacher. But there were eleven of us kids—I was number nine down the line—and that don't mean we were all religious. I kind of have my feelings about religion, but I'm not as strict about it as Daddy was, by a long shot.

"Daddy didn't like the beer business, but his philosophy was, no matter what kind of job you do, if you're gonna be in business you can be honest and square, and run it straight and not do somethin' wrong, whatever it might be. I believe that; I've been pretty strong on that. And I've been very fortunate. We've lived well, and raised our family. We've got thirteen descendants, and every one of them girls. Three daughters, five granddaughters, and five great-granddaughters.That's something, ain't it."

She asked Threadgill if he ever met Jimmy Rodgers.

"Yeah, sure did. I was picking up tickets at a movie house in 1928, and he came there. Now I'd heard him sing before—first at a circus and at two or three different theaters. But I never had met him until then. He was just an old rounder, but he fit my bill, I liked him. Up until that time I was singing all right, but I loved to sing Al Jolson songs."

"When did you first realize you could yodel?"

"When I heard Jimmy. When I heard Jimmy yodeling I just kind of yodeled along under my breath. And I didn't even know I could yodel. And do you know, that's something you can't teach nobody."

"Well I still don't have a very clear picture of how you became a world-famous singer."

"Oh, I'm not a world-famous singer," Threadgill scoffed.

"Oh you are. Of course you are."

"I've got a pretty good following," he conceded. "But the secret to that is the students."

"You've always gotten along well with young people."

"They come to me," Threadgill said. "They come to me, and I love them. I love to be with kids. Imagine now, forty years in Austin and say twenty-five of that was pretty active in music. All right, you figure it this way. A new group of students comes to this university every year and they hear about us from the ones that were here the year before, so they all come out to our place, you see. And when they leave they scatter out all over the United States. Just imagine that going on for twenty-five years. Well, they don't forget where they had a good time. They remember. And so that's it, right there. It builds up around that little old filling station out there . . . Do you like that wine?''

"Yes, very good,'' the interviewer sputtered. She asked if he planned to go on indefinitely with his singing career.

"I just love it,'' he said. ''The good Lord's been good to me. My voice holds up, why and how I don't know. Somebody asked me one time when I was going to retire, and I said when the good Lord gets tired of listening to me.''

She wondered if she would ever hear his album.

"We'll have it out one of these days,'' he said. ''It's gonna come out. If it don't come out nationally then we'll have a limited bunch of 'em on the bandstand that can be bought and heard. You'll hear that album yet.''

looking for a home

As in most college towns, the number of musicians in Austin increased drastically after the rise of Bob Dylan and the Beatles. The performers in Austin during the mid-sixties were very young and had very much to learn, but their sheer numbers and persistence produced an ill-fated boomlet in folk and rock music that had very little regional identity. (Country was still the property of those backward yokels with horse manure on their boots who hung out in Austin versions of the MB Corral.) The boomlet spawned a couple of clubs that failed and few acts that glimpsed false rays of hope on the horizon, but except for those who were persistent and flexible enough to get aboard the swing toward country late in the decade, it ended in frustration and disappointment.

For musicians, the obvious advantage of Threadgill's was its accessibility. Unfortunately, a crowd of 200 at Threadgill's resembled a can of sardines, and hungry mouths went hungry if their only means of support was the tambourine passed around in hopes of charitable nickels, dimes and quarters. The easiest route for an aspiring Austin musician was to lend his or her talent to the rock copy bands which played for fraternity and sorority dances. It was a good way to learn music, and the demand for those bands subsided only during summer or semester breaks, and many of the coveted and comfortable sidemen who accompany Austin's leading performers today went that route. If

31

one was uncomfortable with boisterously drunk young gentlemen who laid Scott Fitzgerald lines on their ladies and exacted rare pleasure from baring their hindquarters in mixed company, then making music was considerably less profitable and not half as steady. There was the student union—where Joplin, St. John, Wiggins and even Boz Scaggs briefly held sway—and a scattering of small clubs around town, but the only place the musicians could reach an audience of any size was outdoors. As a result, in the warm months there was music for the asking on the weekends, though it took divergent forms: rock concerts in a little sunken park near the downtown area, and folk concerts in a larger park on the western outskirts of the city.

An Austin FM radio station operator and road racing enthusiast named Rod Kennedy staged the first Zilker Park folk festival in 1965 featuring Tom Paxton, a UT folklorist named Roger Abrahams who sang children's songs and five young musicians who called themselves the Dallas County Jug Band, two of whom would later play a major role in the country-rock boom. Kennedy was enthused enough about the success of his subsequent outdoor concerts to open a new club in the capitol area called the Chequered Flag, along with a next-door neighbor, the Texas Speed Museum. Showcased were retired racing cars that Kennedy hoped would lure a few dollars from the wallets of tourists headed south in 1967 toward the San Antonio Hemisfair. Fewer tourists than expected made the trip to the Hemisfair, and few indeed were tempted to stop over in Austin for the sake of a bloody Birdcage Maserati and an experimental Smith Chevy.

The decor of the Chequered Flag was standard expresso house derivative, and at first it was chiefly a hangout for Kennedy's rally-racing cronies, but the music was lively enough to excite some interest. Kennedy's working partners, folksingers Allen Damron and Segal Fry, played the first bill. Another native Austin folksinger of international reputation, Carolyn Hester, stopped by occasionally to help out, and Kennedy booked acts as diverse as blues singer Mance Lipscomb and country boy Ramblin' Jack Elliott. He even brought some jazz acts in, but those experiments always lost money, for jazz and folk enthusiasts alike stayed away by the scores. But the most significant performers at the Flag were Townes Van Zandt, a Fort Worth boy who had the audacity to set his blues songs in Texas and went on to record several albums and an itinerant New Yorker, Jerry Jeff Walker. Walker had spent the night in a New Orleans drunk tank once and met a minstrel dancer who inspired the classic "Mr. Bojangles," and he was the archetype of the down-and-out musician: a voice clear as a bell, a temperament erratic as hell. Walker was often surly, all too often drunk, and during summer gigs he commanded the management to turn off the air conditioning so the crowd could hear his quiet songs. In Texas that's an unreasonable demand. But he quickly became the club favorite. Though he looked the part of a folk musician, standing in front of the microphone alone with his guitar, his lyrics smiled out through some inner misery, and an undercurrent in his music fairly begged for bass and drum accompaniment. Though few people realized it, Walker sounded almost country.

In 1969 Kennedy was optimistic enough to stage a concert in the municipal auditorium featuring Walker, Hester, Jimmy Driftwood and Gordon Lightfoot, but the concert lost $5,000. Moreover, the Chequered Flag was operating at a loss. Kennedy and his partners tried everything they could to keep the club afloat, up to and including managerial discouragement of tips in favor of a fifteen percent gratuities fee that never reached the pockets of the waitresses, who were working for a dollar-fifty an hour and free soda pop. "There were some really magical moments at the Flag," Kennedy said, "but somehow it managed to lose fifty dollars a day no matter what we did." Finally Kennedy sold out to Fry and Damron, but they had even less money to lose, and the Flag became a rock & roll joint with a plastic flashing dance floor. It was an unfortunate death, for the Flag had just begun to nurture the seed of what would become Austin country-rock music.

The rock & rollers who got their start in the free concerts in the downtown park traveled an equally frustrating but considerably more exciting path. The first Austin rock band which met with any success revolved around a young Austinite with curly hair and a cherubic expression named Roky Erickson. The 13th Floor Elevators were easier on the ears of their listeners than most hard-rock bands because they restrained their guitars in deference to the adolescent tenor of Erickson, but while his consciousness may have been heightened by the substances he ingested, his lyrics were sophomoric, a whirlpool of philosophical confusion apparently foaming with Karl Marx, the Rig Veda, Bertrand Russell and Bob Dylan. However, the Elevators were the hottest band in Texas during the mid-sixties. When an Austin bar called the New Orleans Club abandoned Dixieland in favor of Erickson's crew, crowds approaching a thousand started showing up, and an AM pop station mobilized its remote broadcast unit. Erickson was audacious in his drug advocacy during those broadcasts, and later he would pay for it, but for the moment he was riding high.

A band of greater long-range potential was the Conqueroo, whose name derived from an old Howlin' Wolf lyric. Powell St. John helped form the group, but then he went off to San Francisco, and the driving forces of the band became Ed Guinn, a black 300-pound bass player of advantaged Fort Worth origin, and a skinny Austin teenager named Bob Brown who started writing songs at the age of fourteen and became the child wonder of the student union set. It was the first time most of the musicians had ever picked up an electronic instrument, and for awhile the Conqueroo was convincingly awful, but Guinn and Brown provided good original material, and soon the Conqueroo had a reputation as the best white rhythm & blues band in the state.

The Austin demand for white rhythm & blues bands was not great, and the Conqueroo wound up playing two nights a week for a year in a squalid little bar on the black east side called the IL Club. Guinn conned the aging owner of the establishment, Ira Littlefield, into the arrangement, which according to Brown, succeeded in running off most of Littlefield's regular clientele. "It was the kind of place where older black people gathered in the afternoons to play dominoes. But here a bunch of cracker hippies marches down and starts playing so loud that food is flying off forks all over the neighborhood." However, the older patrons were replaced by white friends of the band, silently critical black musicians and other young blacks who did their best to make time with the white girls. Everything proceeded smoothly for several months, but then one night the band members and several blacks were discussing the automotive woes of one of the bar patrons. He outlined his plans for repair, and the articulate sound technician for the Conqueroo, Sandy Lockett, said that was a niggardly way to go about it. One of the blacks interpreted that as a racial slur, and despite the peace-making efforts of Guinn, a Hollywood barroom brawl ensued which left a couple of Conqueroo members in need of surgery and ended only when a black's pistol went off in his trousers pocket. The police arrived, surveyed the damage and asked Littlefield what those white boys were doing there anyway. Littlefield said he'd never seen them before. Guinn went to jail, Brown went to the hospital, and the experiment in interracial relations ended on a bitter note.

Lockett was an intelligent, upper-middle-class youth whose head had been turned around by the collegiate experience in Austin. In 1964 he started working sound for the Elevators and later managed them on the road, but he had even closer ties with the Conqueroo. He believed his friends' music deserved a hearing, and he also knew it was going to die if they didn't get one soon. When a group of friends started talking about opening a rock & roll club to serve their musician friends' interests, and another friend stepped forward with enough money to make it feasible, Lockett pitched himself and his money in, and in 1967 they procured a lease to some commercial footage in a seedy part of downtown Austin. They provided their own labor and in five weeks built a club called the Vulcan Gas Company that would gain a minor national reputation and scandalize the Austin establishment.

Inside, the Vulcan was cruder than its successor, the Armadillo. Hurriedly-nailed benches occupied the floor, plumbing poked from the walls and there was no beer. If a club had a beer or liquor license it could take some of the risk from booking entertainment, for two or three drunks could make up for five unsold music tickets. But a club that lived solely by the gate was a precarious enterprise. It operated on the margin above the expenses paid the band, and if no one was interested in hearing that band, there was no money. But the Vulcan had a frenetic light show working on all walls, a patient landlord, a lot of energy and the Elevators and Conqueroo for openers.

It was a wild, wild place by Texas standards, frequented by a few blacks who stopped by occasionally for some jive, sunshaded Airmen trying to be cool, and everybody in Austin who wanted to be a hippie. The managers booked whomever they could afford, which limited them to staple bands like the Elevators and Conqueroo, and the black Texas blues singers—Mance Lipscomb, Lightnin' Hopkins, Big Joe Williams. "As everybody knows," Lockett said, "Texas blues singers have had their asses systematically kicked for thirty years. I grew up in Houston, and when us nice little rich kids decided to have ourselves a low-down nasty party, and got tired of our Ray Charles records, we'd go hire Lightnin' Hopkins. His standard fee was twenty dollars and two fifths of gin. It wasn't quite that bad when we brought him to the Vulcan, but it wasn't much better.''

The Vulcan was primarily a rock & roll joint, however, which made it a threatening presence. The Austin establishment looked on the Vulcan as a social cancer, for the normally deserted downtown area had begun to swarm at night with hippies who were clearly up to no good and were probably selling marijuana. As a matter of fact, they were. One couple used to park their van in front of the Vulcan, turn on the portable television and open their doors for business. Front-page newspaper columnists and every respectable civic leader in town began to snipe at the Vulcan, but artists with growing national reputations like Steve Miller raved about the Austin audiences, and the management held on.

Because it was fashionable in the psychedelic era to channel one's allegiance almost exclusively to one or two groups, the house-band Elevators and Conqueroo soon shone with the aura of Texas holy men. The Elevators were releasing albums through a group of Houston businessmen who called themselves International Artists, and the band was even a favorite at the Aragon Ballroom in San Francisco. And Roky Erickson was a marvel to marijuana smokers. The police busted him, and he responded by insisting publicly that he had done nothing wrong. Eventually he was a kind of local Donovan, striding through a room spewing wisdom while a fellow band member, sure in the belief he was Moses, climbed in a chair and started preaching a sermon.

The Conqueroo were a little more down to earth, though not much. In the early days they lived in an apartment called the Ghetto, but then they met the novelist and reigning cultural hero, Bill Brammer, who by accident of divorce and remarriage watched his friends change from LBJ politicans and journalists to twenty-year-old hippies and musicians. Brammer got a kick out of Guinn and thought Brown had considerable talent as a writer, and after signing on to write public-relations pap for the Hemisfair in San Antonio, Brammer talked his landlord into renting the upper floor of a turreted Victorian mansion to the Conqueroo. The mansion on West Avenue very quickly became the hippie crash pad in Austin. A couple of dozen people often slept on the floors at night, and the object of the game in the daytime was to take as many drugs as physiology and peer-pressure would allow.

The Conqueroo cult even had a brief encounter with the hal-

oto courtesy Burton Wilson

In the late sixties Austin music adapted to national trends. It was guided in the direction of folk by a promoter and clubowner named Rod Kennedy (above left, with partner Allen Damron); toward rock by groups like the Conqueroo, who deified themselves among Austin freaks but found the competition too stiff when they made the rock pilgrimage to Haight–Ashbury. Ed Guinn (below, far left) and Bob Brown (far right) tried to revive the band in Austin.

CLOCKWISE: Spencer Perskin, whose Shiva's Headband became the last cult group at Vulcan Gas Company and ushered in the Armadillo era; Mance Lipscomb, a Texas blues singer who was willing to work for the low Vulcan Gas wages; Doug Sahm, a veteran musician from San Antonio who wasn't quite sure country was the road for Austin music to travel.

lucinogenic big-time. Ken Kesey was a long-standing friend of Larry McMurtry, and when the Merry Pranksters took to the road for one of their wild swings through the country they stopped in Houston to see McMurtry, who directed them to the San Antonio apartment of Brammer, who directed them to the mansion in Austin. The Pranksters descended in grease paint and propeller caps, nursed their young on curbs in five o'clock traffic and stayed for a week. A few of the more impressionable Austinites gathered in awe to watch the lordly Kesey piss, but what the Pranksters had found was a group of young Texans already too stoned to pay them much heed.

Unfortunately, the ascendancy of both the Elevators and Conqueroo was short-lived. The Elevators got very little from their association with International Artists, gained a reputation in San Francisco as a band that failed to show up for engagements and fell into exhausted disarray. Then one night Erickson got busted one time too many. The American legal system couldn't seem to communicate with the fallen rock star, so it sent him to a state hospital for the criminally insane. It was nearly three years before Erickson could win his freedom. During his protracted convalescence he tried to get a hold on things by turning to primitive Christianity. He began to sign his letters Rev. Roky Erickson, and he wrote a book of Jesus-freak poetry called *Openers* that was published by financially endowed friends on the outside. The book contained the standard thee's and thou's, stoned images and wordplay of most Jesus-freak verse—with a little more of the rock lyric brevity—but scattered throughout the thin book were agonized cries of pain. One of the poems was entitled ''Ye Are Not Crazy Man.''

The Conqueroo endured a different demise. Convinced that they had gone as far as they could in Texas, they made the rock pilgrimage to San Francisco, where the drummer promptly freaked out and fled back to Texas, and the others were not so sure they liked what they saw. ''San Francisco started dying about six months before we got there,'' Brown said. ''The scene was really starting to degenerate. Haight Street smelled like piss, and a lot of little stores were closing down. All the people we thought were running around with flowers in their hair were now lying around with needles stuck in their necks.'' Compounding the hassle for Brown were the lack of privacy, a murder rate of two per month in the neighborhood, regular burglaries of musicians' equipment and bereted Black Panthers who scared the living daylights out of him until he cut his hair and they left him alone. Brown was not yet twenty-one. Worst of all nobody listened to their music. "We went out there and played in the park with Santana and Big Brother, and I think we played better than any of them, but people just slipped right over us. 'We want the guys from California, bring on Big Brother.' And man, Big Brother was horrible. Those guys knew two or three chords apiece and couldn't even play those.''

One of the last straws was when a writer from *Rolling Stone* came around to interview Brown. The writer asked about music in Texas, and wanting to spread the good fortune around, Brown told him about a white albino blues guitarist from Houston named Johnny Winter. The writer's eyes flashed white-white, black-black, and shortly afterward Winter headlined the feature on Texas music. Very shortly afterward, Winter signed a recording contract running to six figures. The Conqueroo got lost in the journalistic shuffle.

Weary and discouraged, the band broke up. Ed Guinn became a long-haul truck driver, but Brown and Powell St. John formed another group called the Angel Band, whose name derived from a gospel lyric. Even that led to more indignity. The Hell's Angels came around one night and wanted to know what right the band had to that name, and the musicians had to beg forgiveness. Finally Brown drifted back to Austin and opened an antique shop, bitter at twenty-three.

At home the Vulcan was in trouble too. "It was a giant maw of a goddamn furnace that you had to keep stoked with money,'' Lockett said, but the real problem was that the managers had grown tired, partly because they had simply been doing it too long, but also because the times were changing, and the Vulcan crowds were changing with them. "We had a bouncer who was five-six, a master of tact and discernment,'' Lockett said, "which was all right, because in the first year of the Vulcan's existence it was difficult to tell whether we had a regular money-making gig or a private party. In the last year it was difficult to tell whether we had a rock & roll club or a wrestling match. It got a little rough.'' Tired of the strain, the Vulcan managers started looking for someone to keep the club going, but none of the new managers worked out, and the club died in 1970.

The Vulcan was ill-fated because it sought to import a California scene that was itself short-lived, but its owners had set a precedent that would make things much easier for future rock music entrepreneurs.

They had illustrated that a club could operate on a basis other than beer sales and broken down the Austin musician union's opposition to freak musicians. Additionally, they had provided a training ground for the managers, publicists, technicians and graphic artists who are as necessary to a music industry as the musicians themselves.

In the music business, four years approximates a decade, and by 1973 many of the people associated with the Chequered Flag and Vulcan Gas Company had divorced themselves from commercial music. Lockett purchased a small-crafts shop, and after Roky Erickson was finally adjudged sane, he became another faceless young man in the Austin crowd. A few survived, however, the most spectacular of whom was the businessman, Rod Kennedy. In an effort to recoup his losses at the Flag, Kennedy went into concert promotion full-time, which brought him into traveling contact with Peter Yarrow. Everywhere they went, young writers and singers accosted Yarrow with their material, and he urged Kennedy to think of a way to give some of those aspiring artists a break.

"When I began to be aware of the depth and wealth of the music here," Kennedy said, "I wanted people to be able to hear it outside the smoke-filled rooms." The opportunity presented itself in 1972 when a state arts and crafts fair was scheduled on Memorial Day in Kerrville, a beautiful little town in the Hill Country northwest of San Antonio. Kennedy moved in with a "new folk concert" introducing young performers and a Sunday folk mass on the fairgrounds, and he also rented Kerrville's cozy municipal auditorium for a three-day folk festival featuring more established performers. Yarrow and Carolyn Hester signed on as a favor to Kennedy, but he also sought out the best of the Austin country-rockers. Though the crowds were fairly small, the first Kerrville Folk Festival was a resounding aesthetic success.

Kennedy was a conversational man with a Madison Avenue manner and an abrupt way of ordering his subordinates around, a loyal friend and supporter of Texas' right-wing Republican senator, John Tower. "Dealing with Rod," one of the Austin performers confided, "involves a lot of soul hand-shaking and hypocritical back-slapping." However, Austin artists longed for the chance to appear on one of the night-time bills, and the Kerrville Folk Festival became the highlight of Texas' musical year. Dean Rabourn of Spirit Sound in Austin, who engineered the sound at the Atlanta Pop Festival and was on the team at the Concert for Bangladesh, mixed the sound for Kennedy free of charge, and the spirit of high cooperation extended to the performers. They hopped onstage and lent their talents to their friends in the spotlight, and in 1973, Willie Nelson refused to press charges when a Kerrville woman absconded with his wife's purse. The Kerrville police couldn't fathom that. Kennedy also retained the recording services of a Cuban refugee named Pedro Gutierrez, and all but one of the performers was able to obtain releases from their recording companies to appear on limited-edition Kerrville Folk Festival albums, which became collectors' items.

When I talked to Kennedy he was preparing for the expanded 1974 festival. He had added bluegrass and rag-time festivals on other holiday weekends, but the feature event remained the folk festival, and it had already outgrown the small Kerrville auditorium. In 1973 Kennedy had to turn away scores of families at the door. As a result he purchased several acres of land outside Kerrville and started clearing an outdoor arena with an eventual capacity of nearly 5,000. He was even so confident of the festivals' continued success that he sold his home in Austin and built a cabin on the property. "I've just finished my first 100 hours of chain-sawing," he said. "And I've traded in my racing car for a four-wheel drive jeep. Which is good."

However, his principal worry that day was not the preparation of the site, but the task of convincing the people of Kerr Country that his festivals were not about to ruin the Hill Country. The Texas establishment became extremely wary of outdoor rock festivals after a group of promotors sneaked Joplin, Chicago, Herbie Mann and several other name acts into an automotive speedway barely outside the Dallas city limits in 1969. A *Dallas Morning News* editorialist regretted that he could not welcome young people who refused to work, cohabitated in flagrant infidelity and defied the state narcotics statutes, then summoned a classic conclusion from the depths of his creativity. Whatever happened to the responsible young people of yesteryear? he wondered. Well, they still existed, and that Saturday they would be at home mowing their parents' lawns, while "the lewd and loose [were] swinging in Lewisville." More importantly, the Texas legislature rushed through a statute that made an outdoor music concert an extremely difficult enterprise, for the promoters had to have the blessing of the local county commissioners every step of the way.

"There's a great deal of local trepidation about what we're doing up there," Kennedy said. "We're keeping up a continuing, low-pressure publicity campaign about our moving to Kerrville, about the way our festivals bring young and old people together, about the age-old tradition of festivals in this country. To the uninitiated, the word festival means rock, pot, bottle-throwing, filth. Which is something we're campaigning against."

Obviously, hardcore rock & rollers had no place at the Kerrville Folk Festival, and times in Austin were harder than ever. Their only real home was a club west of town called the Soap Creek Saloon, which was itself beleaguered, for an upper-middle-class school district built a new junior high within a mile of the club, and then started applying pressure to revoke the club's liquor license. And the only name performer in town who seemed truly sympathetic to the rock & rollers was Doug Sahm.

Sahm got extremely tired of the routine with the Sir Douglas Quintet, lapsed into semi-retirement for awhile, then in 1973 enlisted a superstar array of sidemen that included Bob Dylan and Dr. John and resurfaced with a country-rock-blues album. Though he wore a cowboy hat and sat in occasionally with Willie Nelson, he didn't particularly like Armadillo World Headquarters and he told a *Rolling Stone* correspondent, "People are tired of this cosmic cowboy shit. They're ready to rock & roll." Sahm quickly discovered that his name appeared in print more often if he appeared to be a part of the country-rock community, however, and he began to show up at the country-rockers' concerts. He even talked about organizing a tour. But his music was still more a reflection of the diversity of San Antonio than the homogeneity of Austin. While most of the musicians popular in Austin tried to weld several strains of music into a single form, Sahm used a scatter-gun approach. A typical Sahm performance started with the Charley Pride classic, "Is Anybody Going to San Antone," reverted quickly to *chicano* and even Cajun music, descended into authentic black rhythm and blues, then encored with a dead-serious, hilarious parody of Mick Jagger singing, "Honky-Tonk Woman." Sahm was all over the stage in his better performances — plunking a piano with one hand, jamming one-on-one with the drummer, twirling a *sombrero* on the end of his guitar. His second comeback album was aptly named *Texas Tornado*.

One night in a hotel lobby I chanced across Sahm after one of those performances, and he was still damp with perspiration and wired up tight. "Look, look here," he haggled the registration clerk, "I want you to place that call to San Antonio."

"Goddammit man," the clerk finally thundered, "I am busy!"

Sahm backed off a step, trembling. "I-I worked hard tonight," he said to no one in particular, "and I was damn good." Then he flinched and scouted the room for eavesdroppers. "Listen, you'd better make that phone call," he said to the clerk, and then took his lady up the stairs toward his room, muttering to himself.

When Sahm made his Austin debut he chose the Soap Creek Saloon as a forum, and he encouraged the rockers to hang on — the pendulum would inevitably swing back from country toward rock. One of the younger performers he encouraged was Bob Brown, who along with Ed Guinn was trying to revive the Conqueroo. But Brown seemed to know the odds were now against him.

Looking back on the days in San Francisco, Brown said, "We didn't feel like we could play out there unless we were carried in on stretchers. That was the thing; music didn't sound good if it was just good music. It was supposed to blow your mind, mesmerize or milk you.

"We did that a few times, and we'd look out and there'd be people wallowing on the floor, writhing around, eyeballs rolling back in their heads. And that's what we wanted. I suppose a lot of young people took all those drugs because I did, and I really regret it now."

Brown was no more approving of the Austin scene, however. "The stuff in vogue around here is nice, sweet, boring crap. It stinks, it's just as phony as hippie blues. A bunch of funky, loose, spoiled, TV-bred long-hairs are now singing songs about wanting to ride the fence in Wyoming, you know, or retire to the cabin on the ranch. They're full of shit; they don't know what they're talking about.

"I walked in the Armadillo the other night, and it was full of guys with the same length hair and cowboys hats and cowboy boots. It's fine, I guess, I just think it's immature. But I guess that's what fads are: people groping to find mutual identity. Of course, if I were playing hillbilly country-music I'd think things were finally beginning to happen.

"But I don't know where all the magic is. I've been writing country music since I was fourteen, and what would happen to me then is what happens now. You sing a jovial, hah-hah, beer-drinking country tune, and then you sing a very romantic, serious country tune, and the reaction you get is the same. Yee-haw! Country music is whooping and hollering and pouring beer on your head. My experience was that they'd whoop and holler in the middle of a song about your dying grandmother.

"And either consciously or unconsciously," he said, "the Armadillo is quashing all other forms of music. And that really pisses me off; I feel like I invented those people."

But Brown was also aware the magic hadn't returned to the Conqueroo. When I caught the Conqueroo's act one night at Soap Creek, Brown impressed me with his songwriting, though his attempts to sing black blues were as ineffectual as those of most Anglo tenors. Guinn, who had abandoned his bass in favor of a piano, was also impressive — a mixture of blues, jazz and Fats Domino. But they were playing with a lightweight bassist, a drummer borrowed for the summer from one of the country-rockers, a lead guitarist who had been with the band less than a week and two female vocalists who seemed determined to steal Brown's thunder. And the only interested people in the small crowd seemed to be Sandy Lockett, who still liked to fiddle around with the electronics of music occasionally, and their old patron Billy Lee Brammer, who had just missed a deadline for a magazine article about Texas' marijuana dealers because his teeth got so bad they required pulling. Lockett bobbed up and down behind the amplifers, and Brammer grinned encouragement and approval through his new dentures, but Brown and Guinn were pulling dead weight. The best musicians in town had sublimated their rock & roll instincts and jumped aboard the country bandwagon, and they weren't about to stand by the roadside with a disproven band like the Conqueroo. Finally, the Conqueroo performance limped to a halt, which was what many members of the audience wanted anyway. The real attraction at Soap Creek that night was an after-hours party featuring Willie Nelson and Waylon Jennings' band.

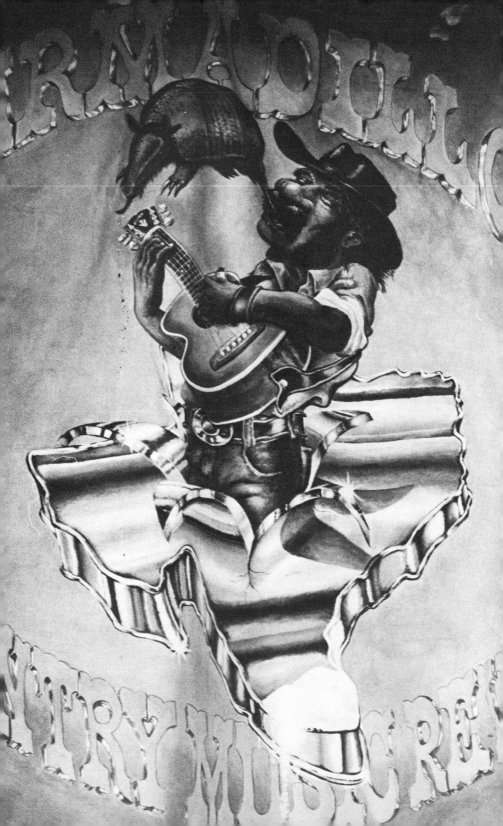

something
to do with age

If an earnest young man had set out in search of a cultural Bethlehem in the autumn of 1963, the campus of North Texas State University would have been an unlikely place to look. It was a suitcase college, an intellectual truck stop for those students who didn't want or couldn't afford to get too far away from Dallas-Fort Worth, and those who didn't quite think they could hack it at the University of Texas. Its territorial benefactor, Denton, was a miserably dull little North Texas town on the rolling plains between Dallas-Fort Worth and Oklahoma, overswollen with too damn many young people and increasingly nervous about it. Several national fraternities and sororities had chapters on campus, but it was thirty miles to the nearest liquor store, coeds had to live in house-mothered dormitories, and the football team was the patsy of the Missouri Valley Conference. There was nothing to do in Denton, and most students went home for the weekends.

But on week nights in the student union, which for some reason was called the Sub, a folk music club of eventual Austin importance was in session. The faculty sponsor of the club was Stan Alexander, the regular at Threadgill's during the days of Janis Joplin and a recent escapee of the University of Texas graduate English program. Alexander was a hillbilly blues singer who performed with another graduate student, Bill Malone, who later turned his dissertation into a fine study published by the UT Press, *The History of Hillbilly Music*.

When Alexander joined the faculty at North Texas he organized the folk club, though he had no great appetite for that kind of music. ''The first great wave of folk-pop music had passed, and the Kingston Trio was like an inexhaustible stratum yielding a single fossil form. They went on and on, with the Brothers Three, Four, Five, whatever it was, until they were rich and tired and had used up the folk music collections in the Eastern universities.'' But Alexander missed the times at Threadgill's, so he sat patiently while the students found out about their voices and instruments. It was an audacious, musically directionless gathering of aspiring performers and hangers-on, but five of them were bound for a musical reunion.

Travis Holland was a scrawny, dark-haired man in his mid-twenties, one of those persistent students who had a hard time getting his degree in math because he couldn't comprehend the sense of language. He grew up in the Red River peach orchard country surrounding Charlie, a lost burg near Wichita Falls, spoke with an ancient Texas drawl and viewed things with wry sociological humor. ''Wichita Falls.'' he used to say, ''that's a weird place, full of . . . suppressed malice,'' Holland was already a subtle, conservative guitar player, and though he could teach himself to play any piece handed him, he was most at home with a rhythm or bass guitar.

Another member, in fact the eventual president, was a teen-ager of transient Texas origin named Steve Fromholz. Fromholz was sleepy-eyed, sardonic, egocentric and thoroughly open to experience. All he knew was that college didn't interest him, and he had a sister who had cut some Sun Records during the days of Elvis Presley. Alexander didn't think Fromholz had a prayer of talent, and neither did Travis Holland, who one night kicked Fromholz's door open and said, ''I'm either gonna have to teach you how to play that banjo or take it away from you.''

Off at an introspective distance was another freshman named Michael Murphey, a Dallas youth so earnest about his Baptist religion that he decided if he was going to make a preacher, he ought to learn classical Greek so he could read the earliest texts. Murphey got interested in the classical poets instead, and when he joined the club he was already a promising guitar player and an aspiring vocal cross between Chad Mitchell and Bob Dylan. Alexander turned Murphey onto the possibilities of country music once it cleared the city limits of

Nashville, and the star pupil itched with impatience when the girls with ukuleles and autoharps had the floor. Murphey was already dead serious about making music.

Eddie Wilson was a barrel-chested sophomore philosophy student, a former "mediocre jock, hot-rodder, and general slob" from Austin. His depression-deprived parents had forced piano lessons upon him at an early age, and as a result he refused to play a note, but he thought about music a lot, and he had become acquainted with Alexander during a brief scholarly fling at the University of Texas. Spencer Perskin was a more advantaged Dallas youth who had been studying violin at the feet of an SMU virtuoso since junior high. Perskin was also learning to sing and play the guitar and harmonica.

After two years Alexander accepted another teaching position at a West Texas college called Tarleton State; the folk club dissolved, and its members scattered. Perskin structured a poem in an underground newspaper which, if read conventionally, said something rather tame, but if read horizontally, instructed the reader to violate himself. A controversial figure in Denton, Perskin headed south to Austin where he put together a group called Shiva's Headband which became the last cult band at the Vulcan Gas Company. Perskin lent his voice, harmonica, lead guitar, electric fiddle and even electric jug to a conglomerate sound which incorporated blues, country and jazzy self-indulgence, and attracted a rabid Texas following and a California recording offer in excess of $50,000.

Wilson's path took him completely away from the music business for a while. He met a pretty girl named Jeannie in a Shakespeare class and married her, enjoyed his stay in Denton, then after graduation moved deep into South Texas where he coached athletics at a black high school while Jeannie taught in the white school across the road. That didn't last long, because, according to Wilson: "The white folks fired me for being a nigger-lover, among other things. They said I had a motorcycle image, and what really got on their nerves was that my football team won district and my track team won second in state, and none of my black athletes would sign freedom-of-choice blanks to go to the white high school the next year. They figured I was a stumbling block."

Wilson stumbled next into a lobbyist trainee position with the United States Brewers Association. Miserable by early 1970, and for lack of anything better to do, Wilson had decided to go to law school. But then

49

Perskin showed up at his house in Austin one day and stayed six weeks, and abruptly, Wilson was managing Shiva's Headband. He knew nothing whatsoever about the music business, which was exactly what the distrusting acid-rockers wanted, and Wilson admitted later that his management probably contributed to the band's early demise.

Wilson was thrown into association with the forces behind the Vulcan Gas Company, among them Jim Franklin, a hardcore freak and eccentric from the Galveston Bay town of LaMarque whose youthful life was almost ruined by interest in theater, art, black girls and drugs. He won first in state in competitive poetry reading, which, "needless to say, was overshadowed by the failure of the football team to win state. That was my first experience with gross mysticism at the football level. The coach called the student body together after the loss and said it was our fault for not supporting the team and afterward broke into tears. He later died of cancer." Franklin also contributed large paintings of African and Galveston black families to the high school library, which naturally enough were taken down when the school integrated. After graduation he painted sets and acted in summer stock in Kerrville for awhile, spent a year in New York, then returned to Austin in the mid-sixties, where one night he took his first tab of acid, asked for a razor intending to shave (thereby frightening the dickens out of his friends), then went for a walk. Accosted by a police patrolman who asked for some identification, Franklin unzipped his pants and wound up in jail. His parents and attorney convinced the authorities he was a good boy who had simply fallen into bad company, and he returned to Galveston, where he hijacked his father's pickup and headed for a Bob Dylan concert in Austin, only to run afoul of the law once again. This time they found a lid of marijuana in the glovebox. After that he fell into the hands of a Galveston County doctor, who administered eighteen therapeutic shock treatments.

(Whether all that has credibility, incidentally, is open to question. Franklin likes to put people on, a habit which, unless one knows him well, renders everything he says suspect. One week he will swear he is a lineal descendant of Benjamin Franklin and boast that he once modeled for Clearasil commercials, and the next forget he ever said it.)

Franklin was a live-in hanger-on and roustabout in the latter days of the Vulcan, but he also provided some of the graphic arts for the establishment and much of the defiant spirit. "The guy who ran the hardware store across the street sold Charles Whitman his ammunition, got all kinds of attention in the national press, and after that his gun business boomed like hell,'' Franklin said. ''The first thing he did was slice up and sell the columns of his building, which was really a fine piece of architecture, then he started complaining about us — we were the bad influence on the community.''

Franklin was out of state when the Vulcan finally went under, and when he came back Wilson had secured the abandoned armory in south Austin, so Franklin moved his mattress into the new attic. Shortly afterward they were joined by Mike Tolleson. The son of an East Texas lumber dealer, Tolleson had bachelor and law degrees from SMU, but he was bitten by the music-business bug at the undergraduate level when he tried to generate a campus radio station, and again at the law-school level when he donated his student-loan check to a demo tape by a Dallas group called the Exotics. Nothing came of the effort, though Monument Records expressed some interest, and Tolleson went off to the University of London to study international law. He found the courses repetitive of those at SMU, and his interests revolved toward R.D. Laing, the Beatles, and the international legal aspects of the communications industry. He designed a study program at the London School of Economics, but soon ran out of money and signed on as an editorial and research adviser for a Mexican diplomat who was writing a book on international economics. Tolleson watched Apple Records, met John Lennon and hung out in an underground arts laboratory for young Britons of artistic interest and intent.

When the book was finished Tolleson fled to Switzerland to recuperate and decided to return to Texas and open a similar arts laboratory in Dallas. Instead, he again contributed his capital to the Outcasts, an offshoot of the Exotics. Tolleson knew Snuff Garrett, the Wichita Falls version of Dick Clark who had moved on to another disc jockey's job in Dallas then migrated to Los Angeles, where he was the producer of Gary Lewis and the Playboys. Garrett relayed news of the Outcasts to one of those playboys, Leon Russell, who hit Dallas with inspiringly long hair, listened sagely and trucked the band off to California. Once again, not much came of it, but one of the younger Outcasts, Marc Benno, stayed on and surfaced during Russell's *Asylum Choir* phase.

In August of 1970 Tolleson went to Austin for a weekend, heard about the Armadillo, and left Wilson a job application form. Though three or four others were involved in the Armadillo's inception and the staff eventually swelled to over thirty, Wilson, Franklin and Tolleson became the cutting edge of the organization. Wilson was the boss-man, the booming voice out front who talked back when Los Angeles wheeler-dealers shouted at him, who treated musicians fairly, who knew what to say to a curious press. Franklin was the house painter, spiritual guru, and *bon vivant* onstage. He decorated his room with remarkable clutter, a dusty American flag, a black cat named Charlie Pride, a five-foot-eight-inch boa constrictor and a feathery bird skeleton trapped in a cage. Franklin also developed an onstage routine and designed the costumes for it — a five-foot cowboy hat, a giant Planters Peanut suit, a suit of unconventional armor with an armadillo mask. "Most emcees don't master any ceremonies," he said. "They don't have any ceremony to master." He also turned his armadillo art into a profitable business. He designed the covers for five nationally-distributed albums, one of which appeared in the Whitney Museum in New York. His murals started appearing on new storefronts all over Austin, and his T-shirts portraying a nearsighted armadillo humping the state capitol dome eventually sold, under consignment, for $4.95. Tolleson was the quiet, thinking man behind the scenes, a balding man who was always running his hand over his scalp as he charted the next day's course of action.

But for the time being there could be no specialization. Though Perskin and Shiva's Headband called the new club home and infused a healthy portion of their contract bonus into the project, the Armadillo was a mad scramble for survival that demanded all hands everywhere. The staff hammered and nailed a stage together, dragged in some carpet scraps, consigned some apple juice and pumpkin bread and opened with three top local bands, but the odds seemed against them. The Vulcan had after all failed, and it had once been a success. What made these people think they could pull it off? How were they different? Moreover, their timing seemed to be all wrong. The summer of 1970 was a hot one in Texas, and a sluggish malaise gripped all sectors of the Austin community. Johnson was out of office, the Sharpstown political scandals were just beginning to surface, the professors were out of town, the everyday people doggedly drove the freeway to work. The malaise even visited the sector professedly seized by the spirit of love. "About the time Armadillo World Headquarters opened," Wilson recalled, "the sub-culture here, the alternative culture — the counter-culture I believe it's called — was really in a kind of quandary. There was a lot of dissension among people who were in basic philosophical agreement about things social and political. There wasn't a focal point — and just very little productive energy.

"That summer we started was really a bad one from my point of view. There was just a lot of unhappy, frustrated people all over town. And we didn't do anything to help it — we gave a lot of people something to bitch about. The Vulcan had been gone for a few months, and we provided the straight people with something to complain about, and we even gave the counter-culture a chance to bellyache, at least the more politically-minded among them. They'd stand back and scrutinize what we were doing and try to decide whether it was politically viable. But we really didn't have time to participate in those discussions because we were working our asses off."

Though the odds were against the Armadillo's success, a few things were working in its favor. Its location was much more fortunate than that of the Vulcan. Now dammed into a polluted town lake, the Colorado River intersected Austin, and the southern side of the river was almost a community in itself, historically relegated to the Mexicans and lower-middle class whites, though it had begun to experience the long-hair invasion. The only neighbors the Armadillo frequents could bother were the young blacks who hung out at the roller rink, a former candidate for county constable who ran the nearby paint and body shop and a few workers in a Social Security office. If Austin had to have its hippies, establishment feeling seemed to run, at least now they would be out of sight and the downtown area. Like the Vulcan, the Armadillo had an understanding landlord, and a happy-go-lucky clique of Austin writers and artists called Mad Dog Inc. gave the Armadillo a thousand-dollar shot in the arm. But most of all, the new rock & roll joint had that name.

The strangest animal this side of Australia, the armadillo was a curious little rodent easily victimized by highway traffic. It had ears like those of a rhinoceros, a tail like that of an opossum, a proboscis somewhat like that of an anteater and a hard protective shell around its vitals that scraped against rocks as it waddled along. It looked like a meek, miniature version of one of those reptilian, prehistoric monsters that Tarzan used to ride into the Lost Valley. An armadillo was either too stupid or too smart to domesticate, and if startled in a roadside ditch it was apt to jump straight up in the air and run headlong into a hubcap, knocking itself out. An armadillo tried to avoid getting too far away from a hole in the roots of a brushy tree, and if it established a handhold on those roots, Hercules himself would have had a hard time breaking its grip. Yet if an armadillo was captured it would sit in total uncomprehending silence in a corner and would not fight for its life.

When Franklin and Wilson chose the armadillo as a motif they ignored the latter facet of its character, focusing instead on its more symbolic qualities. In the early sixties a cartoonist named Glenn Whitehead had employed the armadillo in a university satire magazine called the *Ranger*, and a Texas alumnus responded, "I don't know what you mean by all those armadillos you're using, but you better watch out. I'm keeping an eye on you." But Franklin said he got independently interested in the armadillo. It seemed to embody the plight of Texas freaks — reclusive, unwanted, vulnerable, scorned. And slow-moving, added Wilson: "We're deep enough southwest that there's a kind of *mañana* attitude around here that drives people from New York and L.A. up the wall."

What else? Franklin shrugged. "Something to do with age. I like the way things look when they get real old. New York, for example, has a certain patina to it that you don't find in Houston."

That was the key to it. The armadillo was walking, breathing evidence of times that were different. It was an ancient animal oblivious to modern times. Also, it was a creature whose name had drifted into the Anglo-Saxon tongue by way of Rome, France and Spain, which implied a more graceful way of going about things, and its habitat was the American Southwest. And because of Wilson's rock & roll joint and Franklin's art, the armadillo became a symbol for a regional movement, a virtual state of mind. One freak drifter who had settled in Austin was given to braking to a quick halt when he saw one of the magic animals and sprinting off in pursuit, yelling, " *'Diller, 'diller!''* He said he wanted to export them to North Carolina. Of course, like Franklin, he was under the influence of LSD. An out-of-work television producer visualized a rock movie that would begin with an armadillo waddling across a two-lane rural highway straight into the path of a roaring diesel truck — cut to Commander Cody and his Lost Planet Airmen in full cry — then after several reels return to the same armadillo reaching the end of its perilous journey, with the

In order to stablize the revenue flow, the Armadillos solicited volunteer labor to build an outdoor beer garden and restaurant. Beer sales inside the hall generated more income than apple juice, but it altered the nature of the club.

Stan Alexander (below), a college English teacher and a veteran of the Janis Joplin days at Threadgill's, sponsored a folk music club at North Texas State University in 1963. Members of that club included Michael Murphey, Steve Fromholz, Travis Holland, and Eddie Wilson (right), the booming voice out front at Armadillo World Headquarters.

Jim Franklin became the staff artist, master of ceremonies, and spiritual guru of the new club. His graphic art created a visual cult of the nine-banded armadillo and his murals soon appeared on storefronts all over Austin.

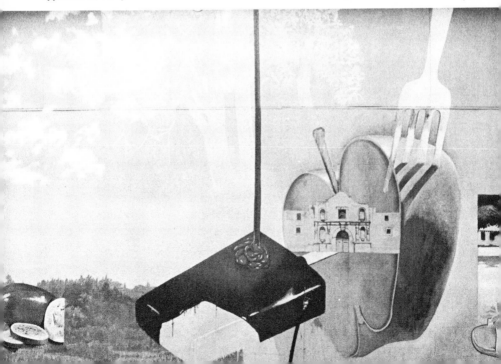

An attorney who once helped a Mexican diplomat write a book on international economics, Mike Tolleson (right) was the quiet, thinking man behind the scenes. He envisioned a community arts laboratory with multimedia potential, but for the moment the Armadillo was still a concert hall, a coveted gig for nationally known artists like Waylon Jennings (below left) and Van Morrison.

semi mysteriously overturned on its side, wheels spinning and radiator heat rising. The armadillo even threatened the University of Texas. A tongue-in-cheek and window-decal movement to change the name of the University mascot from Longhorn to Armadillo got under way, and the University's age-old rival Texas A&M couldn't let that opportunity slip by. At a Thanksgiving Day football game, the Aggies stampeded a herd of orange-painted armadillos into the ranks of the Texas marching band.

Yet Armadillo reality was another matter. The armory was cavernous, filled with acoustical dead spots, universal lack of comfort, atmospheric misery in winter and summer and managerial inexperience. The organizers of the Armadillo tried to run the place as a haven for local talent, but they found if they charged enough for the local bands to pay expenses, nobody came. Yet if they let everybody in for next to nothing, that wouldn't support the overhead either. Finally they took the inevitable, calculated risk. In late 1971 they booked John Sebastian for a one-night stand, and the concert lost $5,000. The Armadillo skinned back down to a skeleton crew and tried to hang on to the roots of the tree.

Murphey, Fromholz, Holland and the other country-oriented musicians didn't come to Austin because of Armadillo World Headquarters. In fact, all but two or three of the major performers now shun the place, or else they are shunned. But because most of them played there at one time or another, and because the Armadillo was the favorite hangout of an Austin audience hooked on their hybrid form of music, the Armadillo gained the music industry foothold: a reputation. It was commended to country fans by Townsend Miller, a Merrill-Lynch stockbroker with a journalistic background who wrote a gratis country column for the *Austin Statesman* and contributed occasionally to *Country Music* ; to rock fans by Chet Flippo, a much more talented writer and graduate student who turned Armadillo journalism into a contributing editorship with *Rolling Stone*.

However, survival in the music business required money more than kind words, and before the Armadillo could get to its feet the management reluctantly had to purchase a beer license, accept a $20,000 gift from a friend and turn the outdoor area into a beer garden and restaurant which kept money coming during off-nights and the summer. Eddie Wilson liked to tell the story of how the Armadillo's neighbor, the body shop operator Doug Scales, watched the construction of the beer garden, said I'll be damned I didn't know hippies would work and marched over to shake somebody's hand and welcome the Armadillo to the neighborhood. What Wilson didn't say, and what the former constable didn't know, was that the artisans were drawing daily wages of ten dollars and free beer and dope.

After that, the Armadillo took off. The stage moved from one end of the hall to the other, the acoustics were improved, heaters were installed. Plans were launched to air-condition the place, raise the comfort level, and in Wilson's words, transform the Armadillo from the world's smallest concert hall to the world's largest club. Jim Franklin went off to tour Europe and emcee for Freddie King, and Mike Tolleson started talking in terms of support systems and Phase II. His dream of an arts laboratory was moving closer to reality. The Armadillo was hosting ballet companies and Mozart string quartets, a new recording studio was under lock and key, publishing and talent management plans were outlined, and Tolleson wanted to move into audio-visual production. He planned to utilize the half-inch videotape talents of an Austin public-access channel and a similar organization of expatriate Houstonites who ran a cable-TV outlet in the rural town of Taylor, serving that community's needs by televising high school football, affording Rose Parade treatment to a local rodeo parade and interviewing every first-grader in town. However, Tolleson's approach to an arts laboratory had changed. "A lot of people have very good ideas and want to put those ideas in motion, but many young people have very negative perspectives toward money and business. Their prejudice limits their potential. I feel now if I'm going to take on something that I feel is very important, the most important thing is trying to see that it works, which entails getting into the financial and business aspects of it."

Wilson said he wanted to throw in the towel many times, and he spent a lot of time apologizing when a band came to the Armadillo for the first time, but he was booking acts that he once could barely afford to phone. He was able to do that because word had spread among performers that the Armadillo was one of the finest places to play in the country. The appeal of the Armadillo to performers might be broken down into four factors: the carpet, the coke machine, the lack of cops and the crowd.

One of the Austin sidemen said of the carpet-scrap onstage, "It's very intangible, very hard to explain. Most places you play you're standing on a hardwood stage and it's all very unfamiliar. It's like the band fragments into separate entities because of the unfamiliarity.But that carpet at the Armadillo gives a band cohesiveness. You can dig your heels into it and make believe you're playing at home."

The coke machine's appeal was very simple. It was stocked with long-necked bottles of Texas beer that cost a dime.

The absence of cops was more of a mystery. The state of Texas was notorious in its intolerance of things counter-cultural. Until recently conviction for mere possession of a seed or stem of marijuana carried a sentence of two years to life, and many Texas prosecutors and juries still looked upon a marijuana dealer as a cross between Satan and a Red Chinese arsonist. (That may have something to do with capitalistic jealousy. A lid of grass cost ten dollars in Texas ten years ago, and it still costs ten dollars.) But though the sight and smell of flagrant marijuana use was known to stop Armadillo newcomers in their tracks, the Austin police left the place alone, possibly because if they conducted a raid a large-scale riot might ensue, possibly because some off-duty policemen and politicians might be among the take. The only time the cops were known to invade the Armadillo was one Halloween night when pumpkins starting flying.

But the most obvious plus was the crowd: mobile, shouting, native-costumed young people beside themselves with beer, music and the thought of being Texans. The hatted, booted, bellowing mobs scared the daylights out of Bette Midler, exacted smiles of karmic delight from John McLaughlin and the Mahavishnu Orchestra, enticed Billy Joe Shaver to play several times for free and lured John Prine from the atmospheric comfort of Chicago to the ninety-degree early-summer heat of the Armadillo. People in the audience said Prine was too drunk to play. Actually he was on the verge of a heatstroke, but he had nothing but kind words for Austin and the Armadillo after his performance.

"I'm not really geared for a full-dress Armadillo rap," Wilson said the morning of our interview. "I'm so damned tired." Looking back at the origins of the Armadillo, he said,"Local musicians were desperate because there were so very few places to play, and they were into an extremely noncommercial sort of music.

"The paradox of all that was Shiva's Headband, because they came very close to being extremely commercial, in the sense that they were, throughout Texas, a kind of Underground Heroic Band. They stood for a lot of things that everybody thought a community band should stand for. It was like a microcosm of the San Francisco scene here. The people on the street needed to feel that their fellow street hippies who were making music were into it in a very pure sort of way. Largely a bullshit rap.

"Frankly, I don't believe in free music. The only free music is when I'm picking for myself on my porch. When it gets any more complicated than that, suddenly it's not really free music anymore. There's no such thing as a free concert. The bands may play for free, but it costs somebody something. The typical scam for a benefit is that, all right, the bands need to do this for exposure — not only exposure before a large number of people, but exposure in connection with a cause. Kinda like Mickey Mantle using Right Guard, so it's okay for everybody to use it. But it's not always what it's cracked up to be. A lot of bands overexpose themselves to the point they have to go months without work because everybody's tired of hearing them."

Didn't that kind of outlook alienate a lot of people?

"We get bad-mouthed just an awful lot, and I'm beyond the point of worrying about it. We get flack about everything from ticket prices to our attitude. We know the source of our problems, and we can't explain them to everybody. People in Austin are so goddamned spoiled that they'll bitch like crazy about paying three-fifty or four dollars to see a show in a place where they can drink beer and be loose and not have cops make them sit in their seats, when the same show in an auditorium would cost them five or six dollars.

"People didn't bitch when we charged four dollars for Mose Allison, and I almost hoped they would. Because if people think four dollars is too high to see Mose Allison, I'll be glad to explain to them that the reason it's four dollars is that we don't want them there. We want people who are Mose Allison freaks, or who've at least paid enough that they don't want to get thrown out."

Why did the Armadillo happen when and where it did?

"In Austin a huge percentage of people are here because they want to be here. And because the university is so large and the off-campus community is related somehow in its distant past to the university, the musical sophistication on a percentage basis is higher here than elsewhere in the state.

"You get 1500 people in Houston who really appreciate an act and you get 1500 people in Austin who really appreciate an act, and those crowds are noticeably different. The people in Austin are looser. They're not as worried about being shot by a cop when they leave the hall. The only place I've ever had a gun pulled on me was in Houston — by a cop — and I've got a lot of friends who left Houston because they didn't feel safe down there.

"The overall mellowness of the situation here is a result, I think, of the power structure here not having the time to jack with the people in the street as much as they do in other places. The power structure here has always been very Washington-oriented, and I think that power structure is ours, or at least it will be in the next two or three years. We've just about inherited it, at least at the street level. In two years, we'll have that city council.

"People start talking about Berkeley and little towns in northern California and Colorado and Kansas where the freaks got the city council. But it never happened in a capital city of 250,000 with a university of 40,000 in a state that has cities like Dallas and Houston. When it happens here it's going to shake the foundations of this country, and it's going to shake them for the best."

What would the development of a full-scale music industry do to Austin?

"The final product is a pretty good reflection of the desirability of the industry. We're not talking about something that will result in new concrete highways and high-rise apartments. It needs to happen. It fact it's got to happen, and it doesn't have to be bad. A music industry would be wonderful for Austin because it doesn't pollute and it doesn't get in the way visually. About fifty million dollars put into the music business over the next few years could be almost invisible. It would take shape in the form of studios and graphic departments and publicity departments all over town, providing work for artists, pickers and any number of hangers-on.

"The main pollutant of the music industry is the carpetbagger. We're going to see a lot of them here in the next few months. We've already seen a lot of them — all kinds of hustlers coming through here looking for a shuck and a jive, a way to get their foot in the door. ''Personally, I'm looking forward to teaching the Austin establishment something about the music business. The bankers here are just as naive and ignorant as we were in the beginning. Big money is going to come in and put that money into Austin and take it right back out again if the people in Austin don't snap to the fact that, goddamn, this is better than a new rock quarry or Westinghouse plant.''

What part would the Armadillo play in it?

''I suppose the key to our whole attitude here is our hope to keep changing as often as we possibly can toward greater quality and diversification. Small businesses are supposed to specialize in order to survive, but the specialty of Armadillo World Headquarters is spreading out and expanding. From a business standpoint, that makes very little sense. Up until recently there was absolutely no reason to try to keep the place open. We had proved definitely, on paper, that the place couldn't make it financially. But we're still here. Somebody must like us.''

What about the trail boss himself?

''I don't want to perpetuate the Bill Graham myth that behind every place like this there has to be one driving personality that keeps it together, and when he quits it's all got to fold. That's rat-race horse-shit. If I can't leave the place and have it still continue to serve a purpose in the community and be run by the people who actually ran it all along, and if the people who work here don't learn and move on and change their interests because they're here, then the place will get just as stale and boring as any place gets when it's manned by people working eight-to-five.''

Jim Franklin made me uncomfortable. I suspected he saw through me as clearly as I thought I saw through him, but then again, neither of us were sure what to make of the other. Probably we didn't interest each other very much. ''Who were the major influences on your art?'' I asked.

''DaVinci, Michelangelo and Rembrandt, in that order.''

A pretentious question deserves a pretentious answer. I groped for a more penetrating query but someone caught Franklin's attention and he excused himself. He paused at the table long enough to show me a cheeping yellow chick cupped in the palms of his hands. ''They just brought in some great food for my boa constrictor, so I'm going up to put it in the cage."

"Where is all this headed?" I asked when he returned. Franklin gave me a blank look. "I don't know."

When I interviewed Tolleson I asked if he thought his Armadillo arts laboratory would ever come about.

"To go into all these other areas," he said, "will require the talents of more people. Right now our operation is about fifty percent out of control, and unless we establish some kind of order, it will be impossible."

Did that mean the helter-skelter, all-hands-everywhere days were over at the Armadillo?

Tolleson didn't like the drift of the question but he met it head-on.

"Yes, when you start defining organization, you have to define who makes what kind of decisions."

Of course, Tolleson was right. A pack of Cub Scouts could pretty well have the run of things in the kitchen of their den mother, but they were liable to get flattened if they got out in the street and started trying to direct traffic. If the Armadillo was to realize its potential, the management had to run it as a business. Friendly freaks waving peace signs could no longer be allowed to crash the gate, and in the interest of introducing a favorite band called Little Feat to an uneducated Austin audience, it became advisable to drop radio hints that Linda Ronstadt would make a special guest appearance, thereby packing the house at three dollars a head, even if she sang only four or five songs. The Armadillo was simply yielding to the demands of bigness and ambition, which was certainly no sin. But with bigness too often came depersonalization. The last time I dialed the number of the Armadillo a pretty voice that I hoped did not belong to Jeannie Wilson assumed control of the conversation from the outset: *"Hello. This is Armadillo World Headquarters with another line-up of fantastic musical entertainment for you. Tonight we have Conqueroo and Lea Ann and the Bizarros. Admission one dollar. Friday and Saturday we have the Cosmic Cowboy himself, Michael Murphey, previewing the songs from his new album. Admission three-fifty in advance, four-fifty at the door . . ."*

She forgot to add, *"This is a recording."*

the music
takes over

The associated success of Austin music and Armadillo World Headquarters spawned a number of music-business ventures, all giddy with hope, all rooted in the reassuring faith that Austin would one day be a major music center. All the people involved in the rush of musical activity were realistic enough to know their ventures were risky, and naive and brash enough to think they could make them work.

The foremost case in point was Larry Watkins, a blond man in his mid-twenties with a sleepy look and easy-going manner who grew up in Waco, attended Abilene Christian College for a year, then transferred to the University of Texas, where the social chairmanship of his fraternity positioned him on the consumer end of the booking business. He crossed over to labor part-time for an Austin booking agency for a while, worked his way into a partnership, later bought his partner out, then threw the agency away. "The key to any business is reputation," he said. "If you perform a service for someone you ought to derive some satisfaction from it, and in return the people you please ought to come back to see you. But if you're booking bands you're just a voice on the phone to a guy at the college or bar. It's strictly first-come, first-serve in the booking business, and I wasn't about to throw my life away doing that."

Eddie Wilson said he didn't manage bands yet because he wouldn't be ready for it until he knew a big wheel in every major recording company on a first-name basis, but Watkins figured that wasn't going to happen unless he made a name for himself first. In early 1972 he launched an enterprise called Moon Hill Management in his little six-room house in north Austin. Though he called himself a manager, he was in truth still a booking agent too broke to pay his bills until he courted and won the business of Rusty Wier, Kenneth Threadgill, Steve Fromholz, B.W. Stevenson, Michael Murphey and Willis Alan Ramsey, the latter two of whom, being temperamental sorts, would only consent to handshake agreements. That was a taboo in the music business, but Watkins had a way of assessing each of his client's eccentricities and gaining their confidence. None of them were stars to the extent they needed a New York or Hollywood big-shot walking point for them, but they all had record deals in the works and were big enough to develop migraine headaches if they tried to handle their own affairs. Watkins was available, and he was ready and willing to do their dirty work for them.

Watkins accepted two other clients—Bill and Bonnie Hearne, a virtually blind couple who whanged the guitar and piano, sang country and appeared almost ready to make their own move—and hired a young woman to book bands which were promising but did not yet require the services of a manager. Watkins gained a moneyed Dallas partner, a Harvard law graduate named Jim Devlin, and as the stock of their clients rose Watkins was able to convert the little house on 45th street into a working office and move his living quarters to a split-level house overlooking the Colorado River west of town. He hired a full-time accountant to keep the books in order, a Phi Beta Kappa English graduate to organize a song-publishing branch and a pretty girl with a flashing smile named Patti Ricker to answer the phone. Patti was a talented and promising singer in her own right, but thus far, the Austin music movement had been largely sexist. Several girls in Austin had band assignments and devoted followings, but a male hippie turned country singer was hard enough to market. Nobody was willing to take a big chance on a freaky female singer. Linda Ronstadt had already cornered that market.

Watkins said that as a manager he was charged with his clients' recording, publishing and general business interests, but what that translated to was staying one step ahead of their lives and keeping things organized. On a typical day at Moon Hill Watkins would be called upon to purchase Fromholz's Texas auto tags and forward them to Colorado; bare every book in the place in order to procure Master Charge cards for his clients; try at the last minute to fulfill Ramsey's belated request for a spring concert tour; and explain to Murphey's band how they were going to be in San Antonio on Monday, Lawrence, Kansas on Wednesday, Northern Kentucky State on Friday, New York City and Hartford, Connecticut over the weekend, Nashville the following Tuesday and Wednesday, Shawnee, Oklahoma on Thursday, and Lubbock, Texas on Saturday, after two weeks of motel rooms, rented cars, airline reservations and a rendezvous with Fromholz in Nashville.

Watkins and his associates seemed to enjoy their work. They were barely old enough to grow mustaches, but they went about their tasks with discipline enough and seemed pretty sure of themselves. Country-rock reeled off the stereo unit in the back room, nobody yelled or hurried, visiting dogs wandered in to snuff at a golden-haired spaniel, Joe Cocker, who had the run of the place. I asked Watkins if he had any qualms about the growth of Austin music.

"As the music scene here grows it's going to bring in a lot of people, and they can't all be good. But for me, right now, it's good. As I grow in my business there'll be people who won't like me because I didn't help them along the way, but you can only do so much for so many people. I'm not into taking on everybody that comes to town. But it's going to get to that. I'm gearing myself for it, but I'm not looking forward to it."

Watkins ushered me into the other room to listen to the new Fromholz album. He wound on a new reel and Fromholz came on backed by too many instruments, sounding like somebody other than himself. Joe Cocker walked in the room and flopped on his side.

"Fromholz takes him right out," Watkins said, nodding at his dog. "Every time we play one of Steve's tapes Joe likes it so much he just sacks out."

"Maybe it bores him," a subordinate suggested.

"No, that's not it," Watkins said. "Watch him. He may look like he's asleep but when he listens to Fromholz, he taps his left hind foot on the floor. Steve's the only one that affects him that way."

Austin radio was rather slow to get involved in Austin music. In the early seventies Austin radio was dominated by the station owned by

Lady Bird Johnson. Scattered around town were one entrenched AM competitor, a less entrenched AM competitor, an excellent public-owned classical music station and several struggling AM-FM stations with limited hours and wattage and programing which ranged from pop to easy listening to shit-kicker country. Then in the spring of 1971 along came KRMH, a twenty-four hour, 100,000 watt FM station positioned between Austin and the nearby college town of San Marcos. Good Karma, as the station was inevitably called, hit the air waves with a lot of money, forties and fifties radio serials and considerable promise, but the programing was limited to Dylan oldies and *Billboard* approved rock, and at first, the advertising spots were enough to send even the most avid listener to the great outdoors. They were the standard pleas to purchase this product or that service, only they were couched in quasi-hip lingo, which made them more obnoxious. KRMH made one premature overture toward Austin music in the spring of 1972 when a new program director named Larry Yurdin designed and aired a "Texas Special." The special was a day-long assembly of rambling interviews interspersed with music that tried to acquaint the audience with Texas' surprisingly rich musical tradition. The man who signed the KRMH paychecks was interested in money, however, not tradition, and when he came back in town he surveyed what had happened to his station and fired Yurdin and his staff. He said they were playing too little Elton John.

KRMH ventured into country-rock, in fact, only when it was rendered advisable by the competition. At KOKE, the mainstream country station whose disc jockey refused to play Janis Joplin's recording of "Me and Bobby McGee" because it wasn't country enough, general manager Ken Moyer had an AM station that was doing all right and an FM station that was going nowhere. Moyer was approached in 1970 by a group of long-hairs who thought Austin needed a hardcore rock station, but he wanted his two stations to bear some relationship to each other, so he sent them over to the easy-listening station manager, who turned his FM turntables over to the freaks for about a year then abruptly locked them out of the building one night.

Moyer first started toying with the idea of an original format after observing freaks who stomped their boot heels to country music at the '72 Dripping Springs Reunion, but one Houston group delivered a tape that was almost entirely rock, and Moyer gave up on the idea until he was approached by Rusty Bell, a heavyset jock for one of the AM pop stations. Moyer was still hesitant. Austinite recorded music would barely fill an afternoon of air time, but Bell argued there was enough enlightened country from Nashville and enough country-oriented rock from elsewhere to launch something absolutely new. Bell treated Moyer to some Flying Burrito Brothers and scouted through a stack of albums set aside by KOKE jocks because the artists on the covers had long hair, and a "Progressive Country" format pioneered about the time the Texas Special derailed. At first the new format was limited to weekends, and it still made way on mornings for a Spanish-language program, but KOKE bumper stickers portraying a goat-roper and goat began to move about Austin streets, and the audacious challenger kicked a healthy dent in the ratings of KRMH.

The pioneers of the new format admitted they had no idea what they were doing at first, but because the Austin audience had begun to respond to the native country-rockers, KOKE's progressive country caught on. "Progressive country evolved as the term for what we were doing because it wasn't country-country, and it wasn't modern-country either," Moyer said. "Actually, progressive is not so applicable to the music, because if anything it is regressive, going all the way back to bluegrass. What's progressive is the delivery. It's not a hard-sell deal—it's an easier delivery with spot clusters and long music segments, which is more of a progressive-type FM format."

The secret to the success of KOKE, however, was that Bell proposed a very liberal definition of country music. What mattered was not the identity or hair length or philosophy of the singers, but the kind of instruments that accompanied them. If anything remotely country could be discerned in a recording, it qualified. George Harrison was sometimes accompanied by a bottleneck guitar, which sounded almost like a steel, and even Paul Simon's "Baker Duncan" song about a youth driving down the upper New England coast toward a first piece of ass was fair game.

Though he was still in his twenties, Bell had been in radio for almost a decade, in enough places to conclude "different geographical spots make for different musical atmospheres." Bell contended that KOKE had stumbled across the right sound for the Austin audience, and added he saw no reason why progressive country couldn't spread. "Janis Joplin is dead, Jimi Hendrix is dead, Jim Morrison is dead," Bell said, "and those were the leaders of rock music. And rock music is just as dead. They left it to people like Three Dog Night and the Osmond Brothers. There's really no such thing as creativity in rock music right now. I don't know what will happen next. Something always comes along, but it's not gonna take anything away from us. As a matter of fact it might be just exactly what we're doing."

Asked if he thought Austin would actually become a major music center, Bell said, "The key to that is the recording companies. Some of the major studios are reportedly thinking about coming in, and if a couple of them actually arrive, then Austin's on its way."

Austin already had one fledgling studio, though it was hardly major yet. Jay Podolnick, a former rock musician with an Austin group called Mariani which signed a contract and recorded an album only to lose it in a legal hassle, wanted a studio for his own group's use, but that required an investment of around $20,000, so he and a couple of partners raised the money and sank it instead into a sixteen-track recorder and later a twenty-four-track machine. Podolnick hung around Los Angeles long enough to figure he had the hang of the recording business, procured an Austin location in an abandoned dry-cleaning establishment, and called the new venture Odyssey.

Odyssey's first major project was a tape of Steve Fromholz which turned out rather badly and proved a waste of Moon Hill Management's money, but then Jerry Jeff Walker, who had a long-standing aversion to sterile recording studios, announced he wanted to record his comeback album at Odyssey. Walker's New York producer and manager, Michael Brovsky, was taken aback by the news Odyssey didn't even have a mixing board, electronic things kept going haywire, Walker and his sidemen usually reported for work about midnight, and part of the album was subsequently recorded in New York. But the roughness and the funkiness of the recordings at Odyssey were the album's virtue. The best cuts on the album were spontaneous, cocaine-crazed yet smooth pieces of music that often seemed to scale the heights of orgasm, only to fall completely apart at the end.

"I'd like for Austin musicians to record here," Podolnick said, "but if they can't, and they can get a gig somewhere else, fine. I don't want anybody in here that doesn't want to be in here."

Podolnick and his partners were trying to work the kinks out of their expensive setup and prepare for the grand opening, at which time the name of the company would change to Lone Star. "When it's finished you won't be able to beat it," Podolnick said. "When it's finished it'll be a dynamite studio. The party we'll have when we open will be really heavy, it'll probably make the *Stone*."

Approaching Austin from another medium were two brothers from East Texas, Alan and Michael Price. Alan was an outgoing Vietnam veteran who looked like Smokey the Bear with a beard. Michael was the older brother, a man in his mid-thirties who was a high-salaried publisher's representative for several companies before he decided he'd better quit lying about his education and get a finance and economics degree at the University of Houston. He started watching the SDS, pulled a hitch in a New Mexico commune, then went back to work with a different outlook. In 1972 both Prices were on the road representing *Rolling Stone*.

"That's when we decided we'd do a magazine," Alan said. "Man, those fools were making a killing."

Michael became the publisher, found a good editor in *Crawdaddy* originator Paul Williams, procured the rights as Timothy Leary's publisher, attracted financial support from a group including comedian George Carlin, and came out in early 1973 with a slick, impressive publication called *Rallying Point*. Though the magazine was based in New York, its editors professed interest in all parts of the country and hoped for a quick nationwide circulation. But instead of the initial printing of 200,000 originally envisioned, they ran into the paper shortage, and were able to put only 5000 copies on the stands in Austin and Boston. "That's the establishment man," Michael said. "He's at the point where he can economize by not doing anything new. And anything new is you and me, so we get economized down. So that means we have to do our own thing. That's why we want *Rallying Point*."

The older Price said he got interested in Austin when he learned of Bobby Bridger's scholarly music project of several years' research. Bridger had been at work for almost a decade restructuring the tale of the mountain man Jim Bridger's travels through the Rockies and had written a fifty-five-minute poem punctuated by songs that he wanted to record as his next album. "What he wants to promote is the story," Price said. "He doesn't give a damn if he sells a record or anything else. That's what really made me think, 'Austin.' "

Price resented any suggestions of carpetbaggage. A New York-based writer named Dave Hickey had written a piece for *Country Music* which maintained Willie Nelson, Waylon Jennings and the other Nashville rebels were different because they were born country on the west side of the Mississippi and often forgot "to go watery at the knees at the mention of Jeff Davis," and moreover were "just about the only folks in Nashville who will walk into a room where there's a guitar and a Wall Street Journal and pick up the guitar." It was a fine piece of writing that generated something of a furor among Nashville country observers, and in response Townsend Miller headlined his *Austin Statesman* column, "Dave Hickey's Country Credentials Are Real," and continued that although he viewed Texans turned New Yorkers with suspicion, he approved of Hickey's article. "I took that Texas-New York bit personally," Michael said. "I started to call the old fart and tell him what I thought, but I was afraid he'd question my country credentials."

Alan still had ties with *Rallying Point,* but he wanted to remain in Austin. He and a partner had purchased some acreage in the hills west of town, and it was a perfect site: a spacious meadow at the base of a hill with a massive, sturdy barn that seemed to have been created for some musical use. "We're gonna work out something small," Alan said. "We'll try to get some laid-back pickers out there and maybe do some recording."

Michael liked the idea of an Austin-based magazine rooted in music, feminism and a new southwestern consciousness, but for the time being he had to return to New York, look for paper and try to make a go of it with *Rallying Point.* "If it's good, it'll happen," he said of the Austin music scene. "If it's not, it won't. You've got to look at it that way."

He said he was still looking to the Armadillo for leadership. "It may be an Eddie Wilson trip, but you have to have an ego to get anything done. I think they're moving in the right direction. What Eddie needs to learn, though, is that the Armadillo can't get a fifty-fifty cut every time somebody comes in from the outside. People from the outside don't understand Eddie has the axe; they don't understand he has the karma. Where would they bank that? They'll give him something, but they don't want to give him half. Personally, I think they should, but what Eddie needs is to get to the point where he doesn't need that.

"I'm going to help him anyway I can," Price said. "Just by talking up the trip, principally. That's the only way I can help him right now."

To some, the thought of a new, local breed of managers, radio pioneers, recording technicians and *Rolling Stone* competitors was fresh as a Texas breeze, but the fact remained Austin wasn't ready for that. The best but still perilous way to make a go of it in the music business was to find oneself a bar, a beer or liquor license and a needy musician.

The Armadillo had created an entirely new perspective in the bar business in Austin. The music came first, the intoxicants second. (Though as time went by at the Armadillo, the former took lesser precedence over the latter.In fact, the two attractions eventually merged into a single entity. What the Armadillo offered was beery music.) Before the new music came to Austin most bar patrons tethered themselves to one or two favorite watering holes depending upon the kind of people they wanted for drinking company. But when the musicians began to make a name for themselves, people began to scout the entertainment pages to find out which of those musicians were playing where. All the talented musicians in town couldn't work at the Armadillo every night. If a man could take advantage of the Armadillo's shortcomings — lack of intimacy, comfort and hard liquor — and book some of that music, then he could overcome some of the obstacles facing a new tavern without a cultivated clientele.

At first the new clubs were small. A veteran manager named Felix Geroud took over a club called the Cricket in a monstrous apartment complex called English Aire in southeast Austin. Most apartment clubs in Austin were havens for student apartment-dwellers who jimmied and jived on flashing-light dance floors to lame rock music and scouted the crowd for bed partners, and the Cricket's location indicated it ought to be one of those clubs. It was positioned between the English Aire tennis courts and swimming pool and offered a view of tiers and tiers of quasi-luxurious dwellings for the wealthier and straighter students at the university. But Geroud took his club in the other direction. Specializing in Fromholz, Wier and Threadgill, and collaring Townsend Miller as a new-talent consultant, Geroud turned the Cricket into a country-music bar frequented not only by the English Aire lessees, but by people who wouldn't be caught dead living in an apartment complex.

More established was the Pub, another small club housed in an A-frame structure on a freeway service road. The A-frame had formerly accommodated a hamburger restaurant, the kind where a customer runs a tiny flag up a tiny flagpole on his table to get the waiter's attention, and at first the club was associated with a chain of restaurants called the Saxon. After disassociation with the Saxon was achieved, the Pub's management found the best way to keep the performers happy was to stop serving food about the time the entertainment began. The seating capacity was terribly small, but it gained a reputation as the most intimate Austin club with the most attentive audiences. Michael Murphey made his Austin bar debut there, and Bridger and Willis Ramsey preferred it because, despite the liquor, its atmosphere came very close to that of a coffeehouse. Its reputation even began to spread among name performers who were not intimately associated with Austin music. Ric Schwartz, the manager of the Pub who had worked his way up from dishwasher, said, "That's the only way that clubs that hold two hundred people can get ahold of the bigger names—by packing in the customers and letting the musicians who play there spread the word."

Schwartz predicted a billion-dollar Austin music industry in a very short period of time. "What I'd like to see, when it gets to the point that it's a major industry and the city itself is making money from it, is a realization on the part of the city fathers and newspapers and radio stations that we are businessmen. Like the newspaper, you have to pay in advance to get an ad, and you really have to push at the radio stations. Things like changing the closing law from one o'clock to two o'clock. The city fathers are dead set against it, but it would help them financially because it would bring in more taxes, and it would give us a break on the weekends.

"This is a business. We pay ten percent off the top on the door, ten percent off the top on liquor; we pay sales taxes. They damn sure get our money, but they don't treat us like businessmen."

Another club with a more far-flung reputation was Castle Creek, a slightly larger bar that was in the building once occupied by Rod Kennedy's Chequered Flag. Castle Creek was intimate and comfortable enough for those who were tired of the Armadillo, but it was large enough to accommodate the rowdy crowds of a performer like Jerry Jeff Walker. Its proprietors, Doug Moyes and Tim O'Connor, had done rather well by the place, and Castle Creek's imported talent was

COUNTER CLOCKWISE: Ken Moyer and Rusty Bell, designers of a "progressive country" radio format that captured the spirit of the new Austin music; Alan and Michael Price, aspiring Rolling Stone competitors who thought the movement was almost ready for a magazine; Commander Cody, whose Lost Planet Airmen became the national house band at Armadillo World Headquarters.

CLOCKWISE: Larry Watkins, a reformed fraternity social chairman whose Moon Hill Management gained a national in-the-trade reputation for proficiency; Bronson Evans, a moneymaker whose Texas Opry House posed a threat to Armadillo supremacy; twenty-four-track recording facilities at Odyssey Studio; the Broken Spoke, a hardcore country hangout invaded by politicians hanging on to Willie Nelson.

almost equal to that of the Armadillo, but they had to pay those performers a measure of what they would draw elsewhere, which usually meant giving them a high-majority percentage of the gate. The price of the Austin performers was also escalating rapidly, and Castle Creek could only accommodate so many people. As a result, some of the performers demanded that the management clear the club and charge admission for two brief shows on one night, which was bad public relations for Castle Creek and critically diminished the liquor revenue. "Two bad weeks in this business hurts," Moyes said. "A bad month can kill you."

Inevitably, a couple of bigger clubs took the plunge. Eddie Wilson said of his aspiring competitors, "I think it's great. Austin needs just as many clubs as it can support." On the northern edge of the city, a restaurant veteran named Ronnie Peterson swung the lease on a large but unsuccessful hardcore country dance hall, remodeled it and opened El Paso Cattle Company. "The bigger you are, the better," he said. "We can half-fill the club four nights a week and make some profit." He said his revenue came from the liquor, not the music. "We're big enough that we can sell our drinks cheaper, but we have to depend on quantity. You can't make anything off a big-name act — the state gets its ten and a big name will get seventy or eighty percent of the gate, so if you break even at the door, you're happy."

Peterson said he was shying away from the more expensive acts. What he had in mind was a large dance hall that would attract both straight and freak customers to the same local country music. "Austin isn't Denver or San Francisco," he said. "It's not ready for a star every night."

Moreover, he doubted that the increasingly selective taste of Austin club-patrons was really good for Austin music. A popular performer like Alvin Crow, a former symphonic violinist from Amarillo who had taught himself to play the country fiddle and sing just like the old Nashville greats, had gained a local reputation and was able to work over two hundred nights a year without ever leaving the city limits of Austin, something he scarcely could have done in the major music centers. In Nashville if a musician didn't have a record he wasn't working, and it wasn't much better in New York or Los Angeles. But Peterson argued Crow was the exception, because he was established. "People here go to see someone they know," Peterson said. "They won't gamble, and that's really sad because there are so many talented groups around that don't even have a chance.''

Asked if the vested financial interests in Austin were willing to get behind a venture like El Paso Cattle Company, Peterson said, ''Clubs are like restaurants and filling stations. The equipment a bank would gain in case of bankruptcy loses its value almost immediately—chairs, drinking glasses, microphones, speakers. They'd get about twenty-five cents on the dollar. The mortality rate of clubs is too high. It's just not a good gamble for a bank.

''Once you get established in this business, the goal is to sell with a very large profit, as soon as possible.''

The most ominous threat to the supremacy of the Armadillo came, however, not from Castle Creek or El Paso Cattle Company, but from a huge new club in its formative stages called the Texas Opry House, one of whose owners was an old Wichita Falls acquaintance of mine named Bronson Evans.

Of all the middle-class war babies I had met, Bronson had always struck me as the one most likely to make a million dollars someday. He was loyal to his friends, but he was most loyal to himself, and he was thoroughly hooked on the idea of getting a new business off the ground, turning a profit and moving on to something else. When I ran into Evans he was a leading figure in a group of social outlaws at the Wichita Falls college who were as cliquish as a fraternity and thumbed their noses at the seething disapproval of the university and law-enforcement establishments. Bronson was also the son of a veteran barkeep and restauranteur, and for one blissful semester he talked his father out of the barroom half of his restaurant and opened Wichita Falls' first college tavern. He sold beer for a dime a draw the first day of the Town Pump's existence, once got in a fight with a customer over the customer's flirting girlfriend, and one night watched his establishment take a turn that could have closed him down permanently and possibly sent him to the penitentiary. One of Bronson's friends, a commodities broker, lured an alcoholic gambling addict of a broker down to the Town Pump's dartboard. The old broker bet twenty dollars a game and accepted all the side bets proposed. It was like betting on the sunup. The old man couldn't hit the wall with the dart, much less the dartboard. Soon the Town Pump resembled a Nevada casino, and Bronson sat down in a corner and got quietly drunk.

Bronson had to join the Air Force Reserve to beat the draft, and when he returned his father's bar was no longer available, so he completed work for his degree and moved to Dallas, where he stocked grocery-store shelves for Campbell Soup Company. When asked about his job, he would sourly respond, "Noo-noo-Noodle-O!"

He finally gave that up and returned to Wichita Falls, where he got a rock & roll joint off the ground, then sold out and moved on to Houston with a wild bunch of cronies — an attorney who had the money, a failed law student, the commodities broker and a wild man known as Whale who had played halfback for Notre Dame, been declared dead at the scene of an accident by an Indiana highway patrolman and crawled up an airplane ramp in his new dress whites when he went off to join the Navy Reserve. Bronson and his gang opened a place called the Abbey, undercut everybody's liquor prices and took the town by storm.

Eventually Evans' cronies opened their own Houston club, Bronson opened extensions of the Abbey in Dallas and Austin, sold those, got into the restaurant and record-selling businesses, and lost $20,000 in 1973. He moved to Austin, allied himself with new partners, and tried to revive a downtown restaurant and club called the River City Inn which had a previous reputation for sky-high food prices, erratic service and rude music audiences. He got a bad rap on his new menu from a *Texas Monthly* restaurant reviewer, and his small upstairs club was going nowhere.

I dropped in to see him one night when he had advertised Ewing Street Times as his entertainment. Ewing Street was an aspiring group led by John Vandiver, a member of the old Dallas County Jug Band who had migrated to Chicago, impressing John Prine and Steve Goodman before returning to Texas. But Ewing Street was not the band onstage.

"I fired 'em," Bronson said. "We sent a waitress up to tell them a car's lights were on outside, and one of them said, 'We don't do that kinda thing. Tell them yourself.' Then this guy says, 'Welcome to another night at Castle Creek.' I informed the guy this was not Castle Creek, and he said, 'Oh, I apologize, we've made the management mad. Let's be serious now, we can't have any sense of humor.' I told him to get his ass off my stage. I shoulda busted the sonofabitch."

Bronson was frankly thinking in terms of challenging the Armadillo: "I went there one night to see Michael Murphey, my wife and I couldn't find a place to sit, and all in all, I hated it.'' He took on three more partners — all with extensive restaurant and club experience in Dallas and Houston — and they risked their necks to lease a huge facility built as part of a motor hotel complex just a few blocks from the Armadillo. Designed as a convention center, the new club had restaurant capabilities,three large barrooms with tiled dance floors, any number of party rooms under lock and key, and an adjacent, unused swimming pool. The decor was that of an uptown theater — plush red carpet, chandeliers, cherubic statues. The overhead had buried a series of investors, the latest a champagne-music director who booked himself to play for his small aging crowd of followers in the convention center's dark empty space.

Bronson and his partners planned to utilize the smallest of the barrooms for a commons area where there would be twenty-five-cent beer, seventy-five-cent liquor, hamburgers, pool tables and no cover charge, even on nights when they booked local musicians. In a larger barroom they intended to book name musicians who needed intimate surroundings, and were dickering with KOKE about remote Monday-night broadcasts from that room. Adjoining that room was the proposed money-making hall — a club with a large dance floor and good acoustics that would seat 1300 comfortably and convert into an auditorium with a capacity of 3000. In order to steady the revenue flow, they were going to make the place available on weekdays to business and wedding parties, but in the first month they booked Ferlin Huskey, Tanya Tucker, the Eagles and Flash Cadillac and the Continental Kids, hoping to acquaint old country folks, hip country-rockers and hardcore freaks alike with the new alternative to the Armadillo. There was no talk of a community arts laboratory in the managerial offices of the Texas Opry House, and the promise of practically wholesale liquor prices and free entertainment was soon forgotten. But the managers had years of experience behind them, and they appeared to have the ideal place — if the music audience in Austin was large enough to support a full-scale Armadillo competitor.

It appeared large enough the night of the new joint's grand opening. The Armadillo drew a good crowd at four dollars a head to hear Boz Scaggs, but lured by the promise of a two-dollar cover charge, free beer and entertainment provided by a local favorite called Freda and the Fire Dogs, Doug Sahm and another talented member of the old Sir

Douglas Quintet named Augie Meyer, the Austin audience was still lined up at eleven-thirty trying to get in the Texas Opry House. Meyer paused between songs, looked at the Armadillo-sized crowd, and said, "Austin just keeps growing, don't it?"

Larry Watkins of Moon Hill and Tim O'Connor of Castle Creek were watching the crowd from the lobby, and both agreed it was a good sign. "People have been wondering for a long time whether a place this size would work," Watkins said. "Apparently it will."

O'Connor nodded, "What this means is that there's audience enough for everybody."

Steve Kirk was unwilling to stay out of the Austin music business simply because he lacked the capital and experience to get a club off the ground. The money for one-shot projects, he said, was in the willing pockets of freaky sons of oil and land-rich Texas families, and they couldn't resist the glamour of investing their money in the music business. Kirk attended Baylor in Waco during the late sixties, managed a locally popular band in Waco, accepted a job with a gospel recording and publishing firm, then in 1970 met Mike Tolleson at a going-away party for Bill Brammer hosted by Dallas Cowboys Craig Morton and Pete Gent. Tolleson told Kirk if he really wanted to get into the music business, he should read *Billboard's* book on the subject first and always keep the legal aspects of the business in mind.

Kirk moved to Austin and worked himself into a partnership in a promotion company called Solar Attractions. He was also working at the Country Dinner Playhouse—one of those middle-class denominators of American theater frequented by scrubbed youngsters who serve drinks then run onstage to sing wholesome folk music, aspiring and sliding actors and actresses in need of work, and theater-goers who pass out in their asparagus during the second act of the light comedy or mystery. Dinner theater was the most popular form of drama in Texas, but the Playhouse in Austin was steadily losing money. Kirk convinced the manager she had nothing to lose by bringing Austin music to the Playhouse on Monday nights, then talked to Michael Murphey. Murphey took one look at the Playhouse — a theater-in-the-round with two stages that appear and disappear by elevator — and agreed to do it.

Murphey's younger brother Mark, an aspiring Shakespearian actor, flew in from Houston, walked up the hill behind Murphey's house and memorized reams of printed material, then they sprung their performance on a modest, unsuspecting crowd. The lights went out, the hydraulic stages moved, and the lights came on Mark Murphey, staggering drunkenly and reciting from Edwin Arlington Robinson:

> *"The bird is on the wing, the poet says.*
> *And you and I have said it here before.*
> *Drink to the bird." He raised up to the light*
> *The jug he had gone so far to fill,*
> *And answered huskily: "Well, Mr. Flood,*
> *Since you propose it, I believe I will."*

Toward the end of the recitation Michael Murphey's music began to be heard faintly, then the lights went out on Mark, the other stage came down, and Murphey was singing one of his songs in a quaint, whimsical voice:

> *Drunken lady of the morning stumbles down the street*
> *Makes a joke of every tipsy minute*
> *Her true love is the garbage man, he sweeps her off her feet*
> *It's not a perfect world but she is in it*
> *She'd like to try to make the morning smile*
> *Hold it to her breast a little while*
> *Rockin' it to sleep just like a child*

Mark Murphey went on to introduce his brother's songs with thematic recitations from Larry McMurtry, St. Francis of Assissi, Geronimo's autobiography, Albert Schweitzer and John Steinbeck, and the older brother said afterward he would have liked to work creative dance into the performance. Murphey didn't play to a packed house that night, and he caught flack before the concert from people who agreed it was a greedy, unprincipled freak indeed who would perform in a place like the Country Dinner Playhouse, and afterward from people who said the performance was just another example of Murphey's intellectual pretensions. But the people at the Playhouse that night were there solely because they wanted to hear Michael Murphey, and Murphey did exactly what he wanted with his music. The other musicians in town took notice.

The suburban middle class was not the only Austin sector invaded by the new music. It swarmed over other beaches as well. The legislature was in town to draft a new constitution for the people of the state of Texas, and while the two bodies of the legislature were sitting together as a single delegation, socially it was business as usual. The delegates acted like the same old politicians, not the new statesmen. Most Texas legislators had something in mind when they ran for office, and a few were downright diligent about their work, but when the recess gavel fell the Texas legislature fragmented into a number of social cliques, each with its own political raiding parties and restricted drunken *fiestas*. Texas was a big state, you see, and the legislators' wives were scattered from here to kingdom come. The Capitol was secretarially staffed by pretty little things off and alone in Austin, and though some eluded the horny legislators' grasp, others clamored for a chance. When a day's work was done, the legislators grabbed their favorite monkey women by the tails and headed for the party of the night.

During the constitutional convention — a supposedly non-partisan affair nevertheless marked by electioneering to determine the next house speaker — the grandest excuse for an all-cliques-welcome party was beer-drinking Austin music, particularly if it was provided by Willie Nelson. The governmental esteem for Nelson shattered political boundary lines. Jumbo Ben Atwell, a Dallas conservative whose influence diminished to almost nothing after House Speaker Gus Mutscher was convicted of bribery during the Sharpstown scandals, followed Nelson everywhere, while at the other end of the political spectrum, one of the state's bright liberal hopes, Land Commissioner Bob Armstrong, was a frustrated guitar player who got a kick out of emceeing Nelson's concerts. At the Capitol, mere mention that Nelson would appear was enough to get everybody interested in a communal party.

Most often, the Austin-music political parties took place at the city's traditional hardcore country hangout, the Broken Spoke. Situated on a roadside in south Austin, the Broken Spoke was Saturday-night country to the last detail — from the dance floor to the plaid tablecloths to the photographs of the heavenly hillbilly hosts on the walls. It was the kind of place where, in 1970, if a customer's hair exceeded the length of his ladyfriend's, the bartender, a large man with a jutting double chin, would keep them waiting for a good while, then say, "Hey, I forgot to tell yaw. We don't serve hippies in here. Yaw get yourselves a haircut and *then* come back. We'll be glad to seeya then."

But that wouldn't work when the politicians and musicians invaded. The musicians were uniformly long-haired, half the Capitol staffers were hip in appearance, and a few quasi-freaks always wrangled invitations just for the music and spectacle. One of those parties took place on a cold misty afternoon in February 1974, and though Willie never made it, it was a sight to behold. A young vested cowboy sat at a table in quiet bewilderment as the party-goers streamed toward the bar to be served by the same old finicky barkeep. Who *were* these people — old men with American flag pins on the lapels of their pinstriped suits, young long-haired men in boots and jeans, young women in moccasins and Mongolian wool coats? There was Atwell, standing by the door with a beer in his hand and saying, "Hi, I'm Jumbo Ben." There was turtlenecked James Street, the miracle quarterback for Texas' 1969 national champions, dancing smartly with some filly, jowlier than he was when he threw the pass that beat Arkansas and engineered the drive that beat Notre Dame. Lieutenant Governor Bill Hobby puffed on his pipe and pumped up the Pearl Beer keg. One small town legislator ran into his hometown newspaper reporter, who nodded in agreement that both their covers were blown. The dance floor squirmed with Texas legislators and their young Austin ladies. A plump, disapproving woman dished out chicken and dumplings. Sitting at a table by himself,one realized after the long-haired country singer welcomed him to the party, was the University of Texas regent, Frank Erwin. Frank Erwin was many things to many people. To some he was a political hero who battled left-wing radicalism all over the state, in all its forms. To others he was the vilest of the establishment sonsabitches, a man who systematically wrecked the university faculty while he drove around in an orange and white Cadillac with UT#1 license tags. To a few he was a complicated man who had once gotten an Odessa Republican's Headliner's Club membership suspended after he called a waiter a nigger and got onion soup thrown in his face. The crowd at the Broken Spoke represented all those viewpoints, but the singer onstage was strictly neutral. He welcomed Erwin aboard and sang sweetly:

Happy birthday to you
Happy birthday to you
Happy birthday dear Frankie

Yes indeed, times were changing. Music had taken Austin by storm, and its appeal was not limited by age, sex or occupation. Its most remarkable creation, perhaps, was the phenomenon of the thirty-year-old groupies. Wellesley graduates with the New York reserve of Gloria Steinem primped in the mirror before going out to meet Willie Nelson, mothers of three wept happily at the sound of B.W. Stevenson's lonely voice, and those were not isolated cases. True, the country-rock fascination was beginning to take on faddish overtones. Everybody's automotive aspiration became a battered pickup truck, and fashionable attire for the economically advantaged became anaconda boots and crushed-beaver hats. (If one suggested that people might stop skinning anacondas and crushing beavers if there were no demand for those products, the standard response was an irritated shrug.) And the craze was limited to the Anglo sector. Blacks and *chicanos* had no part in it, unless one of their political candidates was in need of some Anglo exposure. But the music had been good for Austin. Almost in spite of themselves, the opposing factions of the Anglo community were drawing closer together. They congregated in the same bars and tolerated each other's presence because the music touched something inside them all.

Though the musical activity was frenzied all over town, it was still basically the Armadillo's act. They were the ones with the national reputation. Van Morrison and the New Riders of the Purple Sage were interested in recording albums there, and the Armadillo had a virtual house band which had already recorded a live album there and was spreading the good word everywhere.

Commander Cody and his Lost Planet Airmen were a group of eight musicians who started off in Ann Arbor, Michigan with a trapeze act overhead, migrated to San Francisco and attracted the journalistic attention of every rock journal and even the girlie magazine, *Gallery*. They were an unusual rock band because all members got an equal share of the take, but their namesake and leader was a burly, reformed college jock and graduate student who called himself Commander Cody but liked people to know his first name was George, and his last name was Frayne. Cody's voice was so gruff and unmelodic that it could only be used for talking atrocities like "Hot-Rod Lincoln" and "Smoke, Smoke, Smoke that Cigarette," but he could play the living daylights out of a piano. Cody's vocals were usually released as the band's singles, but three other members actually did most of the singing, and all members could lend a voice if needed. They were often described as a latter-day country-swing band, but theirs was a time-sweep music. It incorporated forties jitterbug, mid-fifties rock, the Sons of the Pioneers and settled finally into a parody of mainstream Nashville country. The parody was all the more devastating because they handled the form better than most legitimate country bands.

Commander Cody was a show band. The only members who didn't move around much were the drummer, Lance Dickerson; the steel player, Bobby Black, who was tired of the road and wanted a studio job in Nashville; and Cody. Bruce Barlow was a fine bass player who would have been more at home with a rhythm and blues band. Andy Stein was a curly-haired man in a Honolulu tourist shirt who stomped his foot in high exaggeration when he played his fiddle and did the bop across the stage when he played his saxophone. Gaunt guitar players John Tichy and Bill Kirchen handled most of the country vocals, but there was yet another lead singer, Billy C. Farlow, who had a painting of Donald Duck on the back of his guitar and destroyed at least one microphone per performance. Farlow was the Elvis-the-Pelvis rock & roll singer of the band.

Commander Cody played one time at the Armadillo with Waylon Jennings and decided it was the place to record the band's first live album. Of course, that was good for Austin music and Armadillo World Headquarters, for the commercially popular country-rock was still coming out of California, yet here was one of the top California country-rock acts who insisted the place to be was Austin. The recording performances were clearly occasions for before-and-after parties, and a select number of musicians and hangers-on feasted on Armadillo nachos and shrimp enchiladas before the Friday night session. Jim Franklin had turned the walls of the backstage lobby into a pop-art exhibit, and Michael Price had contributed his taped interview with Timothy Leary to the Armadillo's closed-circuit television screens. Leary was saying Gordon Liddy worked his way into the Nixon inner circle by busting Timothy Leary. There were only a few groupies, since the Armadillo staff had learned not to invite too many people to a press party, but the rock journalists were numerous. They stood in a group discussing their trade and one said, "Is anybody down here joining the Rock Writers Association?"

As I went back for seconds on the food, I was approached by a girl with an inviting navel and snap-brim hat who said, "Are you with *Rolling Stone?*"

"No, but I'm the sports editor of the weekly paper in New Braunfels, and that's the prettiest little town you ever . . . ."

The girl moved away.

Billy C. Farlow walked by and a girl serving food invited him to grab a plate. "I can't eat before a performance," he said. "I throw up."

One of the Cody entourage was talking with the six-foot-six lead singer of the preliminary band, Asleep at the Wheel, another long-haired country-swing band with an album to its credit. The band had recently moved from California to Austin. "You guys are playing at the Astrodome?" the Cody man said incredulously.

"No," the tall singer said. "The Astro *Hall*. That's right next door to the Astrodome."

The Commander happened by, endured yet another handshake, and I asked him why he liked to play the Armadillo.

"They'll listen if you play country down here," he said. "On the West Coast and in New York, they *demand* that you make them jump and shout."

Asleep at the Wheel took the stage after a while and worked the crowd into the proper mood, then Jim Franklin, who would provide the art for the album cover, went onstage in costume and said, "Ladies and gentlemen! Live at Armadillo World Headquarters, from deep in the heart of Texas, Commander Cody and his Lost Planet *Air Men!*"

The concert was a whooping, hollering good time — onstage, in the audience and backstage. The band was almost frantic — Billy C. bit a chunk out of the microphone after he severed its chord — and the crowd was equally animated, except for one little girl who climbed onstage and went to sleep near Cody's piano stool. The cylindrical beams of red and blue light were almost opaque in the smoke as they played on the musicians, but the most remarkable thing they illuminated was a 35 mm camera that bobbed up and down in front of the stage at the top of a metal rod.

The photographer came backstage after a while, and I asked him what he was doing. "It's a timed shutter release," he said. "I just estimate the setting and focus, then get the camera up in front of them and see what happens."

He said he didn't have an assignment. He was from Ohio, had been staying with a girlfriend and was just trying to hustle some work. I said there was a lot of talent in Austin. "Probably," he said, "but they don't know how to market their work." One of his blind photographs subsequently received prominent display on the back cover of the Cody album.

"The only thing I don't like about this business is the competition," he said. "You come into contact with people that ordinarily you would want to be affable as hell with, but because you're competing against them, you have to keep your distance."

In the rooms behind the stage, a few people were drinking beer and watching the Timothy Leary re-run, but the engineers were having a great time watching the concert by remote telecast and moderating the electronic dance of the sixteen-track recording needles. One of the sound crewmen stumbled into the men's room, took unsure aim at a urinal, and said, "I can't believe this is going down in Texas. I've had bad experiences in Texas."

It seemed like a short concert because it moved so quickly, but suddenly it was past closing time, and the band abruptly exited the stage. "We blew the first set," Cody growled, but outside a beer-bellied man in a Marine fatigue jacket was bellowing, *"More!"*

Billy C. provided the crowd with two rock & roll numbers in encore, then the band went off again. "Is that it?" somebody asked. "Is that it?"

"That's it," an Armadillo decision-maker said. "Turn on the lights."

The Armadillo emptied quickly, and the bands and entourage were off toward an after-hours party in another bar where the beer and cocaine were plentiful, the locked-out wanted in and the locked-in wanted out. But Eddie Wilson was ready to call it a night. He walked onstage drinking coffee, not beer and surveyed his domain. The Armadillo had become a cohesive force. In addition to the Armadillo old-timers, that night there had been a youth with a high school letter jacket in the audience, and another teenager with eye-shadow and glitter on his cheeks. Wilson seemed reflective as he gazed out at the clutter of beer cups and broken glass, the employees skidding folded chairs toward the wall, one couple lingering in a last kiss. By god, he must have thought. We're going to turn this misguided civilization around and make a living doing it besides.

90

PART II

This night life ain't no good life,
but it's my life.

Willie Nelson

beer, cocaine and . . .

The first time I saw Luckenbach was the day they buried LBJ. The weather was miserable that morning, as if the ghosts of Johnson and Ho Chi Minh were waging one last frenzied battle, and once again, Ho had the upper hand. The rain was murderously cold, stubbornly refusing to freeze, and it was more forceful than the windshield wipers of the Pinto. The traffic was heavy in southwest Austin, and god knows why the occupants of the Pinto were a part of it. All of them knew LBJ well, though they had never met him. The driver dodged the draft by assuring the inspecting shrink that he was a crazy writer who often dreamed about murdering his mother. The passenger in the front seat considered overeating himself to a dangerous state in order to avoid having to accept his ROTC commission, then he raised a piteous wail to Senator John Tower to get his assignment changed from infantry to journalism. The passenger in the back seat learned of the Gulf of Tonkin incident in Marine Corps boot camp after three days of rumored Red Chinese invasions and whispered predictions of an international emergency that would require all hands overseas. "No sir," he told his comrades from Michigan. "You fellows volunteer. I'm a reservist."

LBJ was an enigma to most Texans under thirty, an awesome figure full of stupefying contradictions. He and Sam Rayburn were the real powers in Washington during the second Eisenhower administration, yet he humbly accepted an impotent office when John Kennedy offered it. His weight on the ticket possibly carried Kennedy to the presidency, but Johnson hedged his own bet, running for re-election to the senate at the same time. He probably would have been happier the next three years had the presidential ticket lost, for he was shuttled off to supervise the cosmetic space program, endure humiliating rumors of being dumped from the ticket the second time around, and watch helplessly while John Connally and Ralph Yarborough stripped the gears of his beloved Texas Democratic machine. But then Kennedy was dead in Dallas, and Johnson stepped off the plane in Washington, saying he would do the best he could. The country rallied around him after that, and he whomped Goldwater by branding him a bomb-crazed, reckless fool.

Johnson ramrodded almost everything he wanted through Congress, including some social and civil-rights legislation he probably would have resisted had it come down from another president, and in some quarters he was favorably compared to Franklin Roosevelt at the height of his powers. But the blacks were rioting in Watts and Detroit, and Johnson tipped his hand on foreign affairs when he sent troops to the Dominican Republic. He was a reasonable man, but Americans and their friends weren't going to be pushed around overseas. Every winter there would be a cheery assessment of how well the war in Vietnam was going, and every summer several thousand more Americans went over to make sure it went even better. As the war heated up LBJ became less of a distant figure. Just being a student wasn't enough to stay out of the Army anymore; you had to keep your grades up, and if you made the mistake of flunking out they'd nab you before you could get back in. Numerous young ladies got pregnant to keep their husbands out of it for a while, but then that exemption went the way of others. Everybody was looking for a hole to hide in, be it legal or illegal. Nobody wanted to fight that war. It was a war based on the arguments of academicians. But blame must rest somewhere, and from all appearances, Johnson was the one who had brought it about, which made him all the more contradictory to young Texans. He was the most notable Texas politician since Sam Houston, but he was making the lives of young men miserable.

Like many draft-evaders, I prepared for the coming fight with the Communists one weekend a month in Abilene and stamped out tarantulas in the Mojave Desert two weeks every summer. But year after year LBJ seemed to be closing in on me. Finally I sat down in front of the television one evening glumly expecting to be sentenced to the petunia beds of Camp Pendleton while the real Marines went off to die, but a suddenly old LBJ announced he wasn't calling up the reserves. He was stopping the bombing and calling it quits. By god. Johnson had admitted a mistake, the war would soon be over, and Bobby Kennedy was going to be president. I went out and got merrily drunk, my appreciation for the old man already reviving. In the years after his presidency I saw Johnson for the first time: a gigantic Cotton Bowl spectator in a gray overcoat who no longer relished the press of the crowd. He seemed forlorn but almost endearing as he returned to his ranch on the Pedernales. His only real contact with the outside world was Walter Cronkite; he had grown forgetful about his haircuts, and judging from the photographic coverage, he played with his grandchildren in a field of bluebonnets a lot. His health was failing, but he could still be the Man when he wanted to be. One of his last public appearances was at a civil-rights seminar at the public affairs institute named after him on the University of Texas campus. Attacked by a militant black who commandeered the microphone, Johnson talked hard yet emotional politics while Lady Bird fretted about his health. Julian Bond said he had differed with Johnson often in the past but added, *"By god,* I wish we had him now." LBJ had benefited by his successor.

Austin knew and understood Johnson better than Washington ever had, and a hush fell over the city as his funeral caravan moved out toward the Hill Country for the last time. Congressmen and other importants made the trip in chartered Continental Trailways coaches, but they were flanked by various makes and models of vehicles bearing mourners, cynics, friends, enemies and curiosity-seekers from all walks of life. Many of them had cursed and hated Johnson at times, but he was still the mightiest of Texans. At times he had been an almost comic figure, an unwitting butt of those jokes that typecast Texans as blundering, foolish braggarts, but he also symbolized times that were changing, even in Texas. For all his faults, he was one of them. Rest in Peace LBJ, one movie marquee along the way read. Rest in peace, Ho Chi Minh.

Steam rising from their tires, the vehicles moved out Highway 290 toward Johnson City, past the mock-western storefronts, the barbecue cafes, the last-chance mobile home lots, the quasi-luxurious tract residences, a fruit-stand closed for the winter whose owners proudly displayed a pair of pruning shears with the notice: Hippie Clippers. The city was making its move on the Hill Country. Indeed, a few weeks later Lady Bird would sell most of the LBJ Ranch to a developer from Tulsa. The beauty of the Hill Country would be its ruin one day, after the ranchers passed away and their sons and daughters were seduced by the subdividers. But for the moment it was still a garden inside Texas, even on a wintry day. Most of the country west of Austin was unimproved rangeland where deer outnumbered people and sheep and goats outnumbered cattle. The land pitched and rolled like the sea that once covered it until it finally flattened out into West Texas, but until it got there it was heavily wooded, blue-green and shimmering in the distance. The Easterners who ridiculed LBJ's love of the Hill Country never spent any time in Muleshoe.

The grasses on the hillsides were the color of rust that day, but the view was obscured by the ready-and-waiting militia. There were a couple of potential presidents and saints in those buses and the military helicopters swooped low overhead and Texas Highway Patrolmen waited for trouble every mile or so. Texas Highway Patrolmen always seemed to wear sunshades, even when it was practically dark, and we kept encountering their black stares. Many cradled rifles in their laps. "Billy Graham's ass," the driver of the Pinto said. "Let's go to Luckenbach."

Luckenbach was Jerry Jeff Walker's favorite watering hole. Surely we would be safe from state troopers there.

We detoured through Blanco, a small town whose one-time court-house had been turned into a wild-west museum, and followed a narrow winding road bounded on one side by enviable rock houses with working windmills, on the other by a knee-deep river and bluffs that looked like a good place to ambush the U. S. Cavalry. Finally we came to a farm road intersection and a sign that read Luckenbach 18. Luckenbach was a Comanche trading post named in 1849 after the first postmaster, Albert Luckenbach, who later moved a few miles on and settled another village named, naturally enough, Albert. Though natives claimed one of their number got an airplane off the ground four years before the Wright Brothers, Luckenbach was unknown to most people until 1970 when the township was purchased by Cathy Morgan, the gregarious, slow-talking wife of an area sheep rancher, and another rancher named Hondo Crouch. Hondo went to classes barefooted at the University of Texas in the late thirties, excelled on the swimming team, married a landed woman, and years later ran into his old classmate John Connally, who then was governor of Texas. ''You still raising sheep around Fredericksburg, Hondo?'' Connally reportedly asked. ''Yes I am, John,'' Hondo replied. ''What are you doing these days?''

Hondo and Cathy took on a working partner in the enterprise, Guich Kooch (pronounced Geech Cook), a young writer who had turned down a couple of offers to go to Hollywood and make a star out of himself. The point of the Luckenbach enterprise was that there was no point to it. People could make their living elsewhere. They came to Luckenbach for beer, rest and relaxation, and the mock community gained a fairly publicized reputation as a place to get away from it all. Newspaper feature writers were almost as numerous as the chickens for a while. Charles Kuralt of CBS stopped by one day, and Hondo published a poem in the first issue of *Place,* the splendid offshoot of the *Whole Earth Catalogue,* bragging that nothing much happened in Luckenbach except the moon.

The road to Luckenbach climbed steeply and peaked finally with a view that would have extended fifty miles had it not been for the gray winter mist. We veered onto another road, passed a sign that read Luckenbach 2, then turned in what appeared to be a driveway in front of a large stone house. A man on the porch waved like he had known us for years. Whoever was responsible for those roadside markers had paid the highway department off. Luckenbach amounted to that one house, a cemetery off in the distance, a collapsing blacksmith shop, a locked-up dance hall and at the end of the short road, a weathered building with anicent beer and soft-drink advertisements nailed to the walls. Guineas ran along yelling beside the Pinto. A solitary goat returned our stares.

In one end of the building we found a store that apparently hadn't done much business in years. Dusty shelves were laden with products from the past — Icon Flakes detergent, homemade lye soap, Wildroot Cream Oil. In the other end we found the bar, walls bedecked with faded newspaper clippings and photographs, cobwebbed hunting trophies, a hand-carved sign that read Everybody's Somebody in Luckenbach. In the middle of the room a hound and her pups snoozed on the floor near a pot-bellied, wood-burning stove. Four men sat around the stove drinking beer. Guich Kooch scribbled on a notepad with the look of a man who knew something he was about to tell, a dusty, toothless man in a baseball cap nodded often but drank his beer without a word, and Sonny, a pot-bellied young man with a Fu Manchu mustache and broken-down hat, propped his boots on the stove. The gendarme of the community, a high-strung little man named Benny Luckenbach, spun a web of tales with a thick Tex-German accent. It was impossible not to feel like a tourist in those surroundings. LBJ wasn't dead; it was 1937, and he was a young man running for Congress.

Benny was talking about one of his neighbors who had gotten drunk, ridden his horse into his dining room, then shot the fool thing when it panicked and began to wreck the furniture. Benny said the neighbor seemed real sorry the next morning, partly because he had a heck of a time removing the carcass from the premises.

"You mean that bay quarterhorse?" Sonny exploded.

"That's the one."

"Why, that old sonofabitch," Sonny said. "He's the one that shoulda got shot. When he drinks he gets mean as a water moccasin. I've seen it happen too many times."

The four men didn't jump to greet us, but Guich sold us a beer and Sonny worked us into the conversation. Eventually we felt natural enough to move our chairs closer to the stove. The talk strayed toward Johnson, and Benny said, "I knew LBJ a long time. When he was president he used to sneak out on the back roads and lose the Secret Service then come over here and drink beer with us. He was all right."

Hondo stuck his head in the door briefly and Guich asked him if he was going to the funeral. "Nah," he said, "I'm figurin' my income tax."

After Guich and Sonny went to the burial service we fell into the company of another German-accented man who said he was working on the new expressway in Austin but had a little place, about five hundred acres, near Luckenbach. We traded beers with the man and talked about everybody's recent quail hunt, which in my case dated back ten years, then the afternoon crowd began to grow. Three students from Austin came in, followed by a heavyset man with crossed rifles on the lapels of his mackinaw who said he was a trick-shot artist — he had taught Chuck Connors how to play the role of *The Rifleman*. Our friend listened to the newcomer's Chicago accent for a while, then stroked his chin and said, "Well listen here, I've got my thirty-aught-six out in the pickup. I'm not any trick-shot artist, but I can hit what I aim at most of the time. Maybe you can teach me a thing or two."

Luckily, the Chicago man declined the offer and nobody got shot that day. For the next few months I found myself in Luckenbach often, listening for two hours one day to the unfortunate tale of a farmer who lost all recollection of the conversation after he slept it off, recoiling from my first pepper hominy taste of the supposed South Texas delicacy *menudo*, watching tongue-tied as a prematurely grayed-haired girl sauntered about flipping her hair and drinking beer from a long-necked bottled, driving home drunk a few times myself. Music was also a part of Luckenbach. Shy couples just happened to have their accordions in the car; Guich played his guitar on occasion; ambitious amateur musicians sat beneath a shade tree passing the latest Texas songs around. But the star of the show was Hondo. White-bearded and handsome, eyes young and mischievous, he was a wizard with children, a cross between Santa Claus and Gabby Hayes. "Where do you live, little lady?" he would say with a courtly bow, shaking a young girl's hand.

"Downtown."

"Downtown Fredericksburg?"

". . . Just downtown."

"Well that's a pretty good place to live. I been trying to get downtown all my life."

Unlike Guich, Hondo played his guitar and sang Mexican ballads at the drop of a hat, lavishly trilling his *r*'s and performing a slow-motion hat dance to the delight of Mexican wetback laborers who drank their beers at Luckenbach. The town had a few drawbacks. Its economic sustenance was beer, and regardless of prevalent friendliness drunks occasionally turned vomity and mean. And as the weather warmed up the native folk began to be outnumbered by citified pretenders like myself and older, sunshaded vacationers in dark socks and bermudas who demanded this or that cat be ejected from the premises, they couldn't *stand* the things. They also waved their checkbooks beneath Hondo's nose, hoping that a piece of Luckenbach would allow them to move out where life was real. Maybe they could even buy and sell a few modest condominiums.

Hondo handled those customers well. He accepted their beer money but when they inquired about the price of land, he turned his back to them. And if they waxed too overbearing, he climaxed his little Mexican dances with a crazed grin, a crooked elbow and the most obscene of gestures. Like Kenneth Threadgill, Hondo had turned his advancing age to his advantage; he would be mourned by many when he passed on to his next con. Those two had met once, reportedly measuring each other like aged tomcats, respectful but jealous of each other's reputation. Hondo mentioned that he was several years younger. Threadgill countered, "Well I'd a never known it by lookin' at you."

Hondo Crouch was the kind of man Jerry Jeff Walker could relate to. Both were exhibitionists at heart, but both had unhappy things in their lives they preferred to conceal. Both were irreconcilable misfits, unwilling to act their age and play the roles that respectable society demanded. Their philosophy was that they would be dead and gone quite soon enough; they might as well glut their lives on impulse before the last impulse claimed them.

Walker was the leading immigrant of Austin music. He was an upstate New Yorker directed toward music by a sister and mother who sang in an Andrews Sisters-type group and grandparents who played in a square dance band, and he didn't establish residence in Austin until 1971. However, he was a popular man around town long before anyone heard of Michael Murphey. Walker was a favorite in the folk clubs of the mid-sixties, and when he summoned "Mr. Bojangles" from his hungover web of experience, he wrote the song in Austin. He was billed in one of those clubs one night with Hondo Crouch's son-in-law, and Jerry Jeff said he never knew whether Hondo came onstage or the stage got under him. Every year or two after that he tried to get by to see Hondo, but for a long while he was one of the most homeless musicians in the country. Had there been a hint of realism in American television in those days, he could have qualified for a role in *Route 66*, only he rode his thumb instead of a Corvette, and he wound up in jail more often than the bed of some Amarillo debutante. He often hitchhiked alone, and though he recorded two solo albums, he made his reputation in the clubs, playing with David Bromberg. When he tried to settle down he took a hammering, first in New York and then in Key West, and at thirty-two he was a marvel to Austin musicians. He was still on his feet.

Walker was guarded about his past when he talked to strangers, except when he discussed the music experience. Looking back on a virtual lifetime of bitter-lettuce hamburgers and stale beer chased by Alka-Seltzers, he'd remark, "It's damned hard to sing when you're throwing up." His intimates didn't deal in specifics when they talked about his past either, but they grew reflective, shook their heads, and said, man, old Jerry Jeff's sure done some time. Traces of rancor and resentment occasionally cracked the facade of the Austin music brotherhood, but very few of the musicians had anything cross to say about Walker. Some club-owners and paying customers thought he was a prick, but the musicians loved him. He was the closest thing Austin had to Hank Williams.

When Walker was trying to hang on to his sanity in Key West he started thinking about Hondo and the more conventional rural folk of the Texas Hill Country, and longing also for the easy gigs and grateful audiences in Austin, he made his way there along with his companion Murphey and her son. Walker and Murphey lived in Austin for a while before he began to make an impression on local music, but when he surfaced he popped up like a cork. His voice wasn't what it once was — he had been punishing himself for a decade — and he never had been a prolific songwriter. He wrote sporadically, when the wildness subsided, most effectively when he was on the road performing and had nothing else to do. Many of those motel-room songs were dark and moody, depressing to some listeners, human to others. But that kind of song was suited to his style, for his voice was deep and lazy. When he tried to sing rock & roll it was usually a travesty. Though in his Chequered Flag days he was a folksinger by reputation, his voice had always been more country than anything else — verging on a yodel in its highest range, rough as a cob on the lowest — and the minute he added a drum to his act, he became a country musician. He was at home immediately.

Walker had a new record deal with MCA and needed to deliver an album, so he enlisted the aid of Michael Murphey's band and summoned his New York manager and producer, Michael Brovsky, to Odyssey Studio in Austin. Walker didn't have many songs ready and Brovsky was stunned by the unorthodox recording facilities at

Odyssey, but they had the hottest sidemen in town and a couple of borrowed songs that seemed specifically written for Jerry Jeff Walker. The most helpful sidemen were Herb Steiner, a steel player from Brooklyn who had watched Murphey fight for his life in the Whisky á Go Go; Bob Livingston, a tall West Texan who snarled at reporters and once had a record deal of his own before it fell through and he met Murphey; and Gary Nunn, another West Texan who, like Livingston, doubled on guitar and piano and also wrote the most intricate music in Austin. Also helping out were facile, rock-oriented guitarist Craig Hillis, drummer Michael McGeary, fiddler Mary Egan and harmonica player Mickey Raipheld. The borrowed songs came from a Texan Walker had met in Nashville, Guy Clark. One of these songs, "That Old Time Feeling," was as moody and down-hearted as anything Walker ever wrote, and the others fit Walker and his musicians perfectly. Preceded by a lonesome harmonica, Walker started out easy, joined gradually by a country steel, honky-tonk piano, electric guitars that came into their own at the end, and a chorus that sounded like a gospel quartet. The lyrics were both a surrender and a beginning, a nightmarish awakening from the American dream of moving ever westward:

> *Pack up all your dishes*
> *make note of all good wishes*
> *Say goodbye to the landlord for me*
> *sonsabitches always bore me*
> *Throw out those L.A. papers*
> *moldy box of vanilla wafers*
> *Adios to all this concrete*
> *gonna get me some dirt-road back-street*
> *If I can just get offa this L.A. Freeway*
> *without getting killed or caught*
> *I'll be down the road in a cloud of smoke*
> *for some land that I ain't bought, bought, bought*
> *If I can just get offa this L.A. Freeway*
> *without getting killed or caught*

Instrumentally, the cut was a jangling clash of the cultural influences on Austin music: a long-haired Teamster crazed by too much speed and too little sex, too stoned to move but in a hurry to get home. And while

A relic beer joint in the Texas Hill Country was an enticement for Jerry Jeff Walker, who migrated from Florida with his companion Murphey. Proprietor of the establishment was Hondo Crouch, the mayor, foreign minister, and resident con man of Luckenbach.

A transplanted New Yorker, Walker assembled the best band in town and clowned onstage with recorded counterparts like B.W. Stevenson (white hat). But he was retiring, unpredictable, at times indifferent to everything about the trip but the music.

A rare night in formal attire at the Texas Opry House, accepting a rose (lower right) from Luckenbach's Guich Kooch.

The Austin sideman most likely to make a move of his own, Gary Nunn (above) came over from Michael Murphey to orchestrate the Lost Gonzo Band and supervise Jerry Jeff's roller-coaster development. Walker's large, rowdy following included writer Bud Shrake (below, smoking cigarette) and Nashville songwriter Guy Clark (carrying guitar case).

any Depression Okie could identify with the lyrics, so could any freak who had ever made the mistake of driving an automobile under the influence of LSD.

The lead cut on the other side also had an air of pent-up craziness. This one was a Walker song, but like "L. A. Freeway" it started off soft and country, his voice aided only by an exploring fiddle, then it developed into driven, frenzied, deterioration rock:

People tell me take it easy
you're livin' too fast
Slow down now Jerry
take it easy, let some of it pass
But I don't know no other way
got to live it day by day
If I die before my time when I leave
I'm leaving' nothin' behind
'Cause I got a feelin'
Somethin' that I can't explain
Like dancin' naked
In that high Hill Country rain

Except for two or three cuts, the rest of the album was indifferent material, indifferently recorded. Walker had to re-record "L. A. Freeway" in New York with studio musicians, and he wrote three of the songs under last-minute duress. Though the album stood out as an unrefined statement of Austin music and "L.A. Freeway" made one TV-distributed rock-classic album, Jerry Jeff's comeback went virtually unnoticed on the *Billboard* charts. Nationally, his reputation still derived from that one song that he could barely stand to sing anymore.

Of course, a lot of songwriters would have traded lots with Walker. "Mr. Bojangles" transcended artificial divisions of the music audience. It was a song that contended man could never be stripped of his humanity, no matter how low his circumstances. The most unfortunate alcoholic was capable of love, if only for a dog twenty years dead and gone, and art would surface even in a drunk tank, if only in the form of a county-fair minstrel dancer named Mr. Bojangles. Walker's song had been recorded by everybody from the Nitty Gritty Dirt Band to Bob Dylan to Andy Williams, and Walker got a few pennies every time one of those albums sold. The popularity of the song was pervasive. According to a story wildly guffawed around Austin, Richard Nixon once told a trivia-minded reporter that "Mr. Bojangles" was his favorite song; when he heard Sammy Davis Jr. sing that it damned near reduced him to tears.

Consider, then, the manner of man who sent chills up the spine of the president of the United States. A casual interest in Austin music had turned into an opportunity for me to collaborate on a magazine article with an old graduate school friend who wrote about music in the non-pay days of *Rolling Stone,* and when Walker scheduled a four-night stand at Castle Creek during the summer of 1973, my friend and I showed up with pencils and notepads astutely in hand. Walker was preceded on the bill by Guy Clark, who looked a little like George Hamilton IV and played quiet music alone with his guitar. The crowd was boisterous in anticipation of Walker, and Clark quickly lost control of them, but he continued playing. He finally quit, then after a long break Nunn, Livingston and the other sidemen walked slowly onstage and began to play by themselves. Everybody seemed to be stalling.

I knew Walker only by his reputation and his recorded music. I didn't even know what he looked like. But scanning the room as the sidemen played I recognized him instantly. He was propped against the wall by the restrooms, tall and stoop-shouldered, hat pulled low over a stubble of beard, an oft-broken nose, a sleepy look, a cockeyed grin. He looked like a character out of Steinbeck. My magazine collaborator and I were in the you-talk-to-him-no-you-talk-to-him phase of our rock journalism careers, and since I knew he had once tried to communicate with Walker with no success at all, I approached Jerry Jeff, introduced myself, and requested an interview. Jerry Jeff put both hands against the wall and shoved himself upright, scribbled a phone number on my collaborator's notepad, and said "It can't be tonight. I couldn't talk to the sun tonight."

Walker tripped once getting onstage, and he had a hell of a time singing. Then again, he had a hell of a time standing up. Very early in the set he toppled over backward into McGeary's drums. The sidemen played feverishly at first, hoping to pull him through, but it was hopeless. He slurred and forgot the lyrics, improvised to the songs' disadvantage, and finally the other musicians relaxed and stopped pretending. Jerry Jeff was a classic drunk, alternately giggling at his foolishness then feeling sorry for himself: "People get down on you,

108

Murphey gets down on you, hell, you can't ever tell." Halfway through the set he seemed to remember the crowd, doffed his hat to them, and said, "Y'all sure been good to me. If I'd a been in your place I'd a shot myself."

Actually, a grim Doug Moyes had mobilized his waitresses to inform the customers they could have their money back if they wanted, and many were accepting the offer. Those in the audience who could remember being that down on themselves stayed on to witness the spectacle and sympathize, but others hung around to heckle. "Hey, can somebody at the bar bring me a drink?" Walker mumbled into the microphone.

"Whaddaya *want*?" a heckler shouted.

"What?"

Walker peered into the crowd, "Who is that yellin' at me?"

"Whaddaya want?"

"Man," Jerry Jeff responded, "you ain't got no beer, you ain't got no cocaine, and you ain't got no pussy. You ain't got *nothin'* I want."

Walker couldn't be expected to take a break and then come back to play, so he stayed onstage, sinking steadily while what was left of the crowd hurried to get just as drunk. A pudgy, baby-faced girl stood at the rim of the stage motioning for Walker to come to her, and finally he side-stepped over, grinned, and said hell yes, come on up. It was the chance of a lifetime for the girl, and she positioned herself in front of the microphone, wiggled her hips and began to sing "Me and Bobby McGee" in undoubtedly the worst singing voice ever heard in Castle Creek. After she had finished, she expectantly lifted her face toward Nunn, who was playing the guitar, and he dabbed his lips against hers in much the same manner he would have kissed a cobra. They kept her away from the microphone after that, but she stayed onstage, yelling in harmony and breaking into an impromptu can-can routine, a dark bruise glaring from her thigh. Too far gone to care, Jerry Jeff grinned through it all and finally sank to his knees. All in all, behavior outrageous enough to get a good musician's arm broken in Las Vegas.

The next night Walker showed up clean-shaven and hungover, working hard, trying to make it up to the managers of Castle Creek. He was irritable, threatening to walk out when an unfamiliar harp player jumped onstage to jam, and he pointedly ignored the girl he had invited onstage the night before. She had her hair up for the occasion and wore a long white gown, and she stood near the stage waiting to be introduced. When she realized what had happened, her cheeks flushed then drained, and she began to circle the club aimlessly, another casualty of the rock generation. The crowd got its money's worth from Walker that night, but the next evening he showed up in his bathing suit, explaining that he'd been drinking champagne all day. Developing a headache, Moyes looked at Jerry Jeff's dog, an offbreed collie named Cisco Austin. Walker said Cisco had the best version of "Mr. Bojangles" he'd ever heard.

My collaborator called Walker a few days after that, and he gave us directions to a $50,000 suburban-style home situated in the middle of a cow pasture near the highway leading to LBJ Land and Luckenbach. We arrived late in the evening bearing tributary six-packs and found a note on the door advising us to go on in, he had gone out for a hamburger. Walker wasn't as down and out as he sometimes let on. The house was sparsely furnished but equipped with a modern kitchen, fireplace, sliding glass doors. Its floors were even freshly waxed. From what I had seen and heard of Walker I would have expected to find him living in a place with cracked cement floors, unattended dog droppings, flies buzzing around the lefover mashed potatoes from last week.

Walker shouldered through the door after a few minutes carrying a paper sack loaded with his brand of beer, which, apologies to all concerned, was not native Texan. He introduced us to Murphey, a big-boned girl with frizzy hair and a voice almost as gruff as Walker's and ushered us out onto the patio. He pulled out canvas lawn chairs and we leaned back in front of his swimming pool. The setting was upper-middle-class anywhere except for the view — an unfenced wilderness populated, no doubt, by armadillos, coyotes and white-tailed deer. Walker seemed to have the best of both worlds.

I said something to that effect and he said, "Yeah, I've been thinking about rigging up a fountain — a statue of Hondo pissing in the pool." He said he had bought the house from an Austin Volkswagen dealer with no small difficulty. "I'd been wanting a place ever since we moved to Austin, and we finally decided we had the money, but bankers just don't understand the music business. I made $50,000 last year, but they'd ask how long my record contract ran, and

I couldn't make them believe the best record deal is a one-year contract. Their system isn't designed for people who make a lot of money in a hurry and then sit back to spend it. 'Well, what have you got for collateral?' A '47 Packard and a hammock. 'Where do you work?' Well . . . But they understand it well enough to hope I don't have a hit record. They want me to pay all that interest. But this is all right. I wanted a place out in the country, but I didn't want to get too far away from my work.''

"You like those people in the Hill Country, don't you?''

"Oh yeah. Kerrville and Blanco and Fredericksburg, those are the best places in the world. I was in Fredericksburg one time and saw this immaculate 1937 Chevy, one fifty-year-old guy and another seventy-year-old standing beside it. The seventy-year-old said, 'I bought that thirty-five years ago, and it's been real good to me.' I said, you sure turned General Motors around on that one, didn't you? He said, 'What would I do with a new one? They're so big I'd just run it off in a ditch. I've got a '50 pickup you'd really like.' ''

What about Austin? How did he come there in the first place?

"Well, you don't stop in Longview. I was hitching through about 1964 and I saw Houston — zoom, zoom, everybody moving — so I asked this guy the best way to Austin, stuck my thumb back out and hitched another ride. After Dallas and Houston it looked like Mecca.''

How long had he been a performing musician?

"Oh, I didn't start playing for pay until I was in high school. But I was singing long before that, and I was listening to the radio. I met a girl at the hop/she left me at the soda shop — I thought, hell, thirty-five-year-old men are retiring writing that. It didn't look too hard.''

My collaborator observed that he was now billed as Jerry Jeff rather than Mr. Bojangles.

"Yeah, I guess it's better to be known by your name instead of a song you wrote, but if people recognize your face they'll start hassling you. I like what's happening in Austin, but I just want to be in amongst it. I don't want to drive the bus.''

Wasn't he jeopardizing his position by showing up too drunk to play at Castle Creek?

"Oh, I've been a lot worse off than that before. And it seems like everytime I pull something like that my stock goes up. The club owners figure I'm good-time Charlie, so they keep askng me to play. From February to April, I was on the road in Chicago, New York, Philly, Austin, Dallas, Denver, Seattle, San Francisco and L.A., and I was supposed to stop performing in May. But then we did Kerrville and the Pub and it was July and I was still performing. Good times all right, but a string of good times can mean you're getting nothing done. So I misbehaved at Castle Creek. I'll make it up to them. But I had to get to work writing. We're going to do an album in Luckenbach in August."

Walker was one of those performers who froze up when he walked into a professional recording studio. He couldn't clap earphones over his skull, lay down a basic track with his bass player and drummer, then relinquish the work to the mixing engineers and studio sidemen and call that his music, even if that was the way it was ordinarily done. That was the reason he wanted his pieces recorded exactly the way his band performed them, the reason he took his business to Odyssey, the reason he wanted a mobile recording van in Luckenbach. He wanted to make music where he was comfortable, and Hondo Crouch's Luckenbach struck him as the most comfortable place he'd ever been. Livingston and Nunn were exclusively Walker's men by then, having left Murphey amidst rumors of underlying hard feelings, and Walker enlisted most of the other musicians who helped out at Odyssey. Brovsky and the sound truck arrived, and the musicians rehearsed under the Luckenbach shade trees, swapped stories with Hondo and drank his beer, then disappeared into the truck to record another song. On the last night of the session they lifted the ban against outsiders and went into the dance hall to record some more in front of a drunk and frantic crowd of transplanted Austinites.

Walker recorded enough material during the week for a double album, but MCA vetoed that idea. Hondo's reading of his poem got edited out, but the album had a decided Luckenbach flavor — photographs inside and outside the cover, an explanatory essay from Walker, and a title, *Viva Terlingua*, borrowed from a barroom poster advertising a chili cook-off in a West Texas ghost town. But even more than the first album, *Viva Terlingua* was emphatically Walker, emphatically Austin. The album was marked by momentary instrumental brillance, more than a few bad licks, a study of Walker's failing voice, a happy revolt against the established procedures of Los Angeles rock and Nashville country.

Balanced by Nunn's tenor accompaniment, Walker set the tone of the album on the first cut:

> *Hi, buckaroos, Scamp Walker time again*
> *Yeah, I'm tryin' to slide one by you once more*
> *Don't matter how you do it*
> *Just do it like you know it*
> *I've been down this road once or twice before*
> *Just gettin' by on gettin' by's my stock and trade*
> *Livin' it day to day*
> *Pickin' up the pieces wherever they fall*
> *Just lettin' it roll, lettin' the high times carry the load*
> *Just livin' my life, easy come, easy go*

The song wasn't to be taken seriously; as the fiddler and steel player murdered "Rose of San Antone" Walker conceded, "Well, it's not really a monster track, Mike." But it was followed by the best cut on the album, Guy Clark's "Desperados," an emotional song about a boy growing up in the North Texas oilfields while the wildcatter who raised him grew old and died. A couple of throwaways marred the album — an awkward rock piece and a Mexican-flavored song called "Sangria Wine" — but they were offset by a country version of one of Walker's old divorce songs, "Little Bird," and another moody song, a vision of automotive death called "The Wheel." Those were two of Walker's better poetic efforts, but once again other songwriters gave the album much of its raucous, Luckenbach-saloon flavor. One of those was Michael Murphey's "Backsliders Wine," but while Murphey sang the drunken confession like he was at the altar praying for forgiveness, Walker sang it from the gutter. Another, written by a Texan named Ray Wylie Hubbard who drifted between Austin, Dallas and Nashville, was a classic rebuttal of Merle Haggard's "Okie from Muskogee." Walker handled the lyrics of "Up Against the Wall Redneck," but at one point he surrendered the floor to Livingston, who stepped up to the microphone and recited: *"M is for the mudflaps you give me for my pickup truck; O is for the oil I put on my hair; T is for T-Bird; H is for Haggard; E is for eggs; and R is for . . . REDNECK!"*

Walker stepped aside on the last cut of the album in favor of Gary Nunn. Nunn had helped Walker immensely — as arranger, piano player and guitarist, vocal accompanist, and in times of drunken vulnerability, something of a mother hen — but he was also an accomplished songwriter, and he appeared to be the Austin sideman most likely to make a move of his own. Strung out over seven minutes, the lyrics of his song were as sardonic as anything John Lennon ever wrote, but they were the pitiful wail of a Texan marooned in the British Isles:

> *And them limey-eyes were eyeing a prize*
> *that some people call manly footwear*
> *They said you're from down South*
> *and when you open your mouth*
> *you always seem to put your foot there*
> *I wanta go home with the Armadillo*
> *good country music from Amarillo and Abilene*
> *The friendliest people and the*
> *purtiest women you ever seen*

MCA bought full-page space in several magazines to promote *Viva Terlingua*, but it never caught fire nationally. Quadraphonic freaks and radio executives sniffed that it was poorly recorded, and my magazine collaborator, who had gone back to work on his dissertation, contended that Nunn's piece was self-indulgent and much too long for what it was. However, the album assured Walker's reputation in Texas, at least for the moment. Just when Nelson or Murphey released a new album that seemed to establish them as the leaders of Austin music, Walker came out with another funky one and turned everybody around. Though he didn't act like a leader and disclaimed all ambitions to the role, if there was a boosteristic spokesman for Austin music, Walker was it. He wasn't a Texan in origin, but he was a hot act in Texas, if nowhere else. A Jerry Jeff Walker appearance became an occasion.

Walker finally had enough clout to stay out of the clubs more and focus on the less exacting concerts. The Country Dinner Playhouse promoter, Steve Kirk, went out ahead of Walker to set up one of those concerts in Wichita Falls, where he encountered one disc jockey in an ascot who wanted his palm greased before he would play *Viva Terlingua,* another who was just itching to get actively involved in a big-time concert, and a soft-spoken municipal-auditorium manager who said intoxicating beverages were forbidden inside the premises; the city fire marshall would be around to enforce the law.

Well listen, Kirk said, there might be a problem . . .

Extending a carrot, the auditorium manager said the rules might be *bent* a little, but a woman at a nearby typewriter said, "Absolutely not. No drinking whatsoever." Privately the manager told Kirk not to worry too much. It would probably be all right if the musicians were just diplomatic about it, if they poured their intoxicants into paper cups before going onstage . . .

Overzealous to the point of fantasy by the day of the concert, the helpful disc jockey advised his afternoon listeners that Jerry Jeff was at that moment driving around town in a green Volkswagen van dispersing free tickets to the concert. If they'd honk he'd pull over. Entering the city limits at the time in a rented Ford, Walker and his cohorts exchanged curious glances. When the time came for the concert, Walker and his men made several preliminary trips onstage and off carrying paper cups, then the deejay rushed up to Kirk, begging permission to emcee the show, his reputation depended upon it. Kirk relayed the request to Walker, who consented with a shrug, and the deejay gushed with rhetoric, building up to his finale: "And now, here is! *Jerry! Jeff! Walker!*" Walker got off to an indifferent beginning but the show struggled along fairly smoothly, except for the time Livingston held up his empty paper cup and mouthed to a man standing behind a translucent curtain: "Can-you-get-me-some-more-wine?" The man behind the curtain was the city fire marshall.

Vowing never to return to Wichita Falls, Kirk went back to Austin and launched preparations to bring Walker to the Country Dinner Playhouse. The manager of the Playhouse was amenable since Murphey had proved a gentlemen in the first concert and generated some badly needed revenue, but KOKE, which by then had a piece of the action, was wary because of Walker's antics at Castle Creek. But there was little likelihood of that happening again. Walker was riding a crest of popularity, he had the best band in town, and he enjoyed performing for the time being because he had added horns to his sound. Country-rock had gone Dixieland.

On most nights the Playhouse was still a haven for a bored middle class, but on country-rock concert nights it was a fashionable place to be seen. Writers and artists, professors and physicians stood in long lines to get in the Jerry Jeff concert, along with a bearded man who seethed at the thought of people who would sell him an advance ticket but could not assure him a seat near the stage. "I demand to know why not," he accosted one of Kirk's associates. "This is an outrage." Neckties prevailed, not blue jeans. Murphey made her appearance in a comely black dress, the wife of KOKE's Ken Moyer talked with a small measure of distaste about the Commander Cody concert she had recently witnessed at the Armadillo, and the Austin bootmaker Walker had saluted in his Odyssey album, Charlie Dunn, walked slowly to his table accompanied by his wife, who wore a long gown and walked with a cane. Walker's song had made the bald little man locally famous, but Dunn had never seen Jerry Jeff perform.

I had the good fortune of a seat at the table of Hondo Crouch, Luckenbach co-owner Cathy Morgan, and her husband Ken. Hondo had been a character in Austin for years but he became even more of a celebrity now that he was Jerry Jeff's heralded sidekick. Hondo continually showed up at Walker's concerts, and often as not, he stole some of the show. Once in San Antonio he staggered drunkenly onstage, tripped over the microphone cord and hit the floor with a frightening crash, then jumped to his feet and said, "Now that I've got your attention . . ."

If anything, Hondo was a ham. He was also a handy man to have at the table that night, for the Playhouse management refused to sell beer for the concerts. Hondo lifted the tablecloth and peeked down at his feet. "How many beers we got?" he said. "Whose pickup are we in?"

Long-necked bottles of beer materialized one after another from underneath the table, and Hondo patted me on the head occasionally and invited me to take a pull off his. With a reputation of their own by then and the name The Lost Gonzo Band, Walker's sidemen occupied the stage and Nunn said "We're gonna play a few songs before the lead egomaniac comes out." Recently enlisted guitarist John Inmon took his turn in the spotlight, followed by Livingston and then Nunn. As

Nunn finished his last piece Walker slouched onstage wearing a brightly flowered green shirt, nodding and grinning at the flashbulbs that popped in his face. Jerry Jeff was at his best that first show, friendly and accommodating with the crowd but wired into his music, particularly after the horn players came onstage. But as one crowd left and another fought its way in, the performance began to deteriorate. The manager of the place stared wide-eyed as the white-bearded figure of Hondo Crouch trooped by shouldering an immense cooler full of beer, and this time the musicians staggered out of the dressing room. The music wasn't half as tight but the people spitting tobacco juice on the carpet and drinking themsleves to oblivion didn't seem to mind.

"Is Hondo still here?" Jerry Jeff said at one point. "I am, but Cathy's passed out," Hondo shouted in reply. In just over an hour the Country Dinner Playhouse was reduced to shambles. The manager reeled when she saw her place empty, for her Dallas superiors were coming down the next night and her job was on the line. Kirk and his crew spent most of the next day cleaning the auditorium, but it took the manager an equal amount of time to restore order in the performers' dressing room alone. Finally she emerged with two handfuls of stubbed-out reefers and any number of unprescribed pills. "My god," she said. "They were so far gone they couldn't even get these things to their mouths."

It was winter again, and I took my photographer to Luckenbach one Sunday. Hondo and Cathy weren't around, and neither was Guich. His partners had balked when he tried to sell his working share of Luckenbach, and he was off somewhere preparing for nationally-televised tryouts to launch the career of a new Singing Cowboy, where he came in second.Walker wasn't around either, but his presence was everywhere: posters on the wall, albums for sale, a portable phonograph playing *Viva Terlingua* over and over, a hatted young man displaying the snapshots he took that recording-session Saturday, another young Austinite who had the unedited, Saturday-night performance on his cassette player.

The latter young man sat near a drunk farm hand and an older rural man with a Tex-German accent like that of Benny Luckenbach, only this old-timer wasn't so fond of LBJ.

Winking condescendingly at times and cutting the old man off frequently, the young man demanded, "What is it you're trying to say?

117

Do you think Nixon's any better?''

"One side's heads, the other side's tails. Nixon got caught.''

The young man snorted and the old-timer said, ''Listen little buddy, I don't know you, but I knew LBJ all his life.The only time he ever had a lick of sense was when Court Mortimer knocked him off that jackass with his lunch pail.''

The young man patiently explained that all men were human, and so was LBJ. He seemed reluctant to give Nixon the same benefit of the doubt, and I wondered what the arrogant little snip had to say about Johnson when the draft got after him. Then again, maybe I was seeing the first evidence of my own generation gap.Maybe he was too young even for Vietnam. The sun was almost gone, and I was ready to go back to town. I didn't know how long it would be before I would want to return to Luckenbach. It would soon be spring again, the tourists would be descending with their checkbooks, and the real people of Luckenbach would retreat to the hills. I hadn't seen the gray-haired girl in over a year. Somebody told me she had a crush on some guitar player.

Jerry Jeff went off to play Carnegie Hall with the Nitty Gritty Dirt Band, but he didn't have a new album to take along. Most of the leading Austin musicians had come out to help him record another album at Castle Creek, but the recording session didn't work out. Jerry Jeff's band, his pride and joy for so long, threatened to dissolve because of personality conflicts. Murphey and her son went back to Florida. Like the Hill Country he loved, Jerry Jeff's life was a series of crests and valleys. I turned on a San Antonio station one day in time to catch the ending of *Viva Terlingua*'s lead cut:

> *Income tax is overdue, and I think she is too*
> *Been busted and I'll prob'ly get busted some more*
> *But I'll catch it all later; can't let 'em stop me now*
> *I've been down this road once or twice before*

The disc jockey said afterward, ''Hey, Jerry Jeff's playing out at St. Mary's tonight. You oughta go out and see him. He'll be good out there, they don't have anything for him to drink. No, I mean it. He's good when he's sober.'' Disc jockeys can be dreadful smartasses sometimes. Let it slide, Jerry Jeff, let it slide.

just a waltz

Many performers of lesser talent than Steve Fromholz were making a living off their records in 1973, and many people knew that. But that meant very little in terms of dollars, cents and recording contracts. Fromholz was one of the greybeards of Austin music, and his following was large and devoted. People attached themselves to Walker because of his squalor, to Murphey because of his writing, to Nelson because of his smile, but they attached themselves to Fromholz because he was the best entertainer in town. His gigs were comedy acts; his followers valued his wit as much as his music. Unfortunately, stage presence did not always translate into recording effectiveness. The banter between songs of a good stage act got lost in the scratching silence between cuts on an album, and the music had to stand alone. Fromholz had been recorded live and unsupervised on Rod Kennedy's Kerrville anthologies, and he sounded fine on those. The tape he cut at Odyssey was infectious if poorly engineered. But when he got in a professional studio, it never seemed to work out. His music was hard to define, and his producers had a difficult time fitting it into the popular forms. In addition to that, Fromholz seemed the most luckless musician alive.

He laughed and sighed about his misfortune when he talked to his followers, and they kept the faith that his luck would change. He was too good for it not to. In the meantime, they contented themselves with the Kerrville anthologies, an out-of-print album he had recorded as half of a duo called Frummox, and his relatively rare public appearances in Austin, for he was still living in the mountains northwest of Denver.

A knot of these followers stood around one day in Ye Olde Music Shoppe in New Braunfels, a picturesque German community between San Antonio and Austin, ripping the cellophane off the first Kerrville album while a gray-haired lady at the cash register watched in disinterest.

"Which side first?" one of the followers asked.

"The one with Fromholz," said another.

"Who did you say?"

They looked at the woman, surprised. "Steve Fromholz."

"Sure," one of them said. "This is a song about Kopperl."

"You mean little Steve Fromholz is a singer?" she said. "Why, I can remember him riding his tricycle out in the street."

The woman leaned forward on her stool and listened as Fromholz began his "Texas Trilogy." It was an eerie work, long and involved, as rural Texas as a rooster cracking the silence at dawn. Aided only by an acoustic guitar, Fromholz's singing-actor's voice moved slowly through the small town, stopping here and there:

> *Walter and Fanny, well, they own the grocery*
> *that sells most all that you need*
> *They've been up and workin' since early this mornin'*
> *They've got the whole village to feed*
> *Well they put out fresh eggs and throw the bad ones away*
> *that rotted because of the heat yesterday*
> *The store is all dark so you can't see the flies*
> *that settled on round steak and last Monday's pies*
> *Sleepy Hill's drugstore and the cafe are open*
> *The coffee is bubbling hot*
> *'Cause the folks that ain't workin' gonna sit there 'til sundown*
> *and talk about what they ain't got*
> *Someone just threw a clutch in the old pickup truck*
> *And it seems like they're ridin' on a streak of bad luck*
> *The doctor bills came and the well has gone dry*
> *Seems their grown kids don't care whether they live or die*

"Steve Fromholz wrote this?" the woman in the music shop said.

One of the followers nodded as Fromholz began to talk about the demise of Kopperl — the old-timers who remembered when their town

122

was a good place to raise a family, the closing of the cotton gin, the lake the lake dammed on the nearby Brazos River, the construction of a new trestle so the Santa Fe railroad could bypass the town.*"No,"* Fromholz said wistfully, *"the train just don't stop here anymore . . ."*

Electric guitars began to work in behind Fromholz as he sang again, his voice building in intensity until it blared like the horn of one of those fickle diesel engines:

> *But now kids at night break window lights*
> *and the sound of trains only remains*
> *in the memories of the ones like me*
> *who have turned their backs to the splintered cracks*
> *in the walls that stand on the railroad land*
> *where we used to play and run away from the depot man*

The guitars fell silent, and Fromholz spoke again, this time about the young people who came to maturity in a town that offered them nothing:

> *I wonder why it is you never see any young folks around Kopperl?*
> *Seems like as soon as the last part of May rolls round and all the*
> *seniors graduate, they go runnin' off to Cleburne and Fort Worth*
> *and get 'em a good job, you know, and they work at the cement*
> *plant in Cleburne and the telephone company in Fort Worth.*
> *Course there's some that don't leave Bosque County, Texas at*
> *all. Their final reward is being carried down to the Brister*
> *Funeral Home in Meridian, the county seat, and they're laid out*
> *in state and the professional mourners come by. The family holds*
> *court and then that's over and they haul the body back up to*
> *Kopperl where it's laid out in state once again in the Church of*
> *Christ, the Methodist Church or the Baptist Church—any one of*
> *the Big Three. They open the coffin up and drape on the flowers*
> *and the mourners walk by and say, my my, don't he look natural.*

With his final song Fromholz moved his "Texas Trilogy" out into the surrounding countryside:

Mary Martin was a schoolgirl, just seventeen years or so
when she married Billy Archer 'bout fourteen years ago
Not even out of high school, folks said it wouldn't last
When you grow up in the country, you grow up mighty fast
They married in a hurry, in March, 'fore school was out
Folks said she was pregnant, just wait and you'll find out

"He wouldn't write that," the woman said, shocked. "About Mary Martin bein' pregnant when she got married."

Now the drought that came in 1957 was a curse upon the land
No one in Bosque County could give Bill a helping hand
The ground was cracked and broken, and the truck was out of gas
And cows can't feed on prickly pear instead of growing grass
And the weather took the water, and a snakebite took a child
A fire in the old barn took the hay that Bill had piled
The mortgage got the money, and the screwworm got the cows
The years have come to Mary, she's a waiting for them now

"Lord," the woman in New Braunfels said after it was over. "I'm glad he didn't write about me."

It was a masterwork of Texas songwriting. Though Fromholz was no longer a small-town boy, he had been there, observant and intuitive, aware that a way of life was dying out there. "Texas Trilogy" was like a Larry McMurtry novel reduced to song, and though Fromholz wasn't able to stay with some of his fellow Austin writers song after song, none of them had a single work that could match that.

Fromholz had moved around a lot as a boy, but he never strayed too far away from Texas, and out in front of him was that country-singing sister who signed with the same label as Elvis Presley. Fromholz didn't last long when he went to college at North Texas, and he had a long and varied employment history. He sold clothes, cars and washing machines, worked in a bowling alley and made a good living as a bellhop. "Bellhop's a good job," he said. "That's a hell of a good job. I bellhopped at the Marriott in Dallas and at a place called the Carefree Inn in Carefree, Arizona. I made a lot of money as a bellhop, I'd put on my bellhop suit and go onstage, entertain the people. Carry their bags and take their money. Take their money.''

But while in Denton, Travis Holland taught the outgoing young bullshitter to play the guitar and Fromholz spent a lot of time listening to authentic country music — early Doc Watson, Eric Darling, banjo anthologies. In 1965 along with Michael Murphey, Fromholz was a member of the Dallas County Jug Band that frequented Rod Kennedy's Zilker Park folk concerts. He enlisted in the Air Force and spent most of his tour in California, writing songs and playing bingo parlors and still learning. A marriage came along and a daughter, who went off to Alaska with her mother after the divorce. After his military discharge Fromholz started dividing his time between Texas and New Mexico and Colorado, and while in Denver he formed the Frummox duo with Dan McCrimmon, a shy, quiet, young man given to spending long afternoons reading Oriental philosophy. It was a good act, but as the name indicated, it was dominated by Fromholz's personality. McCrimmon was a folksinger who might have stood out in earlier days, but he was the straight man of the act. The flavor came from the manicured, controlled, but Texas voice of Fromholz. An ABC sub-label thought enough of the act to take a chance on Frummox, but the album *From Here to There* got lost in an ABC coast-to-coast shuffle, and after a while Fromholz learned to laugh about it. ''It was the second most obscure album of 1969,'' he said. ''The guy who won first prize is awful obscure. He's dead.''

Fromholz wanted out of the Frummox act. He had met Stephen Stills in Colorado, and when Stills offered the chance to tour with him in the summer of 1971, Fromholz jumped. They went on the road with horns and drugs, and Fromholz grew his hair long and found out about rock & roll, the good and the bad. He was on a hedonist trip but he was miserable half the time. ''I'm not worth a shit at hanging out,'' he said, and one evening in Memphis he sat down and wrote a song about the way that life made him feel:

> *You try not to choose*
> *any particular blues*
> *You stumble and you fall*
> *Don't we all*
> *I found my relief*

(and you must have relief)
in the belief that it's all just a waltz
It's just a waltz
That's all

Fromholz left Stills' tour after a few months, and returned to his three-state stomping grounds and rejoined his old friend Travis. Travis drank coffee onstage and played his bass with his back to the audience, and his sly cracks disrupted many Fromholz acts. Holland wasn't interested in sharing his jokes with the audience, but Fromholz made him a minor folk hero with good-old-Travis anecdotes. "This man here's the wisest man I know," Fromholz would say. "One time we were driving back to Austin from Nacogdoches, and Travis was in the back seat with this girl. It scared me I was so stoned, and I asked Travis how fast I ought to drive the Pontiac. He said slow enough to get us there and fast enough that people can't walk up and look in. So I drove straight on through, fifty miles an hour. By the time we got there the girl was so hungry she was crying."

Travis drew applause when he preceded Fromholz on the Kerrville stage in his Boston Celtics tennis shoes, cut-offs and North Texas athletic shirt, and the Kerrville crowds were the ones which treated Fromholz best. They demanded encore after encore, and when he was finished with his 1973 set, he strode dramatically down the aisle and vaulted onstage to harmonize with Willie Nelson. "I was good up there tonight," Fromholz said. "I won't deny it." Fromholz formed a band that year with Travis, lead guitar player Leonard Arnold and drummer Michael Christian, and it seemed the perfect mix. As word about Austin music spread, it seemed like somebody just had to discover Fromholz.

Advance men from the record companies came around all right, but it was hard for them to decide what to do with Fromholz. His music wasn't folk anymore, though his voice sometimes implied that. Neither was it Stephen Stills' rock, though the influence was obvious. Fromholz joked about that difficulty too. Sometimes he called his music *guacamole* rock & roll, other times existential bluegrass. But if his music was anything, it was vivid. He was an emotional man who fashioned his songs from personal experiences, and since all towns, all locales affected him differently, there was a fine sense of place in his music. Because he was a Texan in manner and idiom, the best musical form for him seemed to be country-western. There were precedents. Nobody threw rocks at Marty Robbins because his songs told long stories, and he didn't particularly sound like a country singer.

Enter at that point Michael Nesmith. Mike had been one of the Monkees, the skinny one with the toboggan on his head and the only really funny one in the group. Nesmith was a Dallas area boy, and his country-boy demeanor was a large part of the Monkees' act. The Monkees were all the junior high rage for a couple of years, and they left a legacy of guitar-playing furry creatures and teeny-bopping comic-strip characters on Saturday morning television, but it all came crashing down when the old *Saturday Evening Post*, too feeble for much muckrakery, broke the shocking story that the Monkees weren't really accomplished musicians. Any musician who had ever watched the show knew that, but the bubble burst anyway. The American television audience wanted its fiction to be real.

The *Post* failed to stress that Nesmith was the exception. He had paid his music dues in Los Angeles long before the Monkees got together, and he had played the outback bars with Michael Murphey. Nesmith was the only Monkee who remained a performing musician. He wrote songs for Linda Ronstadt, recorded some of them himself and developed some strong ideas about the music business. In 1972 he talked Elektra into a distribution agreement that would allow him to sign musicians and record them at his Countryside Ranch in the Valley near Los Angeles. It was a facility designed for musicians. There was a nursery for young children, a first-rate studio, extremely comfortable lounging quarters and nobody to bother them. His records were refreshingly country, and so were the performers he sought. His products weren't making a big impression on the charts, but a lot of people were watching Countryside. It might prove a country Shelter.

It was natural that Nesmith would take interest in Fromholz. They had known each other casually for a long time, and though Fromholz had the better voice, their songwriting and vocal deliveries were similar. He signed Fromholz in the summer of 1973, and Fromholz went to Countryside to record his first solo album under Nesmith's supervision, utilizing his producer's studio musicians.

My magazine collaborator was in California shortly before the album was scheduled to come out, and he stopped at the ranch to talk to Nesmith about Fromholz and Countryside. Nesmith expounded upon his radical views of the music industry, contending that hit-singles charts were ludicrous because nobody bought singles but jukebox distributors, album charts were also a hype because they were influenced by massive shipments by the conglomerate record companies, and Saturday-morning television had created the audience for a video cassette industry. That was the coming thing, he insisted. The recording artist of the future would have to carry visual impact. Turning to Countryside, Nesmith said it was partly for his own artistic purposes, partly a business venture. Also, he wanted recording facilities geared to the needs of artists.

Was he going to stick with country music?

"I'm not going to stick with anything except the real stuff. Whether it's country or not, I don't know. There's another coming trend: the development of *music* music, instead of country music, rhythm & blues music and so forth. The lines are becoming very cloudy, very obscure. It's not the same anymore, so if somebody comes along like Steve Fromholz who is making music that is hard to categorize, I embrace that, because I understand that it's music. But what I've found out is that the top forty stations and the media that support the whole pop trip are not disposed to change. They have very strong preconceptions about what they want to play. And the problem is not just that it's a very unhealthy attitude, which it is, but that it's successful. I mean they're number one in their advertising markets.

"But take a country-music station. They probably have the same sort of tight play list, the same sort of preconceived ideas; they know what country music is and they don't want anything upsetting the apple cart. But they're like number twelve in their market, number nineteen in their market. They really don't have a way to expand their market unless they begin to get mass-appeal records. And so what I'm really in the business of doing is making mass-appeal music with a country flavor. And I use as a marketing power base the weak and small country-western stations. I'm trying to be helpful to them by providing them with a product that is not distasteful to their hardline country audience, but also begins to expand their horizons. I'm hoping they'll be helpful to me by playing my music rather than throwing it away like a top-forty station."

My friend mentioned the success KOKE had enjoyed with its progressive-country format in Austin.

"I know exactly where you're coming from," Nesmith said. "And what I'm doing is pioneering that field. I mean I'm just out there all alone. And I have to tell you: it's tough, I'm not selling a lot of records. I haven't bought a boat yet. But I'm very straight ahead about the purpose of what I'm doing, because I really believe that in terms of mass-appeal music, the country power base is the place to start, and that ultimately it's going to yield results. But what I've got to do is provide them with a product that will satisfy their entrenched listeners and bring new listeners into the fold.

"FM is the place to put it, because of the signal. It's such a beautiful thing that happens on FM when you hear a really fine country record, or a fine record with a lot of country things on it, provided it's well recorded. That's one of the reasons I'm out here instead of in Nashville. Because Nashville says let's get in the studio; it'll be two dates and we'll record an album. Well, in Nashville you have an extraordinary crew of pickers who can do that, because the producers demand that of them. As a result it's clean, straight ahead, no boogie, nothing to it at all. And I want it to be pretty to listen to when you're loaded. Nashville country ain't pretty to listen to when you're loaded. I mean if you're loaded it's an irritant. You say, wow, what is that, get it off there."

Where did Austin fit into his picture of things?

"I don't think you've got something big happening in Austin as much as you've got Austin supporting something that may happen big. You've got a consciousness and you've got a coalition of a culture there, and you've got a marriage just by virture of where it's at and where it's coming from. Injecting that freak culture which all universities have into South Texas is a major injection, and that is probably where some of the synthesis is going to occur. But it's happening everywhere. There's a movement in the Northeast, Boston and Philadelphia and up in there, that's almost identical. Something's happening in Georgia — the Allman Brothers and Marshall Tucker and all that — and when I listen to their stuff, it sounds very similar to what I'm doing."

How had he run across Fromholz?

"Oh, I'd just been familiar with his karma for a long time. A guy sang me one of his songs and I said, wow, that's really nice, who is that? He said that's Steve Fromholz, and then I got a tape I didn't listen to, but in my mind I'd signed him even before I had the record company. I don't know whether he's right or wrong, you know, I don't know whether he's good or bad, but I know that it's music."

What kind of material was on the album?

"Just his stuff. In order to make this kind of music you have to insert what you call a relatable so that you don't totally disorient the audience. Yet you can pull them. You can say come on this way a little bit. I know that artistically you have to insert relatables. It's the old play the hit thing, you know, play the hit so people can identify and say: right, I know, Jesus, I was in Kansas, I remember that, I was driving through . . . and boom, you're there and they connect. So as long as you have those relatables you can go up, down, it doesn't make any difference what kind of music you put on it."

Fromholz fit Nesmith's Countryside scheme perfectly. His music defied categorization, and if the day of the video cassette was indeed coming, the droopy eyelids, Yosemite Sam moustache, wiggling hips and sweat-soaked bandana would not always be lost in the one-dimensionality of a long-playing album. The problem, however, was that relatable.

Side one of the Countryside album would discourage Fromholz's Austin fanatics, for it was designed to entice those redneck listeners outside Austin. The album began with the old Bob Wills classic, "Cowtown." While Fromholz was the only performer in Austin who could get away with starting a set with "John Henry," "Cowtown" was not his kind of song, particularly when he was backed by honky-tonk fiddles, steels and pianos, and he was having to hurry to keep up. Fromholz needed to take his time when he sang, and his voice was forced and awkward on the first cut, and again on the second, one of Fromholz's roadside blues songs called "Maybe the Neon Light Still Shines." One could almost see the bootheels dancing at a trot and the petticoats swishing, but the voice on the album did not sound like Steve Fromholz.

Hopefully having made friends with hard-line country listeners, Nesmith began to slip Fromholz over on them. The instrumentation began to edge toward rock on the third cut, a Fromholz barroom tune called "Mildred's Sin," and again on the next cut, "Rambler and a

Gambler,'' the bitter resentment of a man deprived of a love affair because of his disreputable past, and the relatable Nesmith was looking for leaped out: *"If you people don't like me, you can leave me alone."* Fromholz and Nesmith returned to the country fold on the side's last cut, "Because He's Jesus," a Fromholz tune that appealed to beer-drinking Baptists because it lacked the tongue-in-cheek quality of most Austin gospel songs.

Moving from country toward rock with greater speed, the second side evolved from a love message to Fromholz's second wife to the mournful title cut of the album, "How Long Is the Road to Kentucky," from a sheer rock number paying homage to a lady on the Austin capitol payroll to a song that used nature to laugh at the ways of man:

> *Hate don't exist in the wolverine*
> *He's just uncommonly natural mean*
> *but that's a wolverine's scene*
> *His smell offends but*
> *he don't lie about being friendly*
> *Could it be that you and me*
> *could be that free?*

It might be country music, but it was stretching it. In the last cut Fromholz sang the most emotional song on the album, a letter set to music one day when he wondered whether his daughter, 6,000 miles away in Alaska, still believed he was real:

> *Dear Darcy, can you see the wind blow by?*
> *Covered up with snow like lookin' in a diamond's eye?*
> *Dear Darcy, can you see the northern lights?*
> *Dear Darcy, is it really mostly night?*
> *Are you all right?*

Given Nesmith's approach, it was a subtle, artful album, and Fromholz returned to Texas cocky and proud. In less prosperous times he had resorted to non-stop rum and sodas, turned his back to the audience and plugged into raucous rock & roll when his music was ignored by rich Houston girls with expressions of cameo boredom and voices that cut like knives. But when he came back to Austin from California and a fight erupted in the Cricket Club over whether the freak would loan the construction worker a cigarette or vice versa, Fromholz benignly wiped his forehead with his bandana and talked about his album. Nesmith sold a single offering "Cowtown" and "Dear Darcy" to the Austin jukebox operators, and Austin radio deejays started talking about the album's pending release, but it was a long wait. Lightning had struck Fromholz again. *How Long Is the Road to Kentucky* would never come out.

Nesmith's ally on the board at Elektra had been Jack Holtzman, but he jumped to the chairmanship of Warner Communications; Elektra became Elektra-Asylum, and there was no longer much sympathy in those offices for a West Coast country experiment. Two days before the album was to come out, Fromholz received word that Nesmith was leaving Elektra. A $20,000 investment was stuffed in the throwaway file. In shock, Fromholz went to Hollywood to argue with the recording company lawyers and heard what he expected to hear: there was a petroleum shortage, and vinyl came from petroleum. He retreated to Colorado and licked his wounds throughout the winter, canceled his gigs in Austin and tried to pull himself together. He drew closer to his wife and coached a boys' basketball team. All he had left of his flirtation with success was his sense of humor, and for a while he didn't have much of that.

In the spring he came to Austin and invited me to join him for breakfast at a restaurant near the University. We ordered bacon and eggs, and my photographer came in and apologized for arriving late. She said she had been detained at the Capitol.

"Politicians," Fromholz said as he peppered his eggs. "Do they show up on film? I understand some of them have a hard time making an impression on a mirror."

I asked if he had been playing much in Colorado. No, there wasn't anybody up there to play with. He and McCrimmon had played a couple of gigs together, just sitting in.

"What was McCrimmon doing?"

"He's playing some, writing some. Wondering what he's gonna do, really. He wants to be an entertainer, wants to perform, but his stage presence is hardly there at all. He comes on real weak. A little bit bitter, I think. When we quit playing together he was kinda left out in the storm. Frummox went as far as it could possibly go. We were just dead-ended, and I had that job offer from Stills so, hell, I took it and

132

An album and a tour with Stephen Stills behind him, Steve Fromholz was a writer of haunting songs and a born entertainer. But he was also luckless.

The nucleus of the North Texas State folk club, ten years after. A wisecracking bass player named Travis Holland (left) taught Fromholz to play the guitar and later became the straight man of his act. Though president of the folk club, Fromholz lost some time in the Navy, signed the wrong recording contracts, and found himself playing second act to Michael Murphey (below).

continued to play and kept on growing. Daniel just stopped for a while and took it personally, I guess. You can't take the music business personally at all, because it'll kill you. You have to be businesslike about it. I'm just learning how to be businesslike about it, after a long time of not knowing."

He looked out the window and watched a casually clad, barefoot girl flounce down the sidewalk. "I love Austin in the springtime," he said. "The women don't wear no clothes."

What was the tour with Stills like?

"Working with Stills had a great effect on me, because it was like going to school. I learned how to play a lot of shit that I didn't know before. We went all over and did all kinds of things. We went to England awhile to rehearse, and we played twenty-four cities in fifty days. It was a rock & roll special."

The curtain rattled by our window and Fromholz looked around. "Damn. An electric curtain." Fromholz was a shameful bum of cigarettes, which I couldn't criticize because we shared the same characteristic, but we had run out. He started digging in the ash tray and I said, "Don't smoke butts. I'll get some more."

"Oh, this is a good butt," he said. "This is one I smoked earlier. I never forget a butt."

Clearing his throat, Fromholz went on, "I went to work for Stills the first of June, and quit in November of the same year. I just left him a note one morning and said thanks, I'm going home. We were down in Miami recording and it wasn't my kind of deal. I wasn't where I should have been."

Why not?

"I'm not a surface person. When I'm into somebody I go right in and find out. What I saw I didn't like after I'd spent some time with it. I didn't like the ego hassles, and I didn't like the craziness — it wasn't my kind of craziness. I'm as crazy as anybody else, but it wasn't my kind of shot. I was heavily into cocaine and I was getting real sick."

Nosebleeds?

"I didn't get nosebleeds but I guess I almost died. My skin was turning green, and my joints were swelling up. It was way too fast for me. I never played any rock & roll before I went to work for Stephen. He taught me a lot, but the price was just too much for me to pay. You pay a price for that, by god, and it's very expensive. It doesn't cost money; it costs time and it costs your mind and your friends. I'd rather have my friends than any kind of financial success or critical acclaim, because without them what I do is meaningless. I do it for them, I guess. And working with Stephen was changing my relationship with the people who were my friends. I thought Stephen might be a friend but it turned out we were acquaintances. And I didn't want to lose my mind, so I checked it to him.

"I was a part of Manassas when the band first got together. We'd already started on the album, and we were even talking about doing a Stephen and Stephen record. But it was mostly talk, and working together I would have had to give up a lot. Several times I compromised myself for someone else's benefit. I did things that I didn't believe were true just because somebody said they were. And they weren't. But if you're working with a bunch of people, and you see things that aren't real and are flat-ass wrong, but these people tell you how screwed up you are — we're not wrong, you are — if they tell you that long enough, you'll begin to believe it. I had begun to believe it, then I got real lucky and took another look. Well, I said, that's not for me. I'm not willing to pay the price of my self-respect just to make somebody else happy and please somebody else's ego.

"I've got a pretty strong ego myself, and Stills and I occasionally bounced off one another pretty good. We'd get drunk and holler at one another, almost came to blows one time in Gold Hill, Colorado. But I made a whole lot of money on that gig. Spent it as fast as I made it. I went through $22,000 in six months. And I loved it. I never had any money before; it was fun. Now if I ever have any money again I won't have to do that, I can save it. But I went through it that time. Nobody was gonna outdo me, by god.

"I think I may have been lucky that my relative obscurity has lasted as long as it has, because if anything does happen, and I think eventually something will happen if I stay in the business long enough, I'll be a lot more prepared than I would have been two years ago. I feel better about myself than I did then. And I've got a closer look at it. I've looked at somebody else's stardom, and seen how much it cost him."

Was there any chance *How Long Is the Road to Kentucky* would ever come out?

"I think we could hold Elektra to the contract, but I stopped asking, I stopped wondering about it. Jesus. I fretted and worried and went crazy all October and November. It just freaked me out because I thought, man, the waiting is over, it's gonna come out, and then it didn't. It really screwed me over in the head. I played all kinds of tricks on myself. When something happens that I can't understand I usually blame myself, because I hate to blame somebody else. I'm really hard on myself about things like that. I give myself a lot of unnecessary shit, I guess. But now, if it comes out, fine. If it doesn't, that's fine too. Maybe somebody else will take me on."

Was he dissatisfied with Nesmith's production of the album?

"No, I was very pleased with it. I think it's a good record. But it's not a true example of what I feel about what I do. I don't think I'm captured on that record. I don't feel like what I do is on that record. What I did in Los Angeles those two weeks under Mike Nesmith's supervision is on that record. He definitely produced it, and his ego is felt all through the record. Now it wouldn't *hurt* anything if it came out. There's a lot of people who want it to. I'm the most famous obscure musician in the country. But I quit trying to understand it. I think maybe my karma is keeping it from coming out.

"But it seems to me that recording is taken much too seriously by most of the people who are involved in it. I guess it's the importance put on having a successful record. They say this record has to be good or your career is over. Well, I've proved that doesn't work. When I recorded out there I worked with strangers, dudes that I'd never met before. They were very good musicians, but I'd rather record with my friends. I want it to sound good, but I also want it to feel good, for it to be a legitimate expression of the song.

"The worst thing about recording is spending say, nine to twelve hours in a studio for, say, six days in a row. You lose all perspective of time and people. It's always the same time in a studio — any time you want it to be. It's like a bowling alley. No sunshine, it's not real. Something happens to you. You've got a microphone to sing into; there's no people."

"You like playing for a crowd, don't you?"

"Oh yeah. I love it. The bigger the better. The butterflies came and went a long time ago."

"Even when it's not a good crowd?"

"Well, people go to a concert expecting to get blown away. The music in this country has been so good for so long, off and on, that the audiences expect you to go out there and really hit them. Sometimes I get real bored, not with the crowd so much as with myself, and I get real drunk. But other times I'll be playing with a band, and a song that I think's a nice quiet tune will really start to rock & roll, so I just let it go. It doesn't make any difference. It's just a temporary presentation to a bunch of people who paid a bunch of money. It's show business. It's just like Danny Thomas playing Las Vegas. Realizing that makes it a lot easier, because you can begin not to take it so personally. If you don't take it personally you've got a much better chance of being a success. You can take it personally at home, playing for your friends."

What were his immediate plans?

"Oh, I'm moving down here so I won't have to travel so far to play. And I'm gonna go to work for the management company. I'll be vice-president of artist relations. Don't that sound neat? I have no idea what I'll be doing or how much they'll pay me, but I'm gonna take the job." He laughed and pulled one of Larry Watkins' Moon Hill cards out of his wallet. "They even made business cards up for me. Business cards.

"I make a living doing this," he said. "I'm not in a situation where I can flow as freely as I'd like to. I've got certain commitments that I have to meet, a certain amount of money I have to make each month, and I have to go get it. Nobody says here's your check, Fromholz."

Would he be playing music in ten years?

"I probably will be, one way or another. I don't know what's gonna happen in ten years. I might be playing Las Vegas for five thousand a throw. I've come to accept that this is what I do, and I guess I'll keep on doing it unless something changes. But I'm not planning any farther ahead than this summer. My plans go as far as my next booking goes, and luckily the bookings are getting farther ahead now. To not have any product on the market, I'm critically and financially more successful than I've ever been. I'm making more money and working less, which is one of my goals. But if I start worrying about it and start thinking about what I'll do tomorrow, I think I'll blow it. I'm too old to blow it now; I've been at it too long.

"Sometimes I get in a hurry and think I'm running out of time, but that's silly. Because this is what I do. And promotions come as you keep working. In age Walker and Murphey are my peers, roughly, but I've still got to catch up and qualify, I guess. They started out before I did, and I lost some time in the service, so I guess I have some more time to put in as an apprentice. At least that's one of the rationales I use to keep myself going. Musicians never stop paying their dues, unless they quit playing. And I can't quit playing. I don't know what else I'd do. I wouldn't be happy, I know that. I wrote a song once called 'I'd Have to Be Crazy to Stop All my Singing and Never Play Music Again,' and I would be. Because I do it well. People enjoy what I do. I don't know whether people pay money to hear my music or just to see me work. But when I get onstage something happens to me, and people like to see that, I think. I don't try to overwhelm them, because there're people who can do that a lot better than I can, but they pay to see me and they do it in the weirdest places. I guess I almost revel in my obscurity. I'm nationally known, and in music circles my name is brought up and talked about. People say what the hell is he doing, who is he, I've heard of him, why can't I buy his record? I don't know.

"But in twelve years I'll be forty, and I'd like to have it together by then. I want to be able to sit back and clip coupons, be easy on myself. I take long looks at everybody else's ups and downs. Now Walker's had some ups and downs. But he just stays with it and he becomes more like Jerry Jeff all the time. He may die before he's forty, but he's gonna go out being Jerry Jeff Walker, if it kills him, and it may."

What did he see in the future for Austin?

"Everybody's been saying Austin is gonna be a Texas Nashville, but I don't know. Austin's really laid back. Like if you drive from Dallas to Austin, you can feel the difference as soon as you get into town. It's so easy, and all that hype bullshit doesn't go down here. Nobody buys it. They know it's bullshit and they say it's bullshit. The pickers down here aren't kids. Most of them are pushing thirty, and they've been playing long enough to get that star trip out of their heads. They've seen that it doesn't happen, and if it does, somebody's lying to you and you're believing it. But I have no idea what's gonna happen. I hope it just stays nice and quiet."

Could Austin become another Nashville yet avoid its mistakes?

"Sure. If it happens that's how it'll happen. It won't work the other way. A Nashville hype will never happen in this city, because the musicians won't let it happen."

Dubious, I asked how a musician could prevent it.

"When you hear bullshit you ring your bell. When I had the band together last winter, an A&R man from Columbia came out and caught us on a Wednesday night at Castle Creek, and it was a mediocre show. I knew that. Well, here's this dude from L.A. being the big man, you know, and the first thing he said when we went offstage was, well, your guitar player can't play very well. I said why don't you shove it up your ass? You don't walk up to me and tell me my guitar player can't play. And that was the last word I heard from them. I didn't give a shit if they offered me a deal or not.

"That's what happens down here. People down here move more slowly and drinks lots of Lone Star beer and smoke a whole bunch of dope, and they play good music. They're not interested in limousines. They buy cocaine when they can find it, but those hype days are over, just like the days of the big money advances. Like gasoline, there ain't no more money. To come down here you've got to be truthful and honest and real with the people you're dealing with. You can't lie to the musicians, they won't even talk to you if you lie to them. That's one of the reasons I like it so much. The truth level here is real high. The bullshit is just bullshit among friends. Nobody's lying to each other or stabbing each other in the back. The pickers will not stand for it from clubowners or from anybody. That's why Rod Kennedy is occasionally hard to work for, because he's full of shit, old Rod is."

What about the Armadillos?

"I've known Eddie Wilson for a long time. I enjoy playing there. They perform a really fine service. The Armadillo is nationally famous and a few years ago there wasn't a famous place in Austin. Now there are two or three. The Armadillo's booking major talent; Castle Creek is booking major talent. So is the Pub. You've got to pay money to get these people to come pick, and the folks come back because they enjoy playing here. There are more places to play in Austin than in Los Angeles, and better places.

"What's going on down here is very important to the music business, and the impact has not even been felt in lots of places. In the East, they don't really know what we're talking about. They come from a different world. It's hard for them to relate to a lot of things that the writers down here write about. But it's gonna become easier and easier for it to happen. The glitter rock, the codpiece rock, the naked-man rock can only last so long. Music keeps on changing; it's ready for another change right now. But people will pay to see the damnedest things. Like I think paying to see David Bowie is a very weird thing to do. But I imagine there must be a place for what he does; he's a success.''

If success was to be gauged by the number of people who paid to see him, Fromholz was a spectacular failure one Friday night a few weeks later at Castle Creek. The students were out of town for the spring break, so Moyes and O'Connor closed their place on Wednesday and Thursday, and only a small crowd trickled in to see Fromholz on Friday. Fromholz came in with only Leonard Arnold to help him, but they hooked the crowd early with ''Texas Trilogy'' and another long, involved number that put Arnold to work Chuck Berry-style on his guitar and blended ''Brown-Eyed Handsome Man'' with Fromholz's ''Lanky Southern Lady,'' a tune that lyrically confused a midnight freight back to Texas with a romp in the arms of a black lover.

''How's that mike doing?'' Fromholz asked Arnold after the song.

''You're all right back here!'' a girl shouted in the audience.

''Well you're all right back there too,'' Fromholz said, then ever the cigarette bum, asked, ''Has anybody got a legal smoke they can loan me? Throw it to me.''

A girl near the stage said, ''I will if you'll do 'Yellow Cab'.''

''Okay, I'll do 'Yellow Cab' right now. Woman come all the way from by-god Houston to hear 'Yellow Cab'. He looked around at his amplifier. ''Why is that sonofabitch feedin' back? My patience with inanimate objects should be a lot more than it is, and is a lot more than it was. Hopefully it will be a lot more than it has been.''

Fromholz sang the requested number, then introduced a frivolous *cantina* song, and said, ''We wrote this song in memorium to the car caravans that used to leave places like Denton, Texas and Greenville, Texas ten or fifteen years ago and drive south to the wonderful tropical paradise of Villa Acuna, Coahuilla, Mexico.The boys would leave on a Friday afternoon, cut the last half of school and go down there and drink as much as they could and chase all the ladies in the bars and get generally drunked up and tired. And when it came time to come home they'd take lots of *beenies*. Say man, want a *beenie*?

''I had a stepbrother who was exed off in Vietnam in the recent conflict there. He was one of the leaders of those groups. By the time he was fifteen or sixteen he was one of the instigators of those trips. In fact he probably lost his virginity in Mexico. And he took lots of *beenies*. Larry liked to drive; he'd say sure, I'm all right, I can drive, gimme a *beenie*. He'd take two or three and start driving back, and he said one night this big white Colonial Southern-style home appeared in the highway in front of him. He said he just took a couple of *beenies* and drove on through the door, it was open. Said he had to pull over the time the great huge tiger jumped out and ate the car. Man, he said, I've had enough *beenies*. Anyway, this song comes from that. It's called 'The Mexican Waltz.' Don't you just love a good waltz? I'll do a medley of waltzes.''

When he had finished his tale of *tourista* disease to great applause, Fromholz said, ''We're gonna do a song now that was a hit by a band we used to play in called the Iron Chalupa. We had a big hit down in Del Rio. One side was 'Black Magic Marker.' You mighta heard that. The other side was a song called 'Enchilada de Vida.' They loved it down there. Ate it up.

''No. We're gonna do another waltz dedicated to the Texas Highway Department.'' The song dealt with the time Fromholz and Travis Holland were busted for marijuana possession in Dallas, and the crowd applauded in anticipation. ''Damn, Leonard,'' Fromholz said. ''There's a highway department convention in town tonight, and we didn't even know it. This song is also dedicated to some friends of mine who couldn't be with us tonight. I'm talking about Captain Duck and Dougy Uckling, the hero duo who do battle with the Lizard People. They're so little known that their secret identities are known, and their real identities are not, which makes it real hard to fight crime. It's also dedicated to the United States Customs officials who used to frequent Love Field in Dallas. I hope that when they get home tonight their mothers crawl out from under the steps and bite them on the leg. It's a song called 'The Rest Area Waltz'. '' More applause. ''You're a real good audience. Y'all free to travel? Charter a couple of buses and take 'em with us, Leonard.''

The next night I found Fromholz sitting on a curb in front of Castle Creek. I congratulated him for his show the night before, but he looked up at the sky and said, ''There's a full moon tonight. I'd a lot rather be at the drive-in than here.''

Fromholz's attitude showed in his work. Along with Arnold a dobro player accompanied him this time, but the addition didn't help much. Nothing they tried worked as well as it had the night before. It was a larger crowd, but it was loud, rude and disruptive. "Damn," Fromholz said. "Saturday night spring break in Austin. It seems like I've played every Spring break in Austin for the last twenty years. I've got a friend named Travis Holland who's in Florida eating marijuana sandwiches right now. He used to tell me that I could take the best audience in America and in fifteen minutes turn them into a room full of turkeys. Tonight I feel like I've succeeded beyond my wildest expectations.

An unsure silence fell over the room after a few nervous laughs. "Are you listening? I hear you breathing. I know you're out there." "We're out here," somebody shouted.

"No doubt. Well we're up here too." He eased off on them a bit. "I'm a turkey too. One night in Colorado I got so drunk and rowdy that Taj Mahal shot me the finger. I was just having a good time. I thought he knew that.

"You know there's some friends of ours who help us out from time to time as we go along the roads of our lives. I'd like to pay a special tribute to them now. I'm speaking, of course, of my friends the makers and manufacturers of those delightful Dimmy Jean Pore Puke Sauce Linkages, friends and neighbors. Dimmy Jean's Pore Puke Sauce Linkages, the only pore puke sauce linkages made before your very eyes in Plain-view, Texas, friends; made from only the finest available sows and hostages known to mortal man this side of the Great Beyond. We encourage you, each and everyone of you that is, to rush on down to your neighborhood Hoggy Woggly or A & Poo Feed Store and pick up on some of these fine Dimmy Jean products. Along with Dimmy Jean Pore Puke Sauce Linkages you may also purchase Dimmy Jean Hot Long Foot Dogs, not to mention a brand new product just out on the market, Dimmy Jean Saucy Pattages. We know you'll enjoy them as much as they enjoy being enjoyed by each and everyone of you. And remember friends, added at the factory for your health and well-being is just a touch of horse hide and respoiled cardation, so you know our sauce linkages are fresh, fresh, fresh; from the back of the piggy right to your table every mornin'. You can hear 'em singing in the factory there every Friday afternoon come paycheck time:

Dimmy Jean Pore Puke Sauce Linkages
good for the whole damn family
made from the pig your breakfast loves to be

143

He was born in Oklahoma
His wife's name is Betty Lou Thelma Liz
He's not responsible for what he's doin'
His mother made him what he is
Up against the wall redneck mother
Mother who has raised her son so well
He's thirty-four and drinkin' in some honky-tonk
Kickin' hippies' asses and raisin' hell

With a little help from Ray Wylie Hubbard, Fromholz had disposed of Jimmy Dean and Merle Haggard in one fell swoop, but he still had the Castle Creek crowd in front of him. "Streak for us," a girl suggested loudly.

"You meet me in the back room, honey, and we'll streak together."

"It won't be too hard," Arnold sang out.

"Get back, Leonard," Fromholz cried. "This is ridiculous. You're supposed to be on my side."

Fromholz sang a couple more songs then said, "Here's a song off my recent unreleased album. I won a prize for having the greatest number of unreleased albums in one year. They gave me the Golden Cowpile."

"What's the name of it?" a girl wanted to know.

"What, the album? What does it matter, you're not gonna get to hear it. No. The album was gonna be called *How Long Is the Road to Kentucky*, but as it turned out it was called Exed Out # EP752367."

Was it ever going to come out?

"Shit, the thing couldn't escape the way things are going. It's not up to me. If it was up to me . . . I'd be purty near all you'd listen to. But, it's not up to me."

After he gobbled like a turkey in response to the cries from the audience and struggled through a few more songs, Fromholz said, "Thanks for being with us this first show. We're glad you're here, and if you've got nothing better to do, get up early in the morning about six o'clock and drive to Nacogdoches. There's a festival up there tomorrow."

"What about church?" somebody shouted.

Fromholz looked at him. "That's what I'm gonna do. I'm going to church, only my church is in Nacogdoches. Lord, you can get closer to

God playing music than you can screaming at people who don't believe."

A few people applauded and Fromholz grinned sheepishly. "Whatever that means. God and I have an agreement. I'm not sure what it is yet, but we have a deal. Whole 'nother show coming up in a minute.

> *Six o'clock silence of a new day beginning*
> *is heard in a small Texas town*
> *Like a signal from nowhere, the people who live there*
> *are up and moving around*
> *'Cause there's bacon to fry and biscuits to bake*
> *on a stove that the Salvation Army won't take*
> *Open the windows and turn on the fan*
> *'cause it's hotter than hell when the sun hits the land*

the voice

*(Come with me to L.A., boy,
and we'll make a bundle)*

B. W. Stevenson lived in Dallas, but he was an Austin musician. He hadn't always been. Until he recorded his first album he was just a fat, shy outsider who couldn't buy a gig in Austin. He was another North Texas State student, but he got to Denton about the time the old folk clubbers were leaving, and anyway, he probably would have been suspect in that crowd because he was an academic music student. In a state that tended to abhor the traditional forms of music, North Texas State, which ranked about sixth on the list of state-supported colleges and universities, for some reason had one of the better music schools west of the Mississippi. Perhaps because Denton was dry for so long, and it was easier to keep the musicians straight. Whatever the reasons, very serious youths studied music for four years in Denton and got their degrees in the field, and many had more in store for them than a clankety piano and a classroom of sixth-graders singing "Up In the Air Junior Birdmen." North Texas was proud of its music program. The chairman of the department recruited more selectively than the football coach.

At the age of eighteen Stevenson was a west Dallas face in the crowd; his rock band was called Us. But he had this voice. It had a Texas twang that would have to be ironed out, but it surged from deep in his chest and could rattle the lights if he would let it. He had a soft, favorite range, high in his tenor, that was both winsome and sad, but then he would reach back and gulp more air and the voice would barrel out in an overwhelming baritone. He could take a song with a muttering beginning to a thundering finish. If he had a little more bass and schooling, the North Texas recruiters must have thought, he could probably sing Italian opera. Unfortunately, he didn't take his voice scholarship seriously. He was kicked out of school after a year, for reasons that he preferred not to disclose. Still living in Denton, in a tiny bedroom with a communal refrigerator and a drunk old man in the building who stole his beer, Stevenson drove thirty-five miles north for a semester at Cooke County Junior College, which in those 2-A draft-classified days was the only institution of higher learning in the state that would accept a student who had just flunked out of another institution. (As a result of that, Gainesville became one of the wildest towns in Texas during the years of the Vietnam War.) Stevenson finally gave up the fight and joined the Air Force, but he got out early — again for reasons that he preferred not to disclose.

He was odd-jobbing in Dallas and playing the clubs there when he went looking for work in Austin in 1970 and found nobody was interested. During those struggling days something very important happened to both his outlook and his music. He got jilted. His girlfriend broke off the engagement and he couldn't understand why. In his writing at least, he became almost obsessed with the subject. Either he was doing the jilting or he was getting jilted. Somebody was always on the raw end of things. He was one of the most authentic writers of unhappy love songs since Bob Dylan, but while Dylan's love songs tended to be bitter, Stevenson's songs were just sad.

If you find your true love once again
please don't do the same damn thing to him
Even when I was with you I felt so all alone
So I'd as soon do without you and be on my own
I want to be on my own; it's a long way home
I feel like a baby boy just being born

Those were the songs that made the ladies cry. They didn't help Stevenson much when he tried to market himself in Los Angeles, but they attracted the starry-eyed attention of a regional scout for RCA, and they set the tone for his first album, which was released in 1971. The other imprint on the album belonged to Michael Murphey. RCA didn't think any of Stevenson's songs had hit-single potential, so one of his sad songs became Side 2, and they gave a little Side 1 nudge to a Murphey song that was actually a poor choice. Stevenson did the best he could with "Say What I Feel," but it was a song about songwriting and was as unsuccessful as most novels about writing novels. Like the single, the album went nowhere. Stevenson recorded the album in Chicago and the only identifiably Texas characteristics of the record were Stevenson's nasal pitch and his improved version of one of Murphey's best early songs, a weary stopover in a predawn truckstop called "Five O'Clock in the Texas Morning."

That was enough local flavor for the Austin audiences. B. W. came out of the RCA promo offices dubbed Buckwheat; Austin radio stations pushed and played his single and talked it up. He performed at the Armadillo with Kenneth Threadgill, and the older Austin musicians welcomed him like a little brother. He was identified with Austin music, but RCA didn't see it that way. They wanted a star, and few stars were identified with Austin music. B. W.'s appeal had to be broader than that. B. W.'s producer, a young go-getter named David Kershenbaum, lined up some of the best sidemen in L.A. for the next album, a good deal less of Stevenson's material, and he spread the regional appeal around. The songs were variously set in Pennsylvania, Mexico, Memphis and Jackson, Mississippi. Whoever packaged the product titled the album *Lead Free*, and lined up two introductory epigrams:

> *Some people call me crazy, others think I'm a genius. . . . when in truth I'm just a simple man.*
>
> —the Prophet M

> *And on the seventh day the idea sat back and said, 'Lo, I have created the rhythm, the melody, the words, the copyright, the contracts, the studio and the symphony, the wax, the cover and the cellophane. Now, I will take the seventh day and see if the ears can get it.' Welcome to the seventh day and a simple idea from a man named B. W. Stevenson. He that doth have ears to hear . . . let him hear.*
>
> —Bob Hamilton

149

Bob Hamilton probably thought he was being clever when he wrote that, but he was telling a great deal of the truth. Stevenson was being packaged and sold. He was no longer in control of his own career. Even worse, the album didn't sell much better than the first one. The most commercially appealing cut on the album was his version of "Peaceful Easy Feeling," but the Eagles had already done that so there wasn't even the salvage of a hit single. Yet the people at RCA were still patient. *Lead Free* was slick Hollywood schmaltz, but Kershenbaum had made a significant discovery. If he lined up a chorus, tambourine, downbeat piano and country-rock lead guitar, and if B. W. sang just a little louder, the man could really wail. Kershenbaum found a young staff writer for ABC-Dunhill named Danny Moore who had written a song called "Shambala" that was buried in that factory's vault of rejects. The lyrics vaguely described an appealing never-never land, which was timely since Carlos Castaneda's *Journey to Ixtlan* was very much in literary vogue, and the song gave Stevenson a chance to loosen the reins on his voice.

The single took off quickly and climbed as high as number sixty-three on the *Billboard* pop chart, but ABC-Dunhill quickly rediscovered the song, and they just happened to have a contract called Three Dog Night. An era of flamboyant band names in the sixties had given the world Vanilla Fudge, the Grateful Dead and the Electric Prunes, but Three Dog Night was the catchiest band name of them all, supposedly derived from the Australian aborigine practice of sleeping with two dogs on a normal desert night, reaching for a third when it really got chilly. On top of that, Three Dog Night had chanced upon the perfect commercial formula. Their producer had an uncanny knack for recognizing hit-single lyrics, all the releases sounded the same, and they were all good. As a result Three Dog Night turned out a hit every time. They were the only band in the country that could get away with releasing an easy Christmas-money tune backed up by a chorus of dogs barking Jinglebells. ABC-Dunhill and Three Dog Night "covered" Stevenson, as the saying went in the music business, their version charted the customary top-ten parabola, and B. W. was stuck with number sixty-three and sliding.

Stevenson got some sympathy in the press from the episode, but that was all. He had given his managerial business to Moon Hill by then, and Larry Watkins told my magazine collaborator and me that he was on the road a lot but still living in Dallas. Watkins looked at our deadline calendar and said our best bet would be to make a trip to Dallas one Sunday for B. W.'s benefit for the beseiged at Wounded Knee. To Dallas and back on a Sunday.

Dallas and Austin were separated by 200 miles of interstate highway, the city of Waco, numerous Stuckey's Pecan Shoppes, one sign that said Art Here, and uniformly dull, bald, rolling farmland. After a couple of dozen trips between the two cities one could drive it blindfolded, but it was still 200 miles of monotony. The Volkswagen quit on us once in the vicinity of Willie Nelson's hometown, and I wondered if Willie was trying to tell us something. The trip north proceeded smoothly enough after that, our spirits bouyed by B. W.'s albums on a tape deck in the back seat and one of his original weepers in the front. Lucy was a veteran of Woodstock but more recently a victim of a ministerial marriage, and she was reverting to her old form. She enjoyed meeting the performers we were interviewing, and we were happy to have her along. She was good company, and she behaved herself during the interviews. The skid of estrangement, separation and divorce had made her emotionally vulnerable, and her favorite Austin musician was B. W., for his quiet songs were the most emotional of the lot.

Lucy had lived in Florida, Virginia, New York, Guadalajara and Austin, but she had never been to Dallas. As we passed Waxahachie and moved into the mobile-home suburbs she asked what it was like. My magazine collaborator said, "You're the Texan. You tell her."

"Uh," I said. "Hm."

East Texas extended as close to Dallas as the cotton-farming blackland fifty miles to the east, and nearby Fort Worth was Cowtown, a West Texas city, but Dallas was hard to pin down, for most of its regional flavor had been sterilized by the orderly rush toward progress and prosperity. Dallas still hosted the State Fair of Texas, an event with a prouder past than present, and a stories-high cowboy on the fairgrounds called Big Tex who grinned howdy-you-all and waved over yonder at the downtown office towers. But given the direction of his gaze, they should have named him Big Buck Dollar. Dallas was a working capitalistic model, a tolerable place for those who aspired toward a station wagon, a social wedding for their daughter and a fat retirement check at the age of sixty, for those were the kind of people who made the corporations money. But heaven help those who were unwilling or unable to contribute to the monetary good. Dallas was hard on its ethnics and hippies — unless they were fortunate enough to drive Cadillacs — and the jails were virtual torture chambers, spare of toilet paper and mattresses, chilled to a shivering level even when the heat shimmered off the sidewalks outside.

Most Dallasites were able to stay out of jail, but they lived in one of the most hurried yet deadening cities anywhere. They fought the freeways to work, zipped to the twenty-second floor in the fastest of elevators, zipped down again to take their routine stroll during their lunch hour, zipped up to combat another afternoon's drowsiness, zipped down and hurried to their cars so they could get to the traffic jam. When they got home their liquor or pot was a tremendous relief. They had to hurry to live in Dallas otherwise they'd get run over. There was always some place else to go, something else to do. Some way to beat the boredom.

I doubted Lucy was interested in hearing all that, so I begged the question until we whipped off the freeway onto Central Expressway, which was just another clogged street in the downtown area. We came to a halt at a stop light across the street from the establishmentarian pop station, KLIF, and I looked over at our neighbor in the next lane — a handsome young black with stylish clothes, a pretty girlfriend and a new Chevrolet. Suddenly there was a crash, and the Chevrolet jumped out into the intersection, bumped along several times by a smoking '59 Buick that just couldn't seem to stop. The young black's neck popped with each succeeding collision. Finally the two cars came to a halt; an anguished *chicano* man got out of the Buick apologizing in very poor English, and the young black gripped his steering wheel and stared straight ahead. "God *damn*," he finally thundered and got out of the car with a look indicating he was about to behead some South African Dutchman. His nostrils flared and his eyes flashed as he listened to the unhappy *chicano*, then he sighed and said, "It's all right. It's all right."

"Lucy," I said, "welcome to Dallas."

The remainder of the trip to the Moody Coliseum on the SMU campus was uneventful enough, though the lady in the ticket office with eighteen-inch curls on her head said B. W. would play two hours later than we expected. She also got extremely anxious when we told her we were with a magazine.

152

"You're going to write about this benefit?"

"Well, more about B. W. Stevenson."

She led us through the door, and we followed her go-go boots down a corridor. Looking back over her shoulder, she said, "Before you go in there, I think I'd better tell you this wasn't promoted worth a shit."

Moody Coliseum housed an oval-shaped basketball arena, and one entrance door was hard to tell from another. The woman finally found the entrance to the backstage area, where we encountered a campus policeman who stared grimly at a group of longhaired Ivy-Leaguers singing about their religious experience. The policeman held up a hand and asked us what business we had in the backstage area. I couldn't see that the question made any difference or even deserved an answer. Sprawled on the carpet in front of the stage were about thirty people. The 5000 seats in the coliseum were empty. Apparently the people of Dallas didn't care much for the American Indian Movement.

We retreated to a shade tree outside the coliseum while the first band sang about Jesus and the second band, a rock group from Austin distinguished only by one instrument that resembled a washboard, filled the empty place with raucous noise. We went back inside after a while and finally Stevenson's entourage began to drift in. One of them peeked through the door at the stage, stared at the emptiness, and apparently decided to let B. W. see for himself. Stevenson came in wearing a stovepipe hat, his hair, beard and belly expansive. He set his guitar case on the floor and stood talking to one of the most attractive girls I'd seen in a while. She was red-haired and much too homespun to run in the best Dallas circles, but she had the kind of smile one seldom saw anymore — embracing everyone, singling no one out. Stevenson walked inside the stage entrance, and emerged quickly with a drawn look on his face.

Word got around to the band onstage that the name act had arrived, and they came off angry — they needed the exposure. One of them said a few bitter words to one of Stevenson's associates, who asked his leader, "Who were those guys?"

"I don't know," B. W. said. "They've got a lot of balls."

Stevenson decided his band had made the trip from Austin for nothing; all the accompaniment he would need for that crowd was a bass. He started tuning his guitar, and I approached him and said we were the journalists from Austin. He grunted noncommittally and looked away, rather surly.

My bias against Stevenson was building but he surprised me when he went onstage. He had a shy but humorous manner between songs and his voice fairly echoed through the gymnasium. His voice was bigger than the crowd and I wondered what the people from RCA would have thought about it. "You're a good crowd," B. W. said. "I just wish there were more of you."

After his brief performance, I hesitantly approached Stevenson again, asking if he had time to join us for a beer. An impish grin creased his face making him look like a bearded leprechaun. He was a different man.

Stevenson led the way down Mockingbird Lane in a new Ford van with his smiling girlfriend in the front seat, then detoured through one of Dallas's stuffier wealthy neighborhoods. The citadel mansions sat far back on green slopes manicured by Negro labor, faced toward a little creek and deserted park where cane-pole fishing was severely discouraged. As I watched the back of B. W.'s stovepipe hat, the incongruity of a country-rock musician living in Dallas came down heavily. Positive funk was hard to find in the city of Dallas.

After a stop at a package store for several six-packs of beer, we proceeded north on a narrow, bumpy yet heavily-traveled avenue called Cedar Springs, then pulled into an entrance of a mid-priced apartment complex. It was in a neighborhood that had once nearly driven me crazy. As soon as one DC-7 finished wrecking the TV screen, another appeared on the horizon.

The complex even looked a little like my old abode. As we walked upstairs and followed the railing, a young man in an adjoining yard yelled, "Hey, is that B. W. Stevenson, the rock star?" Stevenson smiled and opened the door for his girlfriend.

In the summer, the only appeal of that kind of apartment complex was its air conditioning. The shallow swimming pools were about as refreshing as a bowl of split-pea soup. We settled into the coolness; the musicians took off their hats, and I looked around. It even looked inside like my old apartment, though B. W.'s girlfriend was a better housekeeper and a sewing machine sat on the floor. B. W. sank into an easy chair, crossed his ankles, clasped his hands on his belly and passed on the cigar-sized joints that his drummer manufactured. At times as we talked he seemed on the verge of sleep. He was easily the most relaxed musician I had run across.

Packaged by RCA as a pop product, B.W. Stevenson was seen with the likes of Leon Russell and was recognized by fellow musicians as a young man with enormous vocal talent.

Welcomed like a little brother into the fraternity of Austin musicians, Stevenson cavorted at a benefit performance with (above, from left) Jerry Jeff Walker, Chequered Flag Folk veteran Segal Fry, and Ray Wylie Hubbard. Managed by Moon Hill's Larry Watkins (below), Stevenson wasn't the most dynamic performer in town, but he was the one who threatened to make a major commercial breakthrough.

My collaborator said he seemed a little nervous before he went onstage.

"Yeah, I get stage fright real bad, no matter where I'm playing."

I asked how one procured a voice scholarship at North Texas State.

"You try out — you stand around like a fool and sing dumb songs. I thought a lot of that stuff up there was superficial bullshit. They destroyed any creativity in music because they tied it down with so many rules."

My collaborator asked if he enjoyed his work.

"I wouldn't do it if I didn't like it. I bitch a lot and I find a lot of things wrong with it, but for the most part it's all right. I'm glad everything has gone as well as it has. It could've gone a lot worse."

Was it extremely important to have a hit record?

"Everybody in the company thinks so. I don't really care if we have one. I'd rather grow in my song writing ability and make it in my own time, when I'm ready to be put up at that level, when I'm sure I can stand right next to people who are considered the best in the business. I'm not right now. Those people out in L.A. are after money. I'm not particularly. I'd rather have some stability of person."

We asked him about the "Shambala" incident.

"That kinda ticked me off. I wouldn't have minded except ABC said they had a freeze on the song. Three Dog Night didn't need that hit. But as far as all the uproar afterward, they made a lot of fuss for nothing. I didn't particularly give a shit. It pissed me off that they thought I would."

Was he pleased with the way he was being produced?

"I don't want to talk about that."

Oh. Well, did he enjoy living in Dallas?

"No, I'd rather live in Austin. Right now I'm here because I can't afford to move." Our faces registered disbelief. "I'm not in the dregs by any means," he conceded. "I'm a lot further along than I was two years ago.

"But I hope to get down there eventually. Austin's the only city in Texas that's worth anything. People talk about the friendliness of Texans. Well, if you go out to West Texas they're not so goddamn friendly. But in Austin it seems like you can get all the different factions together and nobody seems to mind. When you go out on the road you have to submerge yourself in bullshit rat-race — the club-owners and the contracts and the people who come to drink instead of listen. It's such a relief to come back to Austin, because you don't have to be anywhere anytime for anybody."

Would he like to record in Austin?

"No, I like to go away to record. It's a change of scenery, a freshness. But I don't want to move anywhere I've seen. Chicago's populated by masochists; they're always looking over their shoulders. A lot of people have been trying to get me to move to Los Angeles, but that place can really get to you. I went out there before, and that's the hardest town I've ever seen. You can't get any jobs. You take your tape to some club-owner and he says yeah kid, that's real nice, and you know he hasn't even listened to the sonofabitch. It's real hard to get anything done out there unless you have a guy with a cigar in his mouth and a recording contract. They could care less about you out there. They're only interested in the Joe Blow on the charts.

"I guess New York is even worse. The people there are really cold, and at least you can breathe in California and go to the beach. But I'll say this: New York was exactly like I pictured it. It wasn't as bad and tough as everybody said. I kind of enjoyed it. I'd like to go back."

Stevenson was a dull man to interview, but by then our own senses had been dulled by the drummers reefer cigars. The questions got harder and harder to ask, and when the tape ran out it seemed like a monumental task to turn the cassette over, so my collaborator put it away. Everybody always seemed to heave a sigh of relief when we shut down the tape recorder. B. W.'s sidemen went back to Austin, and after a while he got out his guitar and, his voice subdued, began to sing understated, gut-wrenching, backwoods blues. By the time he finished a couple of those songs I was almost a weeper myself, but I knew I'd never hear that B. W. Stevenson on record. I leaned back in his chair, drank his Coors, enjoyed his music, watched his girlfriend and generally envied his station in life. B. W. was no dummy. Somewhere along the line he had learned that if you get a journalist good and stoned and play your guitar for him in private, you've got him.

B. W. seemed on the outskirts of Austin music. He was shy and ungainly, he ranked relatively low on the scale of Austin songwriters, he lived in Dallas. But watching from the perspective of California, Texan Mike Nesmith knew Stevenson was the one who could make it all work on record. A man's speaking voice affected the way he sang. Singers concealed their origins better than television newsmen, but even the Beatles sounded a bit British at times, and the Californians who tried to get commercial country-rock off the ground too often had to work at the country inflections. Much more than the L.A. instrumental slickness — for Nashville instrumentation was just as slick — that vocal defect made the music a mockery to a purist country ear. There was a vague condescension in California country-rock. Hippies listened to *Sweetheart of the Rodeo*, not Utah cowboys, and since the form's rock appeal was limited, it never connected big on the retail level, as Nesmith said. On the other hand, if rock & roll ever became authentically country, which appeared to be happening in Austin, then the market might broaden. Though Stevenson wouldn't last long in an age of video cassettes, vocally he bridged the gap between country and pop. And if one country-oriented Texas rocker could get off, maybe several could. It didn't matter if B. W. was the best or worst songwriter in the country; he had the voice. He was the artist Mike Nesmith needed.

But Stevenson was under contract with RCA, which had no stake in Texas music. They had an investment in B. W. Stevenson, and it was time for that investment to yield some returns. He was preparing to go to L.A. for a recording session when we talked to him, for RCA wanted to follow up on his misadventure with Three Dog Night before the press forgot who he was. He didn't have any songs that RCA considered hit potential, so they called in Danny Moore again. Moore said he hadn't finished any new songs worthy of *Billboard* attention, but he had an interesting guitar piece he'd been working on. Stevenson and RCA liked what they heard, and B. W. sat down to write the lyrics. That way he would get more money, and part of the credit. What, he must have been wondering all along, was the magic formula for a hit song? If he could record just one, and make RCA some money, then he would regain a measure of control over his music.

First of all, a hit tune needed to be short of length and line, preferably it would follow an AB/AB rhyme scheme, and it should carry an oft-repeated chorus that was very infectious and easy to remember. It should tell just enough of a story to capture one's attention. B. W. possibly had all that in mind when he sat down to write "Maria," but then again, it might have been just luck. He wrote the song for his voice, not his poetic audience, and while the story-line was almost nonexistent , a chorus trilled its love for the heroine of the song in the background while his voice ranged high, wide, and handsome: *"Mariiiiiiiiiiah, Mariii . . ."* and so on. To cop a line from Arlo Guthrie, B. W. knew it wasn't the best song he ever wrote.

But it worked. Behind him were a tocking percussion instrument and fine, fluid guitars, very tastefully arranged. And B. W. accented his metric feet with trochees rather than the customary jambs, giving the lyrics a staccato rhythm, countering the instrumental flow. It was vapid in message, but it was catchy, and "Maria" caught on, climbing the *Billboard* pop chart as high as number nine and topping the easy-listening list, spawning an album that sold much better than the first two. "Maria" wasn't a Texas song. It was Southern California, a drive up Highway 101 toward Disneyland with Jay and the Americans on the radio, but Stevenson had done it. He had made RCA a hit.

The next album was equally commercial, but it was suited most to his style. RCA shot the works on *Calabasas,* lined up more top-flight sidemen and enlisted Linda Ronstadt as a vocal accompanist. Stevenson didn't get to use many of his own songs, and the lyrics were again spread out regionally — a love song set in the Georgia pines, a Tennessee musician's plea for his girlfriend to join him in Boston, Denver and L. A. *Calabasas* sounded more like pop country-rock than the albums released by other Austin musicians, but at least the country instruments had returned, and on one cut he sounded like Steve Fromholz at his best. Another cut employed horns to dramatize lyrics that sounded like a mobile-home marital disagreement on the out-skirts of Houston. Perhaps a matter of luck again, the song which most evoked the feel of Austin music was also the best cut on the album, another Danny Moore song called "Look for the Light." A lonesome train whistle blowing early in the song gave it a country setting, but in mood it was sheer gospel, revolving around a Christian sentiment, that equated light with refuge and hope with light. The song was also a fine springboard for Stevenson's vocal talent, for it allowed him to start off easy and build to a crescendo.

RCA couldn't be sure they had pulled it off, but there were indications they had. B. W. showed up on the *Billboard* review page in the company of Paul Simon, Elvis Presley, Gladys Knight and the Pips, Jack Jones, Boz Scaggs and Charlie Rich, but the reviewer spotlighted *Calabasas* as the best release of all and raved: "It is a standout production. This LP is the most significant Stevenson has released in his short career as a nationally known artist. With the proper exploitation, this LP could be a massive seller; it's that good. All the infectious ingredients in pop and rock are perfectly blended here."

RCA burst with pride; one of their promo men called B. W. a monster in Missouri. Kershenbaum could claim that he had reproduced the real B. W. in commercially marketable form. But albums didn't take off with just a big promotional push and a rave review. A well-placed ad or review might attract a record consumer's attention, but artists were so available on tour and television that many people wouldn't buy an album from a new artist unless they'd seen him perform. Accordingly, RCA had Stevenson on the road almost constantly — not in Texas too much, for he was already known in Texas, that was the last place they wanted him — but all over the United States and Canada.

Yet B. W. wasn't happy. He didn't have time to write; he was having an extremely difficult time reproducing Kershenbaum's sound in concert, and worst of all, the red-haired girl was no longer a part of his life. Just when things seemed to get right, they went wrong again. He was making a name for himself, but he was also drinking too much. My photographer had never seen B. W., which was beginning to worry her, but we stubbornly refused opportunities to see him in Lubbock and Wichita Falls. A trip to Dallas for his sake was quite enough. Finally Larry Watkins told us that B. W. was going to play a concert in the gym at Southwest Texas State in San Marcos, just thirty-five miles south of Austin. I called a woman named Mrs. St. Claire in the student services office at the college about our admittance to the concert. A person accustomed to talking down to younger voices, Mrs. St. Claire said the admission price was two dollars each. Yes, fine, but what I was talking about was our ability to get backstage to see B. W. She said I'd have to talk to B. W.'s manager about that. I called Watkins again and he said that wasn't any problem; just ask for him at the door.

Lyndon Johnson went to Southwest Texas once upon a time, and like many graduates he was a school teacher before he ran for congress and became a pupil of Franklin D. Roosevelt. Since that time, Southwest Texas' enrollment had grown to over 10,000, and the college was to San Marcos as North Texas was to Denton. The dormitories emptied on the weekend, for there was not much to do in a town of less than 20,000. The college perched on a wooden hillside in picturesque Victorian limestone until Johnson became the school's number-one alumnus. After that the modern architects went to work on a circular auditorium surrounded by a moat and a ghastly adjoining library. The result was the common architectural mode, American Schizophrenia.

We found a parking space easily enough near the gym, but nothing else was easy. The young man at the door hesitated when I announced our intentions, glanced at a grim white-haired lady sitting in a chair-desk near the door, worried a minute longer, then adroitly asked to see my press credentials. I told him that people who were writing books didn't necessarily carry cards from the Texas Press Association, and he said, "Just a minute. I'll have to ask Mrs. St. Claire."

The white-haired lady came over and said in a voice closed to argument: "No, I'm sorry, you'll have to pay."

Okay. I purchased three tickets from a young man sitting at a card table outside the door and tried Mrs. St. Claire again, hoping to refresh her memory.

A coed popped into the picture with a scrap of paper and said,"I have B. W.'s list. What are your names?"

She read down the list then folded the paper up with an air of finality and said, "No. They're not on here."

"Well look," I said to Mrs. St. Claire. "Can you find Larry Watkins and tell him we're here."

"I don't know Larry Watkins."

"Larry Watkins is B. W. Stevenson's manager. You told me to contact him to set this up."

"Well I've never met Larry Watkins," she said haughtily. "And I wouldn't begin to know where to find him."

"He's backstage."

"I'm sorry. You'll just have to take your seats with everybody else."

There was clearly no point in arguing with Mrs. St. Claire. She had been right for twenty-five years. I knew most gyms had doors leading to the dressing rooms, so maybe we could accept our chastisement, skulk into the gym, then sprint toward the dressing-room door yelling for help. If we were going to infiltrate the building, we had to limit the number of doors. I started into the gym but the coed jumped in front of me.

162

"I'm sorry," Mrs. St. Claire sang. "Your seats are in the balcony. You can't sit down on the floor."

"Lady! I called you long-distance and explained all this to you, and you told me to talk to B. W. Stevenson's manager. I'm writing a book that deals with B. W. Stevenson, I have a deadline, my photographer badly needs some photographs, and B. W. may not be playing in Texas again for months." And the tears of frustration were welling in my eyes, I might have added.

"Well," she responded. "Mr. Stevenson is working for us tonight, and it seems to me that you'll just have to wait until he's finished his work and pose him for your pictures then."

Reeling and answerless, I looked around for assistance. Mrs. St. Claire reproved the coed, "You've just got to learn how to deal with these people without coming to me."

Down the hall I saw a bearded young man in boots and straw cowboy hat, and I played my last card. "Hey, are you with B. W. Stevenson's band?"

He looked at me and nodded, then came over and listened to a hurried tale of bureaucratic tyranny. He gave Mrs. St. Claire a bored look and said, "Sure, it's okay for them to come backstage." Without a word we shoved past the unsure coed and entered the gym, undoubtedly leaving Mrs. St. Claire with a distaste for rock music in general and rock journalists in particular. From the look on her face, it was the most galling thing that had happened to her in months.

I hated to treat Mrs. St. Claire that way, but if you were going to scoop the stars, sometimes you had to get ruthless.

Onstage before a good crowd were a group of musicians singing folk music and playing banjos. Backstage we found B. W., Steve Fromholz and Larry Watkins.

"Did you have any trouble getting in?" Larry asked.

Resisting the temptation to break his jaw, I reintroduced myself to B. W. He didn't remember me. He didn't even remember Lucy. I guessed musicians meet a lot of people. On the other hand, it might have had something to do with the pint of whiskey in one hand and the bleary look in his eyes.

The preliminary band lurched through the door and one of them said, "Damn, B. W., this is fine. People really come out to see you down here."

"Sure," Fromholz said. "He's the Cosmic Asshole."

An awed guardian of the musicians' equipment was trying to strike up a conversation with one of the tribal women, and Fromholz's quip destroyed his line of thinking. Another Southwest Texas student burst through the door and said, "B. W., would you mind if I took your picture?"

"How far you gonna take it?"

"What?"

"Never mind," B. W. said. "Sure, go right ahead."

An Instamatic materialized and a flashbulb popped two feet away from B. W.'s eyes. Pupils wildly dilated, Stevenson muttered, "Thanks a lot," and took another gulp of whiskey.

The equipment guardian said, "B. W., are you from Dallas?"

Stevenson nodded.

"What high school did you go to?"

"I dropped out in the eighth grade."

"Yeah," Fromholz contributed. "His mother carried him that long."

"Oh really?" the student said, casting a wary eye at Fromholz. "Well I'm from Dallas too. What junior high did you go to?"

Stevenson could finally see again. "I was just kidding about dropping out," he told the student. "I went to high school at Adamson.

"Did you see my new guitar case?" Stevenson asked Fromholz, pointing at a red velvet-lined box on the floor.

"Yeah, I saw that." Fromholz looked at the student and said, "B. W.'s left it in his will that he wants to be buried in his case."

A couple of coeds walked past, then scampered away giggling. B. W. staggered a step.

"You've been taking too much acid, B. W." Fromholz said.

"No, I been drinking too much. I wish you'd do something with this," Stevenson said, offering the bottle to his friend.

"Pour it on your dick," Fromholz suggested, then took a swig.

Still trying to strike up a conversation with the disinterested girl, the equipment guardian turned beet red.

Somebody tapped B. W. on the shoulder and said some people wanted to meet him. Standing at the end of the row of lockers were two of the Southwest Texas' finest: braver than the others and prettier, unimpressed as princesses outwardly, starstruck as seventh graders on the inside.

B. W. talked to the girls a minute, then rounded up his band and went onstage, where they played lame rock music in rather dim light. My photographer worked her way through the crowd to the front, where the students punched her in the calves and shouted, "Sit down! Nobody stands up! We have a rule here!"

B. W. sang a couple of songs without addressing the crowd then said, "It sure is nice to be back in Texas. *Hoot*. Give a hoot for Texas."

The students hooted as directed, and Stevenson introduced one of his slow songs. "We released this as a single once but nobody listened to it. You're not supposed to listen to a top-forty record. You're supposed to tap your foot and drive down the highway."

Stevenson sang a couple of his slow songs and the new single, "Look for the Light," then abandoned the downbeat material in favor of more rock & roll, whooping and hollering with the crowd and exhorting them to clap to the rhythm. He was an odd figure, cavorting about the stage, clapping his hands over his head. But that was what they wanted. A young man in the balcony began to play games with the spotlights, pretending he was in the Avalon Ballroom and driving my photographer crazy. Lucy leaned over and said, "What happened to that guy we heard in Dallas? That's not him."

Fromholz had come out of the dressing room and listened briefly then returned backstage, pursued shortly afterward by a uniformed policeman. Maybe Fromholz was going to spend the night in the San Marcos jail. It would probably do him good, and he might write a funny song about it. I watched my photographer plunge out of the crowd, stalk toward the dressing-room door and fling an elbow at a coed who tried to block her path. I followed her into the dressing room and found a smaller crowd around the lesser star, Fromholz, who was playing a borrowed banjo. The policeman hitched up a trousers leg, propped one foot on the dressing bench, and tapped the other on the floor. "Play 'Rose of San Antone,' " he suggested.

the boy
from alabama

Though our Dallas interview with B. W. Stevenson lasted until sundown, and we needed to return to Austin, I prevailed upon Lucy and my magazine collaborator to remain awhile in town so I could touch base with an old friend. "How long have you been in this condition?" she said after she surmised my state.

"Since the minute I walked in the door."

"God," she said, abandoning the sofa in favor of the stereo. "Are you writing about Willis Alan Ramsey too?"

"Who?"

"Willis Alan Ramsey," she said, pulling an album out of a green cover. "He's from Austin." She fitted the record on the turntable, set the needle down in the silence between cuts and said, "This is the only song they play on the radio."

The voice that came through the speakers, backed by a leisurely bass, an erratic fiddle, somebody banging on a coke crate and a yowling vocal accompanist toward the end, was bluesey in a white, Southern kind of way, pressing up against the singer's nasal palate, yet it was whimsical, as if it belonged to a boy shuffling barefoot down a sandy backwoods road. On the national-market scale of things, it wasn't terribly original, but it was refreshingly out of the Austin ordinary. And the lyrics were downright fetching:

North of Waxahachie, east of old Cowtown
them Dallas women standin' up
beat the others lyin' down
God bless the Trinity River
and any man who is unaware
of the Northeast Texas women
with their cotton-candy hair

What red-blooded son of Sam Houston could resist lyrics such as those? I told my magazine collaborator we were going to have to take Willis Alan Ramsey into account, though I'd never heard of him. His record hadn't received any air play in Austin.

The album was easy to find. A glance at the back of the cover indicated it was a Shelter product recorded in Memphis, Hollywood, Nashville and Tyler, Texas from May of 1971 to March of 1972. Ramsey was backed by the likes of Leon Russell and J. J. Cale, and Greg Allmann was thanked for his encouragement.

Ramsey seemed to have borrowed much of his vocal delivery from Russell. It was a fine tenor voice that could have done without some of Russell's affectations, but the songs were more impressive than the singer. The lyrics which best illustrated Ramsey's orientation were a tribute to Woodie Guthrie:

Now I was talkin' to a man that met him
in a bar near Clovis town
He said the whole bar was a shakin'
as they were passin' his songs around
In between tunes my friend asked him
where he'd be when the morrow came
And he said with a grin
'I put my thumb in the wind
and I'm off down the road again
I'm just a boy from Oklahoma
on an endless one night stand
I wander, and I ramble
I drift with the midnight sand
I play the blues and the ballads
and all that's in between

THE BOY FROM ALABAMA

My heart is in the union
and my soul is reachin' out
for the servants' dream'

The blues and the ballads and all that lay in between. Ramsey acted out fantasies in his songs, most of which told far-fetched tales; he weaved just enough of himself into his songs to lift them from the realm of ordinary ballads. The first cut on the album, "The Ballad of Spider John," proposed to take place in a railroad yard. Ramsey's bum introduced himself as *"a supermarket fool, a motor-bank stool pigeon,"* and begged his fellow hoboes' company while he told the story of the way he squandered his only love by continuing to be the kind of man he was, and professing to her that he was not.

And that is all my story
It's been these thirty years
since I took to the road
to find my precious jewel one
Now if you see my Lily
won't you give her my regards
Tell her old Spider got tangled
in the black web that he spun

Though that song could have been set in the Yukon as easily as Texas, Ramsey's music was relatively easy to situate. His songs owed their allegiance to the South, the vanquished confederacy extending into Texas as far as the fertile black-land strip separating the pines from the mesquites. East Texas was lovely country — the red velvet bloom of clover in the spring, the fragrance of running sweet gum in the fall — but it was hidebound by its past. As one proceeded eastward in Texas, the pigs in the pastures began to outnumber the cows, the houses set on blocks outnumbered those set on foundations, and often as not the faces that stared back were black. That was more of a blessing than a curse, but too many of those blacks shuffled up to you in their overalls, 215-pound muscles bulging, and said, "Hello there young mistah. Say, we got a little fund drive goin' on over at the Baptis' Church, and we always had real good luck with the white folks helpin' us along, lendin' us a hand. If you got it in your heart, can you spare us

169

somethin'?'' They would have been easier to like had they spat in young mister's eye.

It was beginning to be better than that. Some of the blacks were going to college, returning to their hometowns, and running for the school board; and occasionally one would find a black farmer, courteous but proud, living in a $25,000 home on 300 acres of productive land with a new pickup in the garage. But just down the road would be a family of poor whites living in a shanty with a broken-down Ford in the front yard, and those whites were seething with resentment. The other regions of Texas were scarcely better. West Texas whites separated and ignored their badly outnumbered ethnic minorities, and a healthy majority of South Texas whites feared and despised Mexicans the way a healthy majority of East Texas whites feared and despised niggers. The whole social and economic structure was designed to keep darker peoples in their place. But while racial prejudice was the cancer of the United States in general, one felt it most in the South. The territory east of Dallas and Houston wasn't Texas. It was another country.

Yet whatever the faults of the South, it was in many ways a more human place than the West. People in the South thought less about animals and machines than people in the West. They thought more about people, whether they loved or hated them, than the land around them. Their passions were closer to the surface; it was the difference between Faulkner and Steinbeck. And though its passions were severely inhibited by the Bible Belt around its girth, East Texas was more sensual than the other regions of Texas. Its summers were sultry, and so were its people.

Ramsey knew that when he wrote his song about Northeast Texas women, and most other songs on his album bore sexual themes. One soft song read human sexual gaming into the mating dance of muskrats. Another called "Watermelon Man" evoked thoughts of a summer day in the plantation South and skillfully turned the old poetic trick of confusing the act of eating with the act of sex: *"Why don't you come to the cabin, bring your watermelon patch/We'll dance in the meadows, what more could I ask?"* The sexual drift of Ramsey's lyrics surfaced most clearly, however, in a coy, playful song about a honeybee entranced by a chrysanthemum.

Oh Geraldine have you forgotten?
I have come for your sweet pollen
I might go crazy, I might go blind
but I'm never goin' back
to the honeysuckle vine
Long as you're alive
I'll buzz around your hive

The artist photographed on the front of the album cover wore a cowboy hat and a crooked, cocky grin; he looked like a talented young smart aleck. Then again, Ramsey had a right to be cocky. There wasn't a bad cut on the album, and when it came to the subtlety of his use of language, Murphey was the only songwriter in town who could touch him.

Ramsey, I gradually learned as we tried to find him, was born in Alabama, the son of deep-Southern parents who moved to Dallas when he was a boy. He was not yet twenty-two, and according to the copyright dates on his album, he couldn't have been more than twenty when he wrote the songs for it. In late summer of 1970 he was playing a coffeeshop on the Texas campus when Leon Russell and the Allmann Brothers came to Austin for a concert on the baseball field. Ramsey had already been discouraged by James Taylor's producer, but he approached Russell at his motel and said he'd like to sign a contract with Shelter Records.

"I'd have to listen to you," Russell said.

"Well I think you ought to," Ramsey countered, and he played well enough for Russell to invite him to California for another audition. Shelter was the American equivalent of Apple Records. It was owned by an artist and designed for artists, thus Russell was practically a god to many struggling musicians, and just as Mike Nesmith had responded to Steve Fromholz, it was natural that Russell would respond to Ramsey. The man with the songs sounded a lot like the man with the record company. Yet the album was already a year old when my collaborator and I found it, and it had flopped commercially. The Pub's Ric Schwartz blamed it on Shelter. He said they failed to promote it, and were just beginning to get behind Ramsey when he made a club appearance.

Ramsey was the hardest of all the musicians to find. We got a phone number that supposedly belonged to him, but a girl answered and said, "He doesn't live here anymore and I don't know where he is." Oh. Ramsey hadn't aligned himself with Moon Hill yet, so Larry Watkins wasn't any help and neither was Eddie Wilson.

"What about Willis Ramsey?" I asked Wilson one day. "Why isn't he a part of all this?"

Eddie grunted. "Ramsey. He's got a terminal case of the kid. He's always running around worried about his attitude. But he writes some damn nice songs . . ."

Shelter Records was no help; their Los Angeles secretary thought he was in Oklahoma City. Finally Schwartz told us the place to find him would be at his makeshift studio in an alley behind a dry cleaning establishment near the university. The cleaners was closed, and a young kitchen helper from the restaurant next door poured his garbage into the can and laughed when we asked if he knew anything about a recording studio. Finally we narrowed it down to one locked metal door, scrawled Ramsey a note asking him to call us, and left it underneath a rock by the door.

Our deadline for the magazine article was fast approaching, and we had reluctantly written Ramsey off when he called one day and said he had just found our note in a pile of dirty clothes. He gave us directions to a small, flat-roofed building surrounded by knee-high weeds. A junked Buick was abandoned in the rear. The young man who answered the door bore little resemblance to the one on the album cover. He was slender, dressed only in jeans, and his hair curled wildly in the humidity. He appeared in a state of shock.

"Oh yeah," he said, shaking our hands. "Come on in." Inside the building was a small recording booth, a beat-up piano, walls insulated for sound by fruit cartons, a large toolbox, a litter of kittens brawling in mock combat and Eddie Wilson. An awkward silence fell over the room. Finally Wilson stood to leave and told Ramsey, "Willis, come see me. You know where we live."

Ramsey sat on the piano stool and stared after Wilson a minute, then said, "Uh, just what is it you're doin' in this article?"

I explained as best I could without saying we really had no idea, and added we were thinking about stretching it into a book. We asked him about his past and he briefly confirmed what we had heard. Was he going to record another album?

172

Suspicious of booking agents, journalists, and most other trappings of commercial music, Willis Alan Ramsey delivered one sterling album then eased back into obscurity, waiting for the second surge of songs to come. He bided his time in his apartment, restoring the woodwork, and in a makeshift studio equipped by Shelter Records.

Ramsey was the child prodigy of Austin music, one of its most poetically accomplished songwriters. But he was independent, moving at his own speed, an idealist who wanted no part of Armadillo oligarchies and performers' pecking orders.

"Not right now," he said. "As soon as I get the material together I will. I haven't written enough new songs to warrant making another record yet. Shelter gave me this equipment, and I'm kind of into foolin' around with it right now."

He led us into the recording booth and showed us a four-track recorder, then flipped a switch and we listened to some backwoods country harmony that sounded like something out of *Deliverance*.

"Who is that?"

"It's a group from Tennessee called Uncle Walt's Band," he said. "They're fine, aren't they? I'm just learning how to work this thing. I'm not very good yet. That you hear there sounds like a drum, but it's really a bass."

We asked why he wanted his own studio.

"It took me a year to make my record. I went through a whole lot of shit that I'd prefer not to go through again. I want this to do any further recording efforts on my part, and also to help some of the other musicians around here — maybe release local singles for the Austin audience. I'd like to do that.

"It'd be small-time again. I want to make it regional instead of national. Bring back Texas color, bring back all those differences between Texas and New York, Texas and Nebraska."

Was he still under contract with Shelter?

"Oh yeah, very much," Ramsey said with a laugh. "A normal record contract runs for five years, with an album a year. If you don't deliver you wind up in one of two places. Number one, you're in trouble, you're liable to get sued. Number two, you can accept their generosity, which I just did. Shelter has said to me, now the second year of your contract is up, we're suspending the contract until you deliver your second album.

"But it's a real lenient type thing, and I really prefer it this way. First of all, my first album wasn't a real hot item, you know, it hasn't sold very much."

Was he satisfied with Shelter's promotion?

"I asked them not to promote it," he said. "And they haven't, except they back me when I go into a gig. Then they say I'm on Shelter Records, and they pay for some of the spots."

Why in the world did he do that?

"I just don't like advertisement. I don't like somebody to feel like they've got to shove something down my throat before I'll find out about it. Because I know that people who listen to records as much as I do will gradually hear one if it's any good. Let it stand the test of time. Just float it out there and see what happens. If the record company can afford it, I can.

"The second reason I like my current arrangement with Shelter is that I'd rather not put out something I didn't write. I don't want to tote my songwriting too much, but right after my album came out I tried to get into writing again; I said I'm going to go ahead and write my second album and put it out at my leisure. But the songs on my first album didn't come out at my leisure, and these didn't either. It just didn't happen that way. I sorta choked on my end. I've started writing some good songs again here lately, but too often people in the music profession nowadays think of a career as, like, five years. Now you see 'em, now you don't. Well I want to make music for a long time. So I'd like to stretch it. I'd like to put out a good one every time, if possible."

He grinned at us. "It's not always possible."

Ramsey produced his letter from Shelter and read aloud: "Dear Willis. Merely a technicality, but since you haven't delivered an LP to us for the current year, we're suspending your contract per paragraph eleven of our agreement, and we are electing to extend the current year until you shall complete and deliver to us a commercially satisfactory LP. Upon termination of the suspension, the third year of your agreement will begin the renewal option for which we are hereby exercising."

I asked him how he paid for his groceries.

"Out of the money I made last year. Also, America recorded one of my songs lately, so I hope to get some living off that for a while. It was the 'Muskrat Candlelight' song. They called it 'Muskrat Love'."

He handed us another letter to read. It was signed by a booking agent in Los Angeles who said he found Ramsey *very* unprofessional to *suddenly* cancel his *first major* concert tour. My partner handed it back and said that was a pretty weird letter.

"It's my fault," Ramsey said. "I screwed up. I canceled out of a tour where I'd of been second act on a coffeehouse tour behind Delaney Bramlett, and granted, it would've been the Troubador and Bitter End, but I don't want to play those places. They're pressure gigs, they're prestige gigs, and they're not gigs that I covet.

"That guy said that the only other performer who ever canceled a tour on him was Van Morrison, then he said of course you never hear of him anymore, do you? Well sure, all the time. So I figure I'm in pretty good company.

"I don't know how those people operate out in L.A. I don't know anything about what an agent does. I've since learned that it's a considerable amount of trouble for them to talk on the phone and get these things set up, because that man told me. But I didn't know you couldn't say you'd do something and then decide not to do it. I told him I didn't want to play that tour, and he said this was totally unethical, you know, it was totally unreasonable and I didn't know what this meant — I didn't want to end my career at such an early date. He was literally saying he could make me or break me, baby, and anytime somebody says something like that . . ."

Ramsey picked up the letter. "And then I don't understand this thing at the end here. 'When you're ready to be represented at a later time, please contact me.' It's just like, you're through, you're finished, *but*, if you ever want to be booked again after a period of lengthy punishment, I presume . . ."

He picked up one of the kittens and grinned. "You all couldn't have come out here at a more opportune time. All of a sudden Eddie and I got into this really heated discussion. I really admire Eddie, the success he's had with the Armadillo. I think it's an amazing place. I also admire him for his integrity in dealing with musicians. He's respected among musicians more than just about any other manager or agent-type person I know of. But I don't agree with everything he says or does. So we were just finding out we weren't agreeing.

"Eddie is very confident about what he's doing. He goes about doing business in a perfectly assured manner; he's just out to get all the kinks out of it. I'm not that way. I'm hesitant, questioning, I admit I don't know everything about it, which is not to imply he does. But he thinks I'm green as shit.

"I said that the booking agent and manager should be at the mercy of the musician. He got real *violent*, you know . . . well, he didn't get real violent, but what I was saying is that when it comes right down to it, the artist, since he makes the music, is the whole reason for the agent or manager being there. He didn't like that at all. People don't realize today how the managers and agents dictate the lives of the performers.

The more you need somebody to handle your money and affairs the more separated you become from the whole thing of getting up and playing for people that come to pay money. That's the first thing that ever went wrong — people getting up and paying money to see somebody. I'll never pay money to see anybody again, I don't believe.

"What I'm trying to do here in the studio is just a compromise, in that the people I'm working with musically are aware there's no set way of doing things. I'm just as amazed and befuddled by the way things come about sometimes, the way they get on tape, the way they're written, as anybody else.

"But people in L.A. are not. Man, they know. So-and-so sits in a room for such-and-such number of hours, and he's going to write a hit tune. Put him out on the road, expose him before so many people so many times, and he'll get known. They just know that, and they also know that's 'good,' whatever that means.

"I don't know. I guess I'm one of those sensitive-artist types that ends up being broke and at odds with everybody in the music industry. It seems like I'm fast working myself there. But I don't give a shit. If I've got something to say I want to be able to say it from start to finish and not have somebody come in and edit it and have somebody decide for me how to present it."

As we left Ramsey asked us to drop back by anytime, but the next time I shook his hand he wasn't so friendly. The *Texas Monthly* article ran impossibly long, and my editor, a sympathetic sort who had once written a novel about rock musicians, called me and started recounting the list of deleted paragraphs and episodes. When he got to the performers' section half of Walker flew away, and then he said they were going to delete all mention of Ramsey. I yelped.

"I expected that," my editor said.

"What about Wier? Are you going to take him out too?"

"No, I was going to leave that in."

"Hell, Wier doesn't even have a record yet."

"Yeah, but I like the quote you got from Wier. Tell you what I'll do. I'll rewrite those two and shorten them so we can keep them both in."

My friend caught the gist of what we said about Ramsey and Wier, but he implied they were starving a little more strongly than we had, and he said Ramsey's contract with Shelter had been canceled, not suspended. Ramsey fired off a letter of protest but *Texas Monthly*'s space problems frustrated Ramsey again: they edited the letter down to one sentence. "Thanks for the mention in your swell article," he wrote, "but I am neither starving nor out of a record contract." Sounded a bit sarcastic.

Shelter Records, which was officed in a little house off Hollywood Boulevard, was actually being very patient and understanding with Ramsey. They took the attitude it was his career and the only thing they could do was re-release the album, though those plans were pending indefinitely. Ramsey's stock as a songwriter was also rising. In addition to America's recording of "Muskrat Love," a Florida singer named Jimmy Buffett had recorded "Spider John," and Rusty Wier, who had finally signed a recording contract, was going to do another song off the album "Painted Lady." But Ramsey was busy in his studio, and he played in public very rarely. I had seen him perform just once, at a benefit for the Free Clinic in a meadow west of Austin. He was nervous as a cat and just before he started to sing, Rusty Bell of KOKE grabbed the microphone and said, "I've got some very heavy news for you. President Nixon has just fired Elliot Richardson and Archibald Cox and positioned FBI troops around the Justice Department." That was a hard act to follow.

Finally Ramsey showed signs of making his move. He agreed to play first act ahead of Murphey and Walker in a large, lavishly designed auditorium on the campus of Trinity University in San Antonio. My photographer and I found Ramsey backstage pacing back and forth in tattered jeans and faded plaid shirt. He looked younger because he had a fresh haircut.

He grinned boyishly enough when he recognized me but his expression quickly fell into a look of hurt and betrayal. "It wasn't just a small misunderstanding," he said. "After the talk we had that day, then it comes out and makes me look pathetic, like I'm starving and my contract's been canceled. I don't understand that. How'd that happen?"

I mumbled something about editorial prerogatives but he said, "Well I hold you responsible. You can't let them do you that way. You've got to tell them now damn it, this is the way it's going to be, from start to finish."

I knew it wouldn't do any good to tell him it didn't work that way, and I wasn't about to tell him that at the time I needed *Texas Monthly*'s money worse than his friendship. He would have thought I was the devil incarnate.

179

"Well I appreciate your coming by and talking to me," Ramsey said, "and I don't want you to think you owe me anything."

He was extremely nervous as he waited to go on. He drummed his fingers on the neck of his guitar, and when a student who wanted to interview him for his television class walked by, Ramsey stopped him and said, "Now just what is it you're going to ask me in this interview?" Apparently he had learned his lesson with reporters.

The student shrugged. "I don't know, what goes through your mind before you go on, that kind of thing."

Ramsey grinned. "Well, I've already been to the john about forty times. I'll tell you that much."

Murphey and Walker had arrived for the concert with large complements of sidemen, but Ramsey went out alone with his guitar and harmonica, took a seat on his stool, and blinked at the audience of nearly 2000. It wasn't an artful performance. He lacked the knack of chatting with the audience when he tuned his guitar, he forgot the name of the author of one of the songs he borrowed and after a few songs he said, "Turn up the lights, I can't see. I'm sorry, I don't know. It's like playing to a big clapping machine."

He was also having a difficult time with the sound system. The Austin sound crew was working with new, unfamiliar equipment, and the performance of all three performers was one large amplified shriek. Walker laughed about it, Murphey got disgusted, but Ramsey turned red and tried to cope with it. He instructed the technicians while the audience squirmed and I grew increasingly anxious standing in the wings. I was surrounded by electronic paraphernalia and deathly afraid of it. I feared that if I hung out at rock concerts long enough I was going to trip on the wrong chord, dance an electrocution jig across the stage and land in the lap of a drummer while the crowd roared its approval, thinking it was all a part of the act.

> I wish I was a millionaire
> I'd play rock music and grow long hair
> I tell you boys, I'd buy a new Rolls Royce
> Pretty women'd come to me, I'd give 'em all the third degree
> I'd given 'em satin sheets, keep 'em off the streets
> Hallelujah, what's it to ya? Let me sock it to ya
> Praise the lord and pass the mescaline
> Pray Jehovah, you'll come over, soon as
> you see me boogie-woogie 'cross the silver screen

A man standing by my side shook his head and sighed. "The boy's a genius," he said, then decided the stage curtain was getting too close to Ramsey. He directed a man at his rear to do something about it, and predictably enough, the curtain moved closer yet to the performer. "Wrong way, dipshit," the man said, and went back to correct the situation himself.

After Ramsey's performance was over he sat down on a sofa in the backstage lounge, squinted into the television lights and talked to the student interviewer.

"What do you think about the Austin music scene?" the interviewer asked. "The Armadillo and all."

"I'm not really a part of that Armadillo scene," Ramsey said. "That's not all the music there is in Austin."

The interviewer quickly ran out of questions and asked Ramsey to play for the make-believe TV audience, then moved closer so he could harmonize. Ramsey glanced at his singing interviewer as he went into his song:

> *Following the stars through the honky-tonks and bars*
> *dream away on a country-music pride*
> *Start the evening by myself, you can bet by the hour of ten*
> *I'm gonna have a pretty painted lady by my side*
> *And I'll tell that woman how it used to be*
> *when the West was wild, and the land was free*
> *How a western word could travel for a country mile*
> *How then one day the drugstores came*
> *and forced my hand to play a truckin' game*
> *Wishin' to be cowboy all the while*

The interviewer sang along most of the way, then his cameraman ran out of film so he said, "Okay, that's enough, Willis. Thank you."

"Wait a minute," Ramsey protested. "Let me finish."

> *Painted lady with your painted face*
> *tell me 'bout your life in this painted place*
> *Tell me with your lovin' lips, and your lovin' eyes*
> *I can feel the pain, I can see the fears*
> *on the painted cheeks that hide the tears*
> *of a lovely, lonesome cowgirl in disguise*
> *Painted lady tell me of your past gone by*

Hold me like the open range and ride me high
Kiss me to the days when your dress
was made of calico or gingham
and a man was a man

the golden fleece

Of all the recorded performers in Austin, Bobby Bridger was the easiest to overlook. He rarely performed, and when he did, few people took interest. His music was intoxicating enough, but it was the intoxication of a thoughtful glass of wine. Austin was a beer-drinking town. Even in appearance Bridger seemed a misfit. He wore a hat to conceal encroaching bladness, but it was the kind of hat one would expect to see in New England, not Texas. He wore hiking boots, not cowboy boots, and the rock & roll influence on his music was negligible. When he performed he sat on a stool with his legs crossed, played an acoustic guitar with nails grown extraordinarily long on his right hand, doffed his hat to applause, explained the circumstances of his songs. In his speech he was afflicted by the nasal twang that marked us all, but his songs told stories set outside of Texas, and his voice was high, soft and silken — too damn pretty for a movement associated with life in Texas. He drove an Oldsmobile instead of a Volkswagen van and spent most of his time with his stepchildren and wife, a university Ph.D. candidate and an English lecturer at the community college. When he made Townsend Miller's country music column in the *Austin Statesman* it was in the context of, "Now Bobby's always been a bit too folkish for my taste . . ."

Yet Bridger was hard to ignore. He had written and recorded two albums for RCA, and except for Nelson, he was the only major Austin performer with a legitimate country career behind him. Bridger's real name was Bobby Durham. He had a natural affinity for Texas as a youth for his father's family lived in the Piney Woods in the eastern part of the state, but he grew up in Northeastern Louisiana. When he enrolled at Northeastern Louisiana State in Monroe he wanted to be a

185

sculptor, but his singing at campus talent shows attracted the interest of a would-be ballad collector who had once assisted the folklorist who discovered Jimmy Driftwood, and who wrote "The Battle of New Orleans" as a history lesson for his students. The Northeast Louisiana folklorist asked Bridger to join him in a project that would take them into the Ozark and Blue Ridge mountain country in search of authentic folk ballads. Bridger spent most of the time opening gates and manning the tape recorder, but occasionally the folklorist delivered a lecture on the influence of Elizabethan language on backwoods music, and Bridger played his guitar and sang to illustrate the lecturer's points. Bridger was gradually realizing he was better at teaching sculpture than creating it, and he was interested in that approach to music. He doubted there were many young men in the United States who were interested in spending their lives collecting story-telling music, so he figured the field was wide open. He was also a talented singer and songwriter, and he was approached with a dozen recording offers, but he turned them down. He didn't think he wanted anything to do with commercial music.

Then he married and started teaching high school art in West Monroe. High school teaching in Louisiana was a one-way track toward semi-respectable poverty and a thankless principal's job at the age of forty, and realizing that, Bridger signed a contract to record with Monument in Nashville in 1967. The West Monroe school administration tolerated the arrangement, though they stressed he was not to allow his Memphis honky-tonking to interfere with his teaching. Bridger had a pretty country voice, which was then all the vogue. A session guitar player named Glen Campbell had taken "Gentle on my Mind" from its rough-voiced author, John Hartford, and made them both a fortune, and Monument wanted a piece of that monetary action. Bridger found himself razor-cut and hair-sprayed, traveling on the weekends with a big band that always featured a pretty, blonde vocal accompanist. If one got married or pregnant, Monument always found another. Bridger recorded an unreleased album and several of his singles received air play — one made the country charts in England — but after three years of drifting away from the kind of music he wanted to play, he abruptly quit. He freed himself from Monument very easily; he tore up his contract and threw it away.

During those Nashville weekends Bridger chanced upon a fishing trip with Paul Simon, who struck him as an egocentric beyond redemption, but a genius in his songwriting. Simon listened to some of

Bridger's songs and said he was telegraphing his lyrical punches; his songs were too predictable. Bridger's songs began to pour out after that, and he decided to record and produce his own finished tape. After borrowing the money and recording his album in Fred Carter's studios in Nashville, Bridger got an address listing of recording companies and went to those offices with his tape, but he had no luck in New York, Nashville or Los Angeles. "RCA rejected it twice because I was dealing with peons," he said. "Rookie producers are afraid to make any decisions because if they make a good decision, the guy up above them's going to fire them because his job's threatened. I found that out very rapidly. Then getting into the offices of the people who could make decisions was just next to impossible, so in essence I'd lost on the thing, and was in bad shape financially."

Bridger went back to Louisiana with little hope left, but then his business manager played the tape for a church-going Louisiana cotton farmer, who liked it and asked for permission to see what he could do. The farmer took the tape to an old classmate who owned a chain of movie theaters based in New Orleans. The theater owner said he didn't know the first thing about the music business, but he forwarded the tape to his son, Jay Houke, who was handling the highly successful distribution of the communal cinematic attempt, *The Legend of Boggy Creek*. Houke took the tape to Los Angeles, talked to the right man in the right office of RCA, and suddenly Bridger was under contract again.

Though Bridger could justly claim he produced the album, he had been ably assisted in the engineering by Jesse Tharp and Fred Carter, Jr. He was backed by as many as six sidemen, two vocalists, and even the Gulf of Mexico on a seven-minute tale about men adrift called "Sea Chanty," and though the material ranged from a collegiate satire called "The Further Adventures of Captain America and Joe College" to a song about terrapins, the tone of the album was set by apparent love songs to Bridger's wife:

> *Knowing that I had to go*
> *She smiled at me*
> *Showing need to say*
> *She wished that she could go with me*
> *So we could be together one more day*
> *The woman that she was*
> *She knew we had already*
> *Shared our span of time*

A beautiful transition
Interweaving into merging of our minds

It was an impressive first album, but it was aimed at a limited audience.
A top-forty radio listener would get tongue-tied trying to sing along
with ditties such as those.

While in Los Angeles Bridger's manager ran into a man who said he
was completing a movie and needed a singer to record the theme.
Bridger played for the man, aware that movie producers were a dime a
dozen in every Los Angeles bar, and was shocked when the man called
three days later and said he wanted Bridger to write and sing the theme.
The Wheel — which was the brainchild of Max Evans, who wrote the
script for *The Rounders* — was set in a junkyard and had only three
characters and twenty minutes of dialogue, so it naturally flopped in
America, though moribund *Look* magazine called it the first serious
American art film, and it became popular in Europe. But the movie was
the vehicle that brought Bridger to Texas. The people behind the film
decided to premier it in Austin, and they wanted Bridger there.

Bridger liked Texas and had heard good things about Austin, and his
wife was able to get a teaching assistantship at the University, so they
moved there in 1970. RCA never seemed to know quite what to do with
Merging of Our Minds, and though Bridger went on the road to
promote it, the album slipped beneath the surface and drowned. Even
in Austin he was practically unknown, though Rod Kennedy put him
onstage at the second Kerrville Folk Festival after Mance Lipscomb's
health forced him to cancel. Still, Bridger's music benefited from his
association with RCA. His second album, produced by Joe Reisman at
the RCA studios in Hollywood, was better than the first. Backed by
three vocalists, mandolin, dobro, arp synthesizer, strings and even
celeste, Bridger's songs were subtly, tastefully done. The album
contained an upbeat soft-rock number called ''Ragamuffin
Minstrels,'' but the quiet Bridger was still in command.

The album clearly indicated the influence of Paul Simon on
Bridger's songwriting, from the introductory guitar licks to the lyrics.
Bridger was frankly awed by ''The Boxer,'' a cut off Simon and
Garfunkel's swan song, *Bridge Over Troubled Waters*. To the very
la-la-la, Bridger fashioned ''The Sculptor'' after ''The Boxer,'' but he
reached a different conclusion. Simon's song was about a country boy
gone to the city, confronted by loneliness, unemployment and hookers

188

on Seventh Avenue, and the weight of the city experience came in the final stanza. A scarred and beaten prize fighter stood alone in a clearing, crying he was leaving the sport, knowing he never would. Bridger thought there was more hope in the world than that. His poor boy from the country encountered the same problems, but Bridger populated his lyrical pasture with a sculptor who "*twinkled in his wisdom, carving love into perfection with his hands.*"

Bridger was still not Simon's equal as a songwriter, but he was learning to economize his language and his writing was much improved, though he still needed to establish his own sense of direction. In truth he already had, but the only evidence of it on the second album was a song called "The Call":

> *A lonesome old Indian lives down deep in my heart*
> *And he speaks without making a sound*
> *And he walks through my forest and hunts for my thoughts*
> *And he knows a man I haven't found*
> *Yes the Indian lives on the plains of my mind*
> *And he sings with the coyotes at night*
> *And he wants me to leave this old city behind*
> *'Cause the way concrete feels just ain't right*

Though the album received more air play than the first one had, it also lacked a big promotional push by RCA. Bridger's songs and arrangements were adequate, but his voice failed to meet the new criterion for success. It wasn't distinctive enough. In order to make an impression, a singer's voice had to be rough as a cob; the listeners had to be able to identify with its imperfections. Ironically, Bridger had already lost his voice once and undergone surgery to remove a collection of calcium nodules on his vocal chords — a singer's occupational disease that afflicted the likes of Rod McKuen, Joe Cocker and Rod Stewart. Yet when Bridger recovered, his voice was still too pretty for the prevailing American market. The melodic voice was a ghost from the past. If Steve Fromholz had arrived four years early, Bridger had arrived four years too late.

I Just Wanted to Sing for the People debuted shortly before the appearance of our *Texas Monthly* article, a source of acute embarrassment since we had failed to interview him or even mention him in the article. Michael and Alan Price of *Rallying Point* urged me to listen to his music and talk to him before I proceeded any further with the book, and Bridger agreed to meet us one Saturday at my photographer's house in Austin. He entered and took a seat on her sofa and removed his hat, which, he told us later, was something he rarely did. He had started wearing a hat as a teenager because he thought it made him look older. Now that he was fast approaching baldness, he thought it made him look younger.

I asked Bridger what he thought of Nashville.

"I became disenchanted with Nashville because I didn't like what was happening there. I think Nashville is a Fascist town. For one thing, it's the Rome of the Southern Baptist Association, and all the hangups of Southern Baptist philosophy concentrate there.

"Most of the writers and musicians in Nashville come from the South, and migrate there. When I went there I was a folksinger, for lack of a better definition. The guy who signed me knew I was a folksinger, knew that my concern was more artistic than commercial. But when I got there the first thing they made me do was start cutting slick country music. I went into country music because of that. I was looking for a hit in order to do what I wanted to do.

"That was my first awareness of the record business. The whole approach is, you do what we want you to do first, and then you can do what you want to do. So I said okay, and after about three years I was wearing my hair the way they wanted me to, singing the songs they wanted me to sing, doing everything they wanted and still going nowhere. So I quit and said I didn't want to have anything to do with this anymore."

I said he differed from many musicians because he enjoyed working in a studio. What made him want to get into the production end of it?

"People are always talking about the sterility of a studio, but I think if a person's music is on his mind, then it doesn't make any difference where he plays it. The studio is a place where I can create a void, a vacuum, where I can eliminate all the distractions and allow my thoughts and energy to concentrate. To me, saying you can't get a good sound in a studio is like a carpenter complaining about this tools. A good carpenter doesn't complain about his tools; he'll build the house anyway.

"I base a lot of what I do on looking at the other side of things. The whole concept of producing is part of that. Most record companies hear about an act that's knocking them dead in clubs, so they send a talent scout out to see them, and if he likes them, they sign them to a contract. Well, when I started thinking about doing my album, I decided that if I were sitting in a chair making a decision on an album, I would much rather have something presented to me that was already showcased, something that other people had already spent the money on, so I only had the choice of saying yes or no. So I decided to take on all the risk myself.''

I observed that although he had been in Austin longer than most of the other recorded Austinites, he was still a musician apart from Austin music. He said he didn't mind that at all. ''The reason I came here was because it was different from Nashville. Quite frankly, I was healing when I came here, because I'd been through a long ordeal with my first album. Austin was so refreshing. There were people in the music business here who were completely aware of the economic structure of the music business, yet they were unaffected by it. They hadn't been stung by it like I'd been.

''I liked that a whole lot, but now I think Austin's being taken over by the other music centers, and that's a very common thing. It happened to Boston in the early sixties when it became a center for amateur folk performers. The next thing you knew Vanguard and Prestige and Elektra and all those labels were signing those acts, and Boston became a real hotbed. But then the next thing you knew, Boston was no longer a part of it.

''I'm afraid that's going to happen here, and that's a real shame because what Austin offered to me was a new approach to the music business — a community approach to cope with economic problems that appear when someone is trying to break in. We've got a lot of talented pickers and writers here and we're collecting a good amount of gadget freaks — studios are basically monuments to gadget freaks. The scene that has developed here will probably accomplish what people want, and people desperately want a music center here. They're supporting it, and that's good and fine. I like that aspect of it. But unless some directional force is given to this then it's going to be a shot in the dark. It'll form a music center, but that's not going to help the people out there starving in the street. What it's going to do is create offices they can't get into. That's all it's going to create, unless Austin has enough foresight to see the mistakes other music centers have made.

''In other words, why do they want a music center here? It's obvious by even wanting to form a new music center they've become dissatisfied with the other ones. So why not make it something that's different? I personally think it's time to examine our motives. Unless

191

we start doing some serious examination of what it is we seek, then we're going to end up perpetuating the same thing we're all up against. But everybody's too busy jumping on the bandwagon to give any thought to where it's headed.''

Bridger said the only reason he was still in Austin was that his wife hadn't finished work for her Ph.D., and added, ''In order to make a name in Austin, you have to play a bar every night in order to get your name in the paper. Either that or you've got to be a member of some clique that associates you with a certain scene. You've got to be one of the good old cosmic cowboys, and I think it's a very dangerous thing to associate oneself with a movement, because the music business is a vacillating, fluctuating constantly moving thing. People may be ready to jump on the maverick cowboy bit right now, the thought of being a conforming rebel. But I think that's strictly a fad. That may be open to argument, but music changes very rapidly, and people who identify themselves solely with country music are going to find themselves wondering in two years how in the world they're going to continue.

''You can hardly go out in Austin without hearing somebody complaining about labels put on their music, yet what they're doing is rigidifying a new label, and they're endangering Austin. An anology might be John Denver singing songs about people raping the mountains. He's singing that to an incredibly mobile public which is looking for some kind of authenticity, so they're going to go to the mountains and rape them. He's perpetuating the whole thing.''

Did that mean he was divorcing himself completely from Austin music?

''No, I'm going to start performing more in Austin, not to sell records particularly, but because I want to get in touch with some of the people in Austin who think there is something besides hip country. I want to be sure that the few people who find themselves drawn to my music will be there to listen when I play it.''

Bridger was responsive but soft-spoken that day, his remarks punctuated by high-voiced laughter, but there was an underlying tension in his manner. In performance, he seemed the most relaxed, retiring musician in town. He responded personally to a crowd's applause and assumed they responded personally to his music, and he was never rough on the ones who stumbled into Castle Creek in search of their fifth tequila sour of the evening. He was too polite for that. But he wanted desperately for them to listen. He took his music more

Assisted in an outdoor concert by Rusty Wier on drums and Murphey's sideman Craig Hillis, Bobby Bridger was personally close to most of the leading country-rock musicians. But he was a solitary performer, and he stood apart in his music. He'd already done his time with country.

Bridger took his music more seriously, perhaps, than any other performer in town. He had a vision of the Rocky Mountains, a wayfaring historical relative, an America at peace with nature.

seriously, perhaps, than any other musician in town. It was a perfectionist's music swimming with ideal loves, ideal places, ideal solutions to universal problems, uninhibited turtles in the creek and butterflies. And most lately, mountain men and Pawnees and coyotes. A suggestion of what he was about to offer the music world, if he could get a company to record it, was laced all through that song on the second album, "The Call":

> *There's a coyote singing down deep in my soul*
> *Throwing all of his pain at the moon*
> *And he sings to the starlight and sings to his mate*
> *With a lonesome and aching love tune*
> *Yes the coyote sings on the plains of my mind*
> *And he howls on my desert at night*
> *And he wants me to leave this old city behind*
> *'Cause the way concrete feels just ain't right*

The project started out as Bobby Durham's reading interest in a historical man who might have been his relative. He had reason to believe the mountain man Jim Bridger was a great-great uncle on his mother's side, and though he never tried to confirm that branch in his family tree, he attached enough significance to the possibility to change his name to Bridger. He picked and poked at Jim Bridger in books from the time he was old enough to read, gaining one impression of the man from juvenile historical novels, another from jingoistic public school textbooks, various others from academic histories. But one day in a rare book collection, he ran across a slender volume called *The Song of Hugh Glass* by John Neihardt. Neihardt's principal claim to fame was the 1932 American Indian classic, *Black Elk Speaks*; but he was also poet laureate of Nebraska, and *The Song of Hugh Glass* was part of a nine-volume epic poem called *The Cycle of the West* which recounted American history from 1820-90. Twenty years old when he found the book, Bridger devoured that work and decided he wanted to write a similar piece of music, though he knew he lacked enough knowledge of the historical material to begin. Through his Nashville and Austin days, he played what music he could, going through hell in his mind as he dealt with music-business professionals whom he considered essentially evil, unearthing more material for his project as he went along. He never communicated with Neihardt, but the example of the older man was always out in front of him. "I wrote

195

Neihardt about twenty letters I never mailed,'' Bridger said. ''If you ever suffered from professor worship you know what I mean.'' Neihardt died before Bridger completed his work, and Bridger was later stunned to learn that he had unknowingly returned to his manuscript after several months' idleness on the exact day Neihardt died in Nebraska.

Finally, by late 1973, Bridger was almost finished with his work, after seven years of research and writing. Though Bridger stood apart from his Austin colleagues in his approach to music, he was personally close to most of them, and John Inmon, Leonard Arnold and several other sidemen helped him record a rough demo tape in a makeshift bedroom studio overlooking a onetime festival site called Hill on the Moon. The new album was to be called *Jim Bridger and the Seekers of the Fleece*, a long narrative poem versed in heroic couplets and interspersed with nine songs voiced by Jim Bridger, Hugh Glass, Jedediah Smith, a Blackfoot warrior, and an omniscient narrator.

The story Bridger had pieced together in his library research was interesting enough in itself. He picked up the trail of American history in St. Louis in 1822 when Jim Bridger, an eighteen-year-old orphan and runaway blacksmith apprentice, joined the Ashley-Henry beaver-trapping expedition west. Also members of that expedition were Smith, a Calvinist minister who pioneered two overland routes to the Pacific before he was killed by the Comanches on the Cimarron River in 1831; and Glass, a grey-bearded loner who had lived with the Pawnees and was later killed and scalped by the Chickarees in South Dakota in 1833. Smith was one of the only members of the hundred-member band who could read or write, and his glowering presence made the others pretend to be reverent, even if they weren't. Glass was a naval captain said to have been captured by Jean Lafitte's pirates, but he escaped and walked upland to Kansas, where he bribed his Pawnee executioner with a piece of vermillion. He lived with those people several years and learned their methods of stalking game, thus he was the expedition's hunter. All those men, Bobby Bridger believed, were men on the run from the civilization east of them. They were anarchists, he wrote in his journal, ''in the finest sense of the term.''

Bridger's story continued that Glass befriended Jim Bridger and trained him as an apprentice hunter, but because Bridger was too slow to react one time, Glass was badly mauled by a grizzly in South Dakota in 1922. Bridger and another volunteer lured into the assignment by an eighty-dollar purse waited for Glass to die, but he lapsed into a coma and hung on. Bridger and the other volunteer were afraid of surrounding Indians, so finally they left Glass to die and took his gun as evidence of his demise to their comrades with the expedition. Glass survived somehow, crawled 200 miles to Fort Kiowa, then made his way another 400 miles to Fort Henry, where he confronted Jim Bridger and forgave him because of his youth, then went off in search of the other betrayer. The story continued that Bridger was driven by the humiliation of that day to strive to be the one out front, the one who volunteered for the most dangerous assignments. Because of that, the researcher continued, Jim Bridger was the first man to the Great Salt Lake, and unlike the others in his company he kept his hair long enough to witness the coming of the Mormons, the death of the buffalo and beaver, the encirclement and theologized extinction of the Indian culture, the submission of the West to a plundering civilization.

It was subjective reading of history, but Bobby Bridger believed in it, and he attached special significance to it. The mountain men, he believed, were the only anarchists in American history who had made their system work, if only for a while. Their flights from ordered society, opened roads that the same society quickly poured over, but they regained what an expansive America had lost: a sense of being at one with nature. Looking around in the twentieth century, Bobby Bridger knew that sense of communion was really lost now, for Americans treated their country like there would always be more land out west to move on to. Soon it would be a civilized wasteland of fetid pools and orange skies and tall buildings founded on garbage, unless there was a revolution in consciousness. Aside from soaring prices and energy crises and the deepening cesspool of Watergate, Bridger believed that the real evidence of ruin in America was the pollution, the gluttony, the enormous waste masqueraded as progress. That was the real message of *Jim Bridger and the Seekers of the Fleece*. The mountain men had procured the fur of the beaver for the stylishly ravenous society east of them, and now that society had fleeced a continent. He was trying to project a nineteenth-century message into the twentieth century.

The trouble of it was, he was locked into a twentieth-century medium. If he was going to disseminate that message among very many people, he would have to do it on record. But there was no market for his music. He wasn't a rock & roller, the folk movement was a thing of the past, and though he wrote about the preservation of the countryside, his music lacked the instrumentation, inflection and suburban obsession that had become the hallmarks of "country" music. RCA rejected the album out of hand at Bridger's first mention of it, and in terms of cold, practical business sense, there was probably strength in RCA's argument. Concept albums were problematic enough even with highly-popular, widely-known artists, for the listening public had been trained to take its music in small doses, four or five minutes in passing. What advertising-minded radio executive was going to set aside fifty-five minutes of programing for an American history lesson from a practically unknown folksinger, and even if they did, how many consumers would rush to their record stores and hurry home to sit still for that? What was American history anyway? In an era of truck-driving snipers, Secret Service men who attacked New York cabbies, homosexual mass murders, and quiet old men who shot up their mobile-home villages because the Astros beat the Giants, who could even remember what had happened the day before? If there had been a memory in popular American music, feelings seemed to run, let it be of the less eventful fifties.

But Bridger said he was going to record his concept album, or record no album at all. He knew his music was good enough to merit release, and he said if he couldn't record the music he wanted he was going to just quit and go back to teaching. This was his last piece of recorded music, he would say, then he'd find himself writing sequels about the Indian vision of Americans moving west, and the more recent siege of Wounded Knee. He had been at his project so long and dealt with it so closely that he began to identify with it. He predicted that the spiritual and philosophical impetus of any movement to turn America around would come from the Indian movement, and his favorite current book became Vine Deloria Jr.'s *God Is Red*. He tried to school himself to think like a mountain man, an Indian, even a coyote. *The Seekers of the Fleece* was more than a piece of music to Bridger. It had become a large part of his life.

Ralph Yarborough, the former Texas senator who was an enthusiastic history student in his own right, exclaimed when he met Bobby Bridger, "My god, you look just like Jim Bridger." My photographer claimed with some seriousness that Bobby Bridger was Jim Bridger reincarnated. Bobby was uncomfortable with that kind of talk, and I shared his discomfort. I never had grasped the metaphysical mechanics of reincarnation, but after listening to Bridger's demo tape at the house on the Hill on the Moon the afternoon of our interview, I came away convinced that at the very least, he was in creative league with the past.

Finally, when Bridger premiered his work, he chose to do it at the Pub. He thought he could draw a more intimate audience there. Still, as he sat tuning his twelve-string in the cramped A-frame office, he was worried. *Jim Bridger and the Seekers of the Fleece* was a moving piece of work but one had to concentrate to follow it. It was long and involved, and if the listener allowed his mind to wander it was easy to lose track of the narrative, for all the characters were voiced by Bridger in similar style. He voiced a more immediate worry as he listened to one of his chords. "I don't know what I'll do if this thing gets out of tune."

As it happened, there were only twenty-eight people, including waitresses, to deal with. Bridger walked onstage, asked for the audience's cooperation and attention, and for the most part received it, though one couple left soon after he began, and another necked passionately at their table from time to time.

Eyes closed as he concentrated, Bridger recited his initial lines of poetry in a well-pitched dramatic voice, enlisting Jim Bridger in the Ashley-Henry company, then went into the theme of the album:

> *I want to see something no man has ever seen*
> *Go somewhere no man has ever been*
> *Find myself alive with every breath*
> *So I will know life when I meet my death*

As he finished that song a new couple walked in and took a corner table, waved hello to the Pub manager who had replaced Ric Schwartz, and lost themselves rather loudly in their conversation. Rod Kennedy was in the audience to help select the songs Bridger would sing at the Kerrville festival, and he lifted his eyebrows over his horn-rims and glared back at the couple but they were too entwined in each other's fingers and emotion to notice.

Bridger's narrative and songs carried his characters through the first weeks of the expedition, Hugh Glass's encounter with the grizzly and then with Jim Bridger, the discovery of the Great Salt Lake, a rendezvous with the Sioux, Jim Bridger's first night with a Cheyenne bride, the arrival of wagonloads of Mormons and other

199

westward-moving settlers. Returning to his narrative voice, Bridger recited loudly:

> *The land began to fill with whites*
> *And talk of land and growth and rights*
> *And talk of hopes and dreams and schools*
> *'These red men are just savage fools*
> *To question this progressive land*
> *We have the will of God . . . Expand!'*

Then in a subdued, quiet voice the narrator surrendered the floor to Jim Bridger:

> *Back in eighteen twenty-two*
> *I signed up with Old Henry's crew*
> *We were the first to find the Sioux's . . .*
> > *precious Yellowstone*
> *This land was just a baby then*
> *Most all the Indians were my friends*
> *Before this land was filled with men . . .*
> > *and broken bison bones*

The blonde giggled and moved her boyfriend's hand from the table-top to her thigh.

Bridger sang his song from the point of view of a Blackfoot warrior, and the work was near its end. Finally Jim Bridger was blind and near death in Kansas City, Missouri in 1875, reflecting:

> *When I was young I left my home*
> *And headed westward, all alone*
> *And I was blinder then than I am now*
> *But still I made it work, somehow*
> *I wonder what Hugh Glass would do*
> *Or any of that buckskinned crew*
> *If they had lived to see old age*
> *And witness this internal rage*
> *of dying in a bed*

Bridger sang a song that likened death to the flight of an eagle, then recited with loud finality, as the couple at the nearby table accordingly raised the level of their voices:

200

Jim Bridger was a mountain man
He walked out into unknown land
Discovered our Great Salt Lake
And lived just long enough to ache
While watching freedom lose the fight
When man pretended he was right
To hate the love of freedom

Bridger repeated his theme, heaved a sigh of relief and leaned back on his stool. The small crowd applauded genuinely enough as he sat there perspiring, but the blonde girl clapped her hands together three times in boredom, and her boyfriend laughed and waved a hand at the performer, then looked back into her eyes. You couldn't reach everybody in a bar.

I rejoined Bridger in the Pub office as the crowd filed out. Many stuck their heads in the door to say how much they had enjoyed it. Bridger grinned and nodded to their compliments, and showed me some letters he had received on his project. One was an encouraging note from a Texas congressman, and another from a U.S. Interior Department bureaucrat interested in the project, but wanted to know how much it would cost. They were frighteningly short of funds, Bridger understood. That was the letter that satisfied Bridger most. If he was unable to find a commercial producer for the album, he was going to summon his old group of backers into session, finance the recording himself, and distribute the albums through the National Parks Service, hopefully in time for the Bicentennial celebration.

Another letter was from an RCA official who said these were the best songs Bridger had written, though this title was weak, that lyric needed work. It appeared the most encouraging letter of the three to me, but Bridger said he was on his way to Los Angeles to demand RCA either produce the album or free him from his contract. Reading the letter again, I wondered aloud if he should go out there with such a negative outlook. Maybe RCA would like it. He might put the twentieth century to work for him.

"Sure, that's a nice letter," he said, taking it back. "It's the first positive response I've had from them. But what I'm going to get from RCA is the vinyl shortage, and that's what the damn thing's all about."

I asked if he thought he would ever find a commercial outlet for his album.

"I think so. It just seems like there are people somewhere who would be interested in this kind of thing, and there ought to be some company, somewhere, who would realize that. I don't know. I've pushed all my earnings into the middle of the pot and I'm going to say, deal. It's option time again, and I found RCA in the phone book.''

Bridger severed his ties in California and went to the Grand Tetons for the summer, where he resumed his writing and enlisted Slim Pickens as narrator for his album. Plans for that recording proceeded, along with plans for a film, but the financing came from Bridger's church-going, cotton-farming friends in Louisiana. He was back where he started.

the ballad of evelyn goose and donna dumbass

Rusty Wier was second to no one in the dues that he had paid. He had lived in and around Austin all his life, working his way into the music spotlight for half of it. He was talented, ambitious, energetic and stubborn, but success always seemed just beyond his grasp. Younger musicians got the breaks he needed and passed him by while he adjusted to a life spent in roadside taverns in towns he'd never seen until he passed the city limits sign. Each new gig was a breakthrough, for he had mastered the art of making music in a bar, and the next time he came to town he would be worth a little more. Some day, he thought as he smoked and drove, he would encounter the right recording scout in the right bar in the right town. Then again, maybe he never would. It was easy to imagine Rusty Wier toppling off his stool in some suburban honky-tonk with a heart attack at the age of forty-nine.

In 1973 Wier was twenty-nine years old. He had grown up near Manchaca, a tiny farming community near Austin. Wier received a set of drums at the age of ten, and accordingly turned up his nose when the band teacher invited him to bang his drumsticks against the rubber pad provided elementary school drummers. In later years he would regret that snobbery, for he never learned to read music. He was a tall, gangly youth, all elbows and knees and Adam's apple. In high school he concentrated on football, basketball and track, and like many Austin area youths intimidated by academic bigness, he went to Southwest Texas State rather than the University of Texas. While in San Marcos in the early sixties, he started playing drums in a country troupe called the Clyde Barefoot Chester Show.

But the monotony of country music bored him. He wanted to be a rock & roll drummer, and he got his chance when a disc jockey named Mike Lucas decided to form and promote an Austin version of the Monkees. Lucas wanted five minimally proficient musicians who could all sing well, and Wier got the job as the drummer. The Wig was a hot act in Austin during the mid-sixties — a locally produced and distributed single called "To Have Never Loved at All" topped the Austin charts in 1966, largely through the help of Lucas, and finished the year at number five. But those were the years when Roky Erickson and the Elevators were leading the rock & roll freakout, and the Wig members told Lucas they were tired of playing the role of straight buffoons.

Lucas let his ungrateful charges go, and the band quickly fragmented. Wier and the bass player, Jess Yaryan, allied themselves with a guitarist from Temple, John Inmon. Guitar players Layton DePenning and Leonard Arnold came over from a group called the Baby Cakes, and they were joined by a versatile musician and arranger named Gary Nunn, whose latest assignment had been with a popular West Texas group called the Sparkles.

The Lavender Hill Express was more of a copy band than the Elevators and Conqueroo, but it had an excessive reputation in Austin until 1969, when Wier realized he was going to have to get out front with a guitar if he was ever going to make a name for himself. Most of the Lavender Hill members, along with Donnie Dolan, a drummer from Temple, formed another popular rock group called Genesee, but Wier traveled alone as a folksinger. At first he had a hard time of it. He was plagued by cowboys who demanded that he sing Hank Williams, and he had his first experience with a heckler in the Swingers á Go Go, a club which later became El Paso Cattle Company. A girl maintained she could sing better than he ever could, and flustered and unwise, he invited her onstage. She was terrible and when she refused to leave the crowd showed signs of holding Wier accountable. Finally he squeezed her arm to about the size of a nickel, grinned out at the crowd, and said out of the corner of his mouth, "Ma'am, we're both gonna get in trouble if you don't get down off this stage."

Wier was more accomplished and confident by early 1971. He was the most popular solo performer in town, making too much in the pizza parlors and off-campus clubs to help Eddie Wilson out when he went looking for local talent for his new place, Armadillo World Headquarters. But popular as he was, Wier badly needed a band. He had a good voice, but couldn't carry a solo act. Crosby, Stills, Nash and Young were all the rage in those days because they had toned down the electric guitars and rediscovered vocal harmony, and later that year Wier and two of his old band fellows formed their own trio of names.

Layton DePenning was a songwriter blessed with a fine, high tenor voice, John Inmon was a songwriter and a fine guitar player, Rusty was a songwriter with a way of winning a crowd over. Brimming with material, Rusty, Layton and John invaded clubs in Texas and Arkansas at rock-bottom wages, courted and seduced most of the audiences, and were good enough to attract some record-scout interest. The trio parted amicably a year later, and Wier went on his own again, this time with a band, and he soon developed a hometown Texas routine that went over well. Just being himself was his act. He laughed and grinned and kicked in the air when he finished a song, and he became the most backwoods boy in town when the Austin music taste turned country. Jerry Jeff Walker's fabled boot maker Charlie Dunn made Wier a pair of boots that became locally famous, and his low-crowned, western-villain hat became a popular model when the craze for stetson's took over.

Wier was making more money in the clubs than B. W. Stevenson was making with RCA, and some friends in the lower echelons of the recording industry were trying to sell his talent to several labels, but with no success. One of those middlemen took Wier and John Inmon to Nashville to cut a demo tape, where like most Austin musicians they were amazed by a breed of studio musicians who by some magical process converted music to a number system and played anything perfectly after four or five runs-through. Wier was Larry Watkins' first client of any real worth and he was one of the most familiar names in Austin, but nobody from *Rolling Stone* came around to interview him. Austin had been invaded by newcomers and Wier had been bypassed.

Though the new arrivals accepted Wier as an equal and said it was just a matter of time till he made it, he was left standing in the court of the newcomers' reign. Jerry Jeff Walker stumbled in out of the wilderness like John the Baptist, Michael Murphey arrived amidst whisperings that he was the messiah, and Willie Nelson smiled down on the new Jerusalem like the benevolent being above, but Rusty had been there all along. Wier's old associates were doing all right. They were members of the "Interchangable Band," the sidemen who jumped from country-rock leader to leader and would staff the studios if Austin realized its musical potential. Inmon drifted between jobs with Wier and Walker, DePenning drifted between Wier and B. W. Stevenson, Leonard Arnold drifted from Murphey to Fromholz back to Wier, Donnie Dolan drifted from Wier to Stevenson to Jerry Jeff, Gary Nunn was an indispensible assistant to Murphey and Walker, Jess Yaryan played bass for Bill and Bonnie Hearne. But Wier wasn't going to be comfortable backing anybody up. He had to make it out front, or he wasn't going to make it.

When my magazine collaborator and I went in search of Wier, we found him in the new Cricket Club, which was trying to crack the country market by bringing in performers during an afternoon happy hour. Wier was all elbows and knees and Adam's apple as he played for the crowd, and he was the sort of performer Texas club owners would love. He came across as a good old boy not too affected by all that counter-culture nonsense, and he plugged the most expensive drinks in the house, promoted tobacco sales with a song called "The Cigarette Man" and the theft of Brother Dave Gardner's line, "If I could light a chain I'd smoke it." He didn't question the bar-music procedure, in fact he thrived on it. He sought the level of the crowd, which he apparently thought was reasonably low. Homicidal grammar and the joys of growing up in Manchaca. The down-to-earth fellers he met on the highway construction crews. A song called "I Heard You Been Laying My Old Lady." Shucks, Rusty.

The Cricket crowd wasn't too large that afternoon but it was enlivened by a soiled construction crew from Temple who raised an amiable uproar until the price of drinks went up. "God damn it, Rusty," one of them said as he left. "Goodbye."

After Wier finished he joined us at a patio table overlooking a swimming pool and the cluttered landscape of English Aire apartments. I asked if he had ever lived in Temple.

"Nah," he said. "Those guys just come down to see me ever once in a while."

He punctuated his sentences with laughter, dipping his chin down inside his shoulders as he cackled. My collaborator asked why he had made such stark transitions from country to folk to rock and back to country.

"Well, I'm really not much of a guitar player," Rusty said. "I found that out when I was doing all those folk gigs. I figured that country was the easiest way to get where I wanted to be. What I do is not really country, but it's got a lot of country flavor. I appreciate straight country, but I just don't like to play it all that much. I've written a lot of country songs, but I wouldn't even think about recording a lot of them. Now if somebody else wanted to record them . . ."

"Like 'I Heard You Been Laying My Old Lady'?" I suggested.

Wier laughed. "No, I'd love to record that. That came about one time when I was on my way to Colorado. We were listening to a country station and three really hokey songs came on one after another, and one of the guys in the truck said Rusty, why don't you write a song called 'I Heard You Been Layin' My Old Lady'? I had it finished by the time we got to Denver."

Onstage Wier advertised the charms of Austin more than most performers, and we asked him why he liked it so much.

"The musicians around here are good — if you need a band, need some pickers, you can find them. It used to be that you had to just fend for yourself, really look. But now we know so many people — all of us pick together. That's the thing I like about it. Everybody sticks together. Murphey and Jerry Jeff and all the guys that have records out try to help the ones who don't. They put in good words for us every place they go, and we do the same."

My collaborator asked Wier if he had ever played in New York or L.A.

"When we were doing the Rusty, Layton and John thing we were gonna do the Bitter End in New York, and they said we'll give you thirty minutes. Hell, it would've taken us that long to set up, so we blew it off. It wasn't worth it. When we were in L.A. we also blew off a guest set at the Troubador. Those guest sets, if you're nobody just coming in out of the cold, they treat you like a dog."

Wier talked about song-writing and his wife and small son. I asked him if being on the road all the time was hard on a marriage. Rather defensively, Wier said, "My wife figures it's my business. It's almost like I go to work at eight o'clock in the morning and get off at five. She looks at it that way. And I'm not on the road too much. We try not to go out for more than three weeks at a time."

My collaborator asked if out-of-state audiences were responding to country music.

"I think they like rock & roll more in Colorado, but in Michigan they really like country. They like the accents and the boots and the hat, the whole trip. They'll spot you a mile off up there."

Did he agree that Austin audiences tended to be more responsive than those elsewhere?

"Yeah, but I'm prejudiced. I've been here a long time, and they like me. I've been to other places that were pretty cold. When that happens you've just got to warm them up. You look for that button to punch to get them off. If you can get them off the first time, then they'll listen to music they wouldn't have listened to before."

Did he think Austin was going to become the creative force everybody was talking about?

"It's gonna be a center, I really believe that. All it needs is the studios . . . there is a studio here," he added quickly, "and while I can't knock it, those people in Nashville blew my mind. They know what they're doing. They've got the equipment down at Odyssey, but they need to practice at it and get it down to a science instead of a hit-and-miss situation."

Was it possible to content himself with a leading role in Austin and a good income playing the clubs, or was there always an overriding pressure to make it big?

"There's always that pressure; it just depends on how far you want to go. The pressure's definitely there, or else you wouldn't be doing it. You want to get better and you want to get to know more people, and to do that you've got to sacrifice so much. That's the reason I do a lot of songs I wouldn't ordinarily do. I figure if they'll listen to that, then more than likely they'll listen to what I've got to say. I play games with them. I have to because I don't have an album out. So I do other people's stuff, when I'd really like to be doing my songs, Fromholz's songs, Jerry Jeff's songs, B. W.'s songs."

My collaborator mentioned that we had seen Fromholz turn his back on an audience because they wouldn't listen. Was he ever tempted to do that?

Jamming with Michael Murphey and drummer Donnie Dolan, Rusty Wier was an Austin performer who had been around when times were harder. With his stylized hat and boots, Wier adapted easily when the Austin taste turned country, but for a long time he was a saloon performer, his music in conflict with his domestic instincts.

Overshadowed at first by the immigrant talents of Willie Nelson and Michael Murphey, Wier finally got the break he needed. He was still on the road performing, away from his family, but now he had a record that guaranteed him serious consideration. It had been a long hard road.

"I started out in a beer joint. The first gig I ever had was in a place called the Old Playboy Lounge. Nothing but cowboys, and I got off to it. I did some songs they'd like and stuck some of my stuff in there and over the years I've been putting more and more of it in. I like a place like the Cricket, because I don't like a crowd that's dead. A lot of times when people go out to a club they're not really in the mood to listen to the band. I can sympathize with these people, because they're not musicians. I'm a musician. I can go out and get off to a lead guitar player, a good singer or bass player, but they can't take it apart like that. They take it as a whole, and if it's not exciting you lose them. I can also sympathize with Steve — he's one of the best talents around — but I like to get out amongst them and mix it up."

Still, didn't he ever get discouraged?

"Oh yeah, I've been discouraged. But the only times I get discouraged are when I've been playing around here a lot, and I feel like they're gettin' tired of me. That's a fear anybody has at any level. But this is the only way I can do it. If you don't start off at the top, you've got to make yourself take it slow, take your time and hope for the best."

When things finally broke for Wier, they broke in a hurry. Shortly after we talked to him, a disc jockey in Houston put him in contact with Californians Lee Lasseff and David Chackler, who had an agreement with ABC-Dunhill similar to the one Mike Nesmith had with Elektra. Wier signed his contract with their company, Chalice Productions, which meant he could encounter the same fate as Fromholz if ABC-Dunhill soured on the arrangement, but that didn't appear in the immediate offing. Wier requested the assistance of DePenning and Inmon in the L.A. recording session and called in New York producer Jim Mason, who had earlier expressed interest in producing Rusty, Layton and John if that act ever got a break.

Mason imported sidemen who had played with Buffalo Springfield, Poco, Manassas, the Byrds, the Dillards and Van Morrison, and after eight weeks in the studio, the results were surprising. Wier's voice was still country — a recorded mix of Gordon Lightfoot, Tony Joe White and Buddy Holly — and much of the material was country, but it was more of a rock album than anyone expected. Much of the credit for that went to Inmon. For a long time the instrumental difference between country and rock had been the lead guitar. In country it complemented the vocalist, while in rock, particularly in the excesses of acid-rock, the lead guitarist became the most important member of the band, and the singer had to shout to be heard. *Stoned, Slow, Rugged* was a raucous mixture of the two forms. Inmon was one of the younger members of the Interchangeable Band, but when he picked up his instrument other guitarists set theirs down and listened. He wasn't as introspective as Leonard Arnold, and he didn't strive for as much as Murphey's guitarist, Craig Hillis, but he was more inventive than either, and he covered more ground. Inmon's guitar play, DePenning's tenor accompaniments, and all that commercial rock talent surrounding Wier's rough-edged voice resulted in a sound so wildly hybrid that it was almost disorienting. There was no pattern to the album, it had a split personality.

In material, Wier borrowed Ramsey's "Painted Lady" and Murphey's "Five O'Clock in the Texas Morning" and gave them the barroom treatment they had not been afforded before, but he also utilized two of Inmon's songs which were unabashedly rock-oriented. The best cut on the album, "Easier to Hurt," came from a Nashville songwriter, Wayne Berry, but Wier used just enough of his own material to give the album a personal imprint. One of those songs, a ballad called "Jeremiah Black," began as an idea for a screenplay before Wier decided to turn it into music. Accompanied by a backwoods fiddle and banjo, the song began with a boy's reminiscences of his father, who sang for the passengers of paddle-wheel riverboats, but abruptly, as Inmon's guitar turned reflective then almost savage, the lyrics took a darker turn:

> Now Papa was a man who made a bad hand at the table
> Somebody told me
> Mr. Black was dealing from up his sleeve
> Well my papa drew his knife
> Old Jeremiah he took his life
> He was buried in the forest
> by the river that runs to the sea
> Jeremiah Black found a knife in his back this mornin'
> Somebody told me
> He was dead, a layin' there in his bed
> I guess I've wasted too much time
> I'd better let my legs unwind
> and run into the forest
> by the river that runs to the sea

214

It was a simple song about murder, not an uncommon theme in American songwriting, yet it seemed to contradict everything that Austin music proposed to stand for. But it was a commerical song, and that jarring, repetitive *somebody told me* was what Michael Nesmith called a relatable. It wasn't too country for the pop audience, and it wasn't too pop for country.

The album was hard to assess. Maybe it was good, maybe it was mediocre, maybe it just hadn't worked, but the different sound was often the one that caught on, and the nationwide air play quickly afforded Wier's album surprised even his devoted Austin followers. With that pivotal album behind him, Wier began to look like more than the supporting character he had been. Time and again, Michael Nesmith's music-business theories came to mind. Wier was a visual performer, he didn't run and hide at the mention of commercial music, he was acceptable to a hard-line country audience. B. W. Stevenson might disperse the Austin message by way of the pop charts, Michael Murphey might spread the gospel with his songwriting, Willie Nelson might dazzle them in New York, but Wier might be the one who would make the personal impression in the beer joints. He was the only one who accepted them for what they were.

After the album's release I met Wier once again in the Cricket Club. The Cricket was prosperous enough that country-western happy hours were no longer a necessity, and loyal to old friends, Wier elected to premier his album there. As we sat at a table he sent his new band through warm-up drills for that evening's performance. Inmon was unavailable because he was playing with Jerry Jeff, DePenning had moved up from bass guitar to lead, and Arnold was playing banjo, lead and steel. Filling out the band were two newcomers, drummer Jimmy Marriott and bass player Bobby Smith, who had played with Gary Nunn in the old West Texas days of the Sparkles. They ran through "Five O'Clock in the Texas Morning" and sounded better than the cut on the album, though Wier said afterward the new band had never played it before.

Wier, my photographer and I retired outside to the same table overlooking the English Aire swimming pool where we had met before, and we talked about Wier's new band, his album and his record contract.

"I always wanted to do it with ABC-Dunhill," he said. "They've got the promotion. It happened just like that, after waiting fifteen years. And I'm happy as hell so far. They said it would be out April thirtieth, and they hit it within three days, so I can't complain.''

"How was L.A.?''

"Eight weeks in a motel room. I nearly climbed the walls. L.A.'s not one of my favorite places, but I wanted to do it out there. I thought I could come closer to what I wanted to do there than in Nashville. I was kind of surprised by the way the album came out though. It's different for me. I'm going back a few years. It came out more rock & roll than I expected. But that's fine. Everybody else is getting more country. It's all one big cycle, I guess.''

How was his promotion being handled?

"I'm my own promotion man. The first album is really hard to break, it's just kind of a feeler. The second, third and fourth are the ones that tell the tale. But we're going out on the road with it, just like we used to, only this time we're not going in cold. This time I've got people to call when I hit town, this time we know who's who.''

A middle-aged man in white shoes and modern wire-rims stepped out on the patio and clapped Rusty on the shoulder.

"Hello C. L.,'' he responded.

C. L. asked Wier how his voice was holding up.

"I thought I was about to lose it. But it's all right now. I've got a good doctor. He keeps me shot up with cortisone.''

"They have to shoot that into your larynx, don't they?''

I choked on my beer and Wier said, ''Naw, he shoots me in the ass.''

C. L. leaned against the railing and looked out at the panorama of apartments. ''See those units over yonder?'' he said. ''They're a lot purtier than these.''

"Yeah, they look a lot better,'' Wier said unenthusiastically. Glancing at me, he explained, ''C. L. and I've sat out here many a time. We've watched it rain, watched the apartments burn.''

C. L. returned inside for a drink. Wier said, ''You know, what I really like is an outdoor concert. It's like sittin' on your back porch pickin'. Concerts are good too. You've got more room to move around in. But I don't mind playing places like this. Actually, what you're doing is magnifying your personality, trying to project a feeling that you're like them, let's all drink a beer and have a good time. You've got to fight 'em on their own ground. I've been there. I was a redneck myself for a long time.''

He lapsed into memories of the olds days of the Wig and the Lavendar Hill Express, which must have seemed a long time distant,

216

and told us about one of those band fellows, "a great drummer, now a TV repairman. He's one of those guys who just quit."

Why did he quit, my photographer asked. Wife and family?

"I don't know if she's his wife or not, but she may have had something to do with it." He looked at her. "Playing music is not good for a marriage relationship at all. Our kind of life is hard on a woman. I have to do it though. I couldn't sit back and be a songwriter or studio musician. I enjoy the crowds, I love to work with audiences. See what I can do with them."

I said much had happened to Austin music in a year's time, and the movement seemed to be steamrolling. What did he think of that?

"We're telling everybody now to go to Dallas, that's where it's at. It's gotten out of hand. Groups are now coming *here* to get discovered. We've had a real good thing for a long time. But there's fixing to be some backstabbing and undercutting. I can feel it already."

My photographer wondered if the scene was peaking out.

"Oh no," Wier said. "It hasn't reached its peak yet. Austin may well be another Nashville. But I hope to hell not. I'm moving to Dripping Springs, or at least I'm gonna try to. I want some land. I want out."

A typical Wier crowd packed the Cricket that night: rowdy, profane, prone more to ratted hair and white patent loafers than boots and straw stetsons, more demanding than a Walker crowd, for they were used to getting what they wanted from Wier. He slouched in, calling many of them by name, pausing to shake their hands, making them feel at home. He tuned his guitar with his back to the audience then DePenning came onstage, and Wier turned around and said, "Hi, how y'all doin'? The rest of the band's gonna be up here in a minute. In the meantime we figgered we'd just pick a little, so get your cigarette and drink or whatever it is in front of you, and let's get this show on the road."

Wier was at his calculating best that night. He began with a straight country tune called "The Lonesome Highway Blues," then tilted his audience in the other direction with a song that extolled the merits of smoking dope much in the country-boy manner of Terry Southern's short story, "Red Dirt Marijuana." Reminding them he was on their side, he railed in their behalf against snobbish Northerners: "You ever go someplace where they make fun of the way you talk? The farther you get away from Texas, the more it happens. And you get to worryin' about it; you become self-conscious, and you train yourself to *enunicate*. That way you'll be acceptable company. Only trouble is, you wind up soundin' like a faggot."

He played some of their country requests, but before they knew what was happening he had them squirming in their seats to rather loud rock & roll, and when he wanted them to listen to a song off the album he quieted them down with an entertaining story: "Have you ever woke up on a Sunday morning and said man alive, who is that, where'd she come from? What have I done now? That's what this song is about. It's off my new album, which oughta be in the stores any day now.

> *Still fellin' tight I remember last night*
> *Just like I was sittin' there*
> *Tall, dark and slinky*
> *Wearin' long black shiny hair*
> *Well I'd like to say*
> *she's that pretty today*
> *but I finally got her in the light*
> *It's just a stoned, slow, rugged Sunday mornin'*
> *after a good-time Saturday night*

The crowd loved him; he spoke their language. But they didn't know how well he spoke it. My photographer and I found a table along the wall, and just a few feet away, in the darkest of corners, was a representative sampling of the audience. A tall, dark-haired man in his early thirties looked at me with a glint of recognition in his eyes but failed to place me. However, I placed him. A recent graduate of the UT business school he had a wife and family, a mortgaged home, and a ranking midway up the ladder of an automotive sales department. He valued those assets, but he was a man torn between security and infidelity. Nothing so risky as an affair, now, just an occasional stray piece of ass. When I knew him, he told his wife that he had to spend his evenings in the library, and apparently she never checked into the business school library hours, for every night he turned into a hunter of secretaries, topless dancers, beauticians and particularly hippie girls, for he figured they had to be ever so much easier. He wasn't too finicky about the game he stalked in the bars of south Austin, but when he scored his chest ballooned. When he failed, the pressure to prove himself increased. He was the kind of guy who would pull out the ten-gauge if he ever caught his wife in bed with the next-door neighbor.

He was accompanied by a platinum blonde with long legs and a pointed bra, who cooed a lot while he stared at the blue lights on the Cricket's ceiling. They had arrived separately, the car salesman leading a man who looked like one of C. L.'s fellow contractors, the blonde leading a shy dumpy woman who jumped when Wier said shitfire.

"This is Evelyn," the blonde said to the older man, whom the car salesman introduced as Everitt.

"Evelyn?" Everitt said, nodding politely.

"Yeah," said the blonde with a wise acre giggle. "Evelyn Goose."

After drinks arrived the car salesman and the blonde fell into a long embrace, tongues thrusting wildly, while Everitt drummed his fingers on a glass of Scotch and ventured, "Well, ah, Evelyn are you new to Austin?"

"No, I've been here a long time!"

Driven back by Evelyn's spooked response, Everitt attacked his drink. "Do you come here often?" Evelyn ventured, looking over her shoulder at Wier, who was singing Dave Dudley's truck-driving classic, "Six Days on the Road."

"Oh no," Everitt said. "This is the first time I've ever been here."

Cheeks flushed by the long kiss, the blonde turned to Everitt and attacked him coyly. "*Everitt* you're telling a *lie*. I've seen you here before, that time you brought that secretary from the office, what's her name? Donna Dumbass?" Everitt drank in abashment.

"He raises hell and dances every night," the blonde told Evelyn. "But sometimes he's not too careful about the company he keeps. I think it's called lack of couth."

What the hell was wrong with the company he kept, Everitt wanted to know.

"I saw you the other night with that Lester guy. He's queer."

"Well, he never queered me."

"He was *touchin'* you," she persisted, "and you was *enjoyin'* it."

"We were talking business," Everitt said in disgust. "He needed a damn floor."

Alarmed perhaps by my crazed grin and frenzied note-taking, the car salesman, the blonde, Everitt and Evelyn fell into a drinking hush and aimed their chairs toward Wier, who was singing one of the crowd's old favorites.

Well Joe, I thought we'd just sit down and drink a beer
I know you're wonderin' why I called and asked you here
It's around the town that you've been seein' Sue
So I called you here to ask you if it was true
I heard you been layin' my old lady
Time must be gettin' hard everywhere
I hear you been layin' my old lady
Well I like you Joe, but wives are hard to share

the quota on singing texas jews

After nearly a year, I was sick and tired of talking to musicians. They didn't have any more answers to the world's questions than I did, and they were a damn sight harder to contact. Most were reclusive as snakes. They had either just moved, or they had an unlisted phone number, or, if one plied that number for a sympathetic intermediary, the number had been disconnected or changed. The only alternative to all that was to attend one of their performances, wait until after the final set, and hog-tie them as they stepped off the stage. The pleasant exception, or so it seemed at first, was Kinky Friedman.

Friedman was a University of Texas graduate and former Peace Corpsman who insisted he introduced the Frisbee to the island of Borneo, and while working at his family's camp for children in the Hill Country, he learned he could make youngsters laugh when he sang. He directed his aim at an older audience and tried to sell himself in Los Angeles. He failed and went to Nashville, where he attracted the attention of Tompall Glaser, who produced his album and sold it to Vanguard in New York. When Friedman came to Austin he stayed in his family's home, and his father, a university psychology professor and speech therapist, was listed in the directory.

"Ah yes," Dr. Friedman said when I called. "I read your article. He's in New York now, negotiating for a new contract. A lot of money and lawyers involved. Are you going to the KPFT benefit in Houston?"

"Um, I hadn't planned on it."

"Well for the moment that would be the best place to contact him. I believe he's flying in for the concert then flying right back out to New York again. You could probably catch him there. Otherwise, I'll take your number and have him contact you when he gets here."

I left Dr. Friedman my number and reluctantly concluded I had to subject myself to the freeways of Houston and several more hours of country-rock music. I should have qualified for a degree in it but then, I had never seen Friedman perform, and he was getting to be quite a star. For all I knew his next concert might be in Bangkok.

The drive from Austin to Houston was pleasant enough — a two-lane road along the Colorado River past a misplaced pine forest, down through rolling Spanish-moss country onto the flat coastal plain, a short road race with Continentals and Mercedes on an interstate highway, and then we were there, or at least within the city limits. Houston was Guy Clark's L.A. Freeway come to Texas. It sprawled out among the neon signs toward infinity and its atmosphere was a source of wonder for boys from West Texas. The biggest news in Houston that day was a couple of dozen homosexually-motivated murders that Truman Capote said could have only happened west of the Mississippi. I was interested in hearing his defense of that statement, but it would have to be good.

Most people from the northern part of the state were aghast at the thought of living in Houston, yet if one didn't want or couldn't conform to the Anglo-Saxon, middle-class norm, Houston was a much better place to be than Dallas. In one short block on our way to the Hofheinz Pavilion at the University of Houston, we passed a likely carload of dope-dealers, a transvestite street-walker, and a Chinese antique shop next to a taco stand, all this on a street once barricaded when blacks rioted at Texas Southern University. Nobody stood out in Houston. It was easy to escape into its diversity.

KPFT was an FM station in Houston with a colorful history. It originally made an impression when it became a public-affairs station with a left-wing viewpoint, and got promptly bombed by right-wing vigilantes. Lately it had pioneered a format, considerably more rock-oriented than that of KOKE that was the radio talk of Texas. The station was trying to survive through listener subscriptions rather than advertising, but as the benefit suggested, it wasn't making it. In order to raise money, the station managers had enlisted most of the big-name

Austin acts, Commander Cody and Floridian Jimmy Buffett, lumping them all under the heading Cosmic Cowboys, a promotional tactic which infuriated Michael Murphey, since he had coined the term and therefore had to be there. The young, newly-elected mayor of Houston, Fred Hofheinz, had purchased a large block of tickets for the show, which supposedly meant the Houston establishment was making overtures to the counter-culture. From the look of the crowd in the Pavilion, which was an overblown basketball court, it meant nothing of the sort. The concert-goers were uniformly young, long-haired and hip to rock & roll country. All they knew was that it was time to smoke dope and boogie, even if it was in the middle of a sad Willie Nelson song.

The manager of the concert, a hustling young man with a company called Wild West Productions, let me in free but denied me access to the performers. Banished to the crowd I had made the trip for nothing. I would only be able to get close enough to Friedman to shout at him, and from what I'd heard about the man, he'd probably misinterpret what I was shouting and invite me to commit a homosexual act. Jerry Jeff Walker and his band had already played and caught a plane to Phoenix. Glumly I endured Buffett, Asleep at the Wheel, and a KPFT jock turned folksinger who said, "I'm sorry I'm not as much of a Cosmic Cowboy as the others." There seemed a trace of resentment in his voice, an air of indignation that the musicians on the bill hailed from Austin, not from Houston. Houston was by-god Texas and proud of it, and its only rival for leadership in most Texas departments was Big D. Another jock identified himself as Rockin' Bobby Aiken and said, "We are a listener-supported station. No ads. We are asking 4000 people to subscribe at thirty dollars a year. But we only have 2400 subscribers. Now there's 6000 people here, and simple subtraction indicates that some of you people are falling down on the job." A most unfortunate choice of language, as far as my Austin pocketbook was concerned.

The Austin audience amazed me. They would pile in cars and drive all over the state to see the same performers they had seen in Austin the week before, and the Houston concert was no exception. A whoop went up every time somebody mentioned Austin, and the visitors were dressed in pioneering get-up in order to pull rank on the directionless Houston freaks. Just after Rockin' Bobby finished his spiel, one of the mobile Austinites, dressed in a straw cowboy hat and Lone Star beer

T-shirt, abruptly vomited on the girl next to me, wiped his chin and staggered toward the area normally reserved for the basketball bench. "God," the girl said. "God."

All I really knew about Friedman was that he was marginally famous in places other than Austin, and he pissed a lot of people off. He had played in Austin just once to my knowledge, and I passed up the opportunity. The only cut I'd heard off his album was "Ride 'em Jewboy," the song which prompted some people to say he was a Hebrew heretic:

> *While ponies, all the dreams were broken*
> *rounded up and made to move along*
> *The loneliness which can't be spoken*
> *just swings a rope and rides inside a song*
> *Dead limbs play with ringless fingers*
> *a melody which burns you deep inside*
> *Ah, how the song becomes the singers*
> *May peace be with you as you ride*

That didn't strike me as very offensive. Friedman was writing rather about the reality-myth of the dispossessed Jew, which in Texas was more reality than myth, for the Ango-Saxon greater Southwest dispossessed its Jews by stripping them of their ethnic identity. It seemed to me that Friedman had turned the tables on Texas by seating his myth in the saddle of the honored Texas myth, the cowboy. Of course I was a Gentile, so it was probably none of my business.

Billy Joe Shaver came out and said, "Hi, I'm a songwriter," then sang his song about his good Christian raising and eighth-grade education. Shaver was too country for that crowd. They were stingy with their applause, and he abruptly left the stage, though his band hung around. Jim Franklin, who had come down from Austin to emcee the benefit, waltzed onstage in costume and introduced Friedman. "His Jewboys couldn't make it tonight," Franklin said, "so we lined up a good Christian band to back him up."

Friedman didn't look much like the Lenny Bruce of country music. His hair was short, he wore sunshades and a flat-brimmed western hat, and he smoked a cigar. He looked more like a young Groucho Marx. Friedman sang two or three songs in a mock country voice, and he tried once to alienate the audience, but it didn't work. He tapped his cigar like Groucho and said with an exaggerated drawl, "What do you get when you cross a prostitute and a leprechaun?'' Almost as if there were a censor in the sound booth, the microphone went off and Kinky lost his pale punch line. He didn't offend the crowd. Mostly he bored them. ''Who is that?'' a girl near me said. ''Kinky Friedman,'' her boyfriend yawned.

Friedman caught his flight back to New York, and I didn't get away from Houston till nearly two in the morning. It was a harrowing drive back to Austin, punctuated by hallucinatory giraffes which continued to bound out in front of the Volkswagen, and a bitter cup of coffee and a rubber-meringue piece of chocolate pie in an all-night truckstop cafe. All day long I had been listening to people roar their approval when one of the singers said, ''We're gonna do another truck-drivin' song now.'' Apparently none of them had done any time in a truckstop lately. Rancid grease crawled up the walls of this one, the waitress appeared on the verge of tears, and the four truckers in the place were swapping tales about their latest coon hunts. Everybody in the place looked like death. A truckstop cafe at 3:30 in the morning was the most depressing place in the world. I wished somebody would write an honest song about it.

I decided I'd better listen to Friedman's music before I talked to him, so I bought the album and he fulfilled my wish with a song called ''Highway Cafe.'' He crooned about a waitress in an all-nighter on Route 64 who served up corned beefs on rye and counted the minutes until her trucker came to take her away forever. Then Friedman started talking:

> *And the hours passed by even as the trucks passed by out on the highway. And then two grim highway patrolmen came into the place, shook the rain from their hats, and as the poor girl brought them their coffee she overheard the words that they said:*
>
> *Voice 1: 'Hey Curly, did you see that old diesel flattened out like your damned nose up by the Predicament tonight?'*
>
> *Voice 2: 'Yeah, he jackknifed that sumbitch slicker'n owlshit.'*
>
> *Voice 1: 'Get me a chilidog over here, honey.'*
>
> *Voice 2: 'Hey, you don't suppose he had a little old hog waitin' on him somewhere down the line here, do ya?'*
>
> *Voice 1: 'Aw hell, Curly, don't you know? Those truckers, they got a little filly in every cafe from here to Las Crudas. Haw haw haw.'*

227

That might have been an affront to a hardline country-music fanatic, but little more. I had to turn the album over before I found a song that seriously encroached on the boundary between humor and insult:

Early in the morning you're out on the street
passing out pamphlets to everyone you meet
You gave up your Maidenform for Lent
and now the front of your dress has an air-scoop vent
Every great man who's ever come along
has had a little woman telling him he's wrong
Eve told Adam, here's an apple you hoss
and Delilah defoliated Samson's moss
Get your biscuits in the oven and your buns in the bed
That's what I to my baby said
Woman's liberation is a goin' to your head
Get your biscuits in the oven and your buns in the bed

Like most absolutists, doctrinaire feminists were a remarkably humorless lot, and when Friedman sang that song in Buffalo, the stage was soon swarming with protestors, one of them weeping hysterically. What they objected to, they said, was not the song, but the pleasure Friedman derived from insulting them. Kinky didn't help matters by telling the weeping girl, "Hey honey, come on over here and lick my salt block." That time the crowd almost turned against him.

But the song designed to endear Friedman to no one was "The Ballad of Charles Whitman." Nobody was quite sure why the University of Texas had that tower, though J. Frank Dobie called it the phallus of an impotent administration. Except for the fact that it turned orange at night when the Longhorns won and could be seen for miles around, it served no useful purpose. It housed one of the best libraries in the country, but whoever heard of a library with fourteen floors and one matchbox elevator? The observation deck of the tower offered a grand view of the campus, the Capitol complex, and the steep hills to the west, but apparently Texans couldn't be trusted with that kind of height. The tower served the self-destructive needs of many a despairing Austinite; one time I was reading Jung in a library carrel when a young body plummeted by. But the Whitman murders were too much to comprehend. Anyone who had ever fired a rifle knew that what he did was practically impossible, even with a scope. Yet he shot a man out of a barber's chair several hundred yards away, and people

Onstage at a Houston radio benefit, backstage in Austin with Gary Nunn, holding court on his parents' patio, Kinky Friedman was the persona. When he took off his sunshades he became Richard.

In the company (from left) of Jim Franklin, Roger "Captain Midnite" Schutt from Nashville, and Willie Nelson's daughter Lana, Friedman was a man of many poses. His animosity toward the Austin performers was overstated, a part of the hype, but like many men he was no longer comfortable in his hometown.

died out in the open because even the most heroically inclined were afraid to leave their cover to help them. In his derangement, he must have been inspired.

After it was over, and the shock wore off, the topic became a conversational taboo in Austin. Passersby still glanced up at the tower and remembered, but three months after the incident, it was something that nobody talked about. Thus when Friedman started cracking jokes about it one night at a party, the Associated Press reporter, who was himself wounded by Whitman and wrote his story of the bizzare affair from his hospital bed, stared a hole through him; and when Friedman sang his song at the Armadillo, a girl wept long after the performance was over. "I just can't believe someone would write a song like that," she told one of Friedman's sidemen.

Some were dyin', some were weepin'
Some were studyin', some were sleepin'
Some were shoutin' Texas number one
Some were runnin', some were fallin'
Some thought the revolution had begun
The doctors tore his poor brain down
but not a snitch of illness could be found
Most folks couldn't figger just why he did it
and them that could would not admit it
There's still a lot of Eagle Scouts around

Texans were clearly not ready for a sarcastic Jew with an exceedingly black sense of humor. When Friedman teamed with Jerry Lee Lewis in a concert billed in Killer and the Kink at the Western Place in Dallas, his choice of language so offended the manager that he took his family home then, tembling with rage, accosted Friedman in his office. "What about nigger?" Kinky said. "Is that an objectionable word?" Friedman was pushing his luck when he said that, but a Dallas newspaper reporter was in the office with a tape recorder, so he figured he was on safe ground.

In Austin, Friedman was a marginal character. He had, after all, abandoned its charms in favor of Nashville and New York, and he was, well, pushy. Many people believed he never would have made it if he hadn't had a telephone and a brother who could sell an Alaskan husky to a camel-driver. The country instrumentation on his album was Los

Angeles slick, radio programers in Austin wouldn't touch most of his songs, and in songwriting ability, most Austinites ranked him near the bottom of the recorded heap. He wasn't serious enough about his music. Yet elsewhere, Friedman was a minor phenomenon. Though Vanguard failed to do much with his album, it had drawn rave reviews almost everywhere, and when he played the clubs on the West Coast, Kris Kristofferson, Allen Ginsberg, Bob Dylan, Roosevelt Grier and even Ken Kesey dropped by to chat. A filmed segment of one of his performances appeared on Sally Quinn's morning shows on CBS, *Playboy* mentioned him as a young man of note, and he was in New York trying to free himself of Vanguard so he could sign a $250,000 contract with another company. None of the other Austin performers could say that.

When I finally contacted Friedman, he gave me directions to his parents' home and told me to come out that afternoon. Yes, he said reluctantly, I could bring my photographer. The Friedman residence was perched on a hillside in northwest, upper-middle-class Austin. His brother met me at the door, and said I would find Richard out back. Inside was a thoroughly middle-American scene — opera on the stereo, Friedman's father shuffling about in disheveled pants, his sister convalescing from the flu in front of a television set. I found the star drinking beer and sunning himself in a lawn chair on the back porch, along with his lead guitar player, Danny Finley, a slight man with short red hair and the general appearance of an adolescent, except for a cigar and forty-year-old eyes. Friedman called him Panama Red.

Friedman led me over to the porch railing and showed me a map of Texas carefully laid out with polished white rocks on the ground below. "My mother did that," he said. "Ain't it purty?" We winced as an airplane shuddered overhead. The Friedman residence lay below an approachway to the Austin Municipal Airport.

The keys to Friedman were the voice and sunshades. When he lapsed into a heavy Texas drawl he became crude and arrogant. The rest of the time he spoke quietly and intelligently. He rarely took his sunshades off, but when he did he revealed squinting, sensitive eyes. Kinky Friedman was the persona. Under that, I suspected, Richard Friedman was a marshmallow.

"We've been readin' yore magazine article," he said. "I see you gave us part of a sentence."

I said the reason for that was that my collaborator thought the best way to handle Kinky Friedman was with a ball peen hammer, so we avoided the subject.

"You didn't go along with that?"

I said I didn't know.

"Well, shake my hand and have a seat."

I said I'd heard he was putting together a new band.

"It's not really a new band. It's really the driving forces of the old band, with a little more ethnic presence, I believe. We're gonna have a coon in our band, and get rid of our Chinaman. We're kinda keepin' the sound under raps, strictly on the q-t until we get this new album out. Nothing like what we've been doing."

Friedman belched loudly and sneaked a glance at my photographer to judge its effect. I asked him about his contract negotiations.

"That's the most exciting part of the whole musical scene. It's not the music, it's the machinations behind the music. At least it is for me. Ninety-eight percent of the other people involved in it seem to have a laid-back attitude. They just like their music, and if you let them they'll jam all night, wine and T-shirts and stuff. We dig our music too, but we — "

He looked at my photographer, who was moving around the porch. "I'm a little bit self-conscious about being shot without my hat," he said. "Oh go on, I don't give a shit." She asked him why he was self-conscious. "I was quitting the music business a while back so I got a haircut in Mexico.

"We've been trying to get off a label we were very happy to get on," he continued. "Cody told us not to trust them but we signed anyway. And god, the trouble we've gone through — it was incredible to get off the label. And every person of any human worth in my operation has departed. All the good, innocent people are gone. That's true of any act in the business. The ones you see, the Dinah Shores and the Jack Bennys, those are the hard ones. Their career was more important to them than anything else. You don't hear about the ones who couldn't stick it out. . . . I know a girl in Austin, kind of a sad case. She's the Janis Joplin who didn't make it. Then again, Janis Joplin is the Janis Joplin who didn't make it.

"Country Joe McDonald's also on Vanguard. He can't get off the label and he's very bitter about it. His first problem is that he's not Jewish. Another problem is that he doesn't have a Jewish dad and a

Jewish attorney. He's got a laid-back attitude. The secret to it is hanging in there. I never believed we'd be off Vanguard Records, but now that we are, we've got a whole new lease on life.''

Who had helped him get off Vanguard? He credited a New York attorney who also handled Led Zeppelin, and a New York manager whose other clients included the Moody Blues and John Denver. ''There are a lot of people a lot groovier than John Denver,'' Friedman said, ''but few of them are worth as much.''

Wasn't a $250,000 contract rather outlandish in the current record business?

''It's almost ridiculous now. It's based on a number of things. It's not just that we're a great act or that I write good songs or something. It's based on the new label's belief that we have a lot bigger reputation than Vanguard was able to work with. They think Vanguard blew it the first time around. Whether they're right or wrong, we'll find out, but hard promotion will get it off. I mean, anyone of us here could get off a big album with the right push. I'm sure of that. I think we're going to do it this time without question. It's just a question of how big it will go.''

Didn't the contractual infighting bother him?

''It did at first, because our original negotiations with Vanguard were on a very personal level with people who were very decent and honest with us. I'm not as close to the people at the new label, and I don't want to be. In fact this label has already had a couple of things that were pretty ugly — a lawsuit involving the Mamas and the Papas, for one thing. But what this label has is promotion cash and interest. And that's all it takes, I think. I knew all the people intimately at Vanguard, and it didn't do me any good.''

I asked him another question about his working past but he said, ''It'd be better if we didn't get into clinical recall. I'd just repeat what I said in Montreal.''

Kinky had me there; I hadn't kept up with his rock & roll press. I asked him what he thought of Austin music.

''I'm very ambivalent about Austin. There's a Chamber of Commerce attitude around here that I don't like a lot.''

Did he mean he liked Austin as a place to live, as opposed to a place to play?

''No, I'm not putting the music scene down. And I don't like Austin as a place to live. When I come here I stay at my parents' home and until I signed this contract I was on an allowance — which was kind of tedious. You know, I'm twenty-nine years old but I come in and ask my father for five dollars.

"Austin to me is just some guy pulling a boat behind his car. It's nice in a lot of areas, but the Armadillo and all that stuff has always left me pretty cold. We did a show out there once, and though the people who run it are nice — I like Eddie Wilson and Mike Tolleson and particularly Jim Franklin — the people who go to the Armadillo are nerds. A lot of people think it's a very warm place, but to me it's an airplane hangar. We were about five hundred yards from the audience for one thing, which is ridiculous, particularly if they're not sure where you're at. Geographical distance from the stage to the audience is murderous with an act that is satirical and sometimes downright hostile as we are. I mean, there's a difference between us and Asleep at the Wheel.

"But I've got to ask whether the scene is really here. Something's happening because of the interest in the press. The *Washington Post* called me in Nashville a while back and wanted to know about the Texas scene. But the question really is, does that mean anything? Remember a couple of years ago when Mickey Newberry and Kris Kristofferson were saying Nashville was the Paris of the thirties? Paris of the thirties, my ass, it was one big con man."

Finley interjected, "Every ten years or so they start talking about a metamorphosis in country music. There's no such thing. After the dust has cleared, control rests in the same hands that always had it. Everytime somebody says there's a new phase in country music, invariably it doesn't get absorbed by country, because those people reject it. It gets absorbed by pop."

"Now if Willie Nelson can get off as a big, national, commercial pop star," Friedman said, "with his angelic attitude intact, it'll be very interesting to see. Somebody behind him has got to do some ball-cutting though, because you get hosed by people as you go along.

"But I wonder if it's going to become a localized thing like Cajun music, which I suspect. I don't really think people in Madison, Wisconsin and Berkeley are going to get off to it. Everybody keeps talking about Waylon Jennings crossing over and becoming a pop superstar, but the only way he'll do that is with a big TV thing or movie.

"Personally, I think all the talk about the brotherhood of country music is a lot of baloney. When Skeeter Davis pulled her stunt at the

Grand Ole Opry, not one of the people who'd been singing with her for twenty years would stand up for her when they threw her off the Opry. It was a stupid thing for her to do there, talking with the Jesus trippers, but her career was just nipped in the bud, for whatever it was worth. None of those people would help her.

"I really think the best thing to say about these people in Austin is that if at any time they wanted to be a rock & roll star and make a lot of money, and they didn't make it, then they just like their music. That's the difference between me and Michael Murphey. You called him an intellectual in your article. Well I hate intellectuals, and I am one. He may be more of an *artiste* and his music may be a way of life, but I look at it as a business. If I had an old lady and a dog and a house by the lake and a child I really liked, I might be able to settle into that kind of thing.

"But what does it matter if we have 200 or 400 country bands in Austin? Seven years ago we had that many rock & roll bands, and even the best ones like Roky and the Elevators, they couldn't get off, right? A guy like Roky, one of the original crazy guys, wound up in wig city with a patch over his middle eye. People are so goddamn fickle it's just ridiculous. I really question the whole thing. My father was telling me I ought to play for the Temple Teens tonight; these kids would really enjoy seeing me. But I really question whether you owe anybody anything. You keep doing this shit and then one day you're like Sonny Liston — people notice the fourteen newspapers piled up on your porch. That's how they know you're dead.

"It's a question, hell, life is a question of how long you can keep putting up a front. You're putting up a front until the day you die. You never know who's your friend and who ain't. And you never know what your situation with reality really is. You get to a point where you say reality is bad enough, tell me the truth. Your life could be going to hell in a handbasket, and you're doing some show for the Temple Teens. Really, your life can be sad, depressing, a total driving bore, and you're rushing around doing a sound track for people you despise. Jerry Jeff's the exception to these Austin schmucks, I like Jerry Jeff. He and I were playing a radio gig down in Houston recently, and he and I were both really embarrassed by the way people were acting. Rod Stewart, Alice Cooper and those people — if they have any intelligence, and Alice does — they develop a very strong dislike for their audiences."

I asked Friedman about the benefit he had played in Houston.

"I don't want to do any more benefits," he said, "pot prisoners or anybody. I don't like to jam either. 'Jewboys don't jam' has been our motto. I play on bills with these bands, and they say come pick, let's jam. We never use the word pick when we're going onstage. A lot of bands say they're going to pick at nine o'clock. We say we're gonna go on. We're more realistic, I think, about the whole damn thing."

"The word pick," Finley said, "indicates some kind of imbecilic joy at being able to get your hands on a guitar."

"That's the negative side of it," Friedman said. "The positive side is that we take pride in a trade that's being demeaned by a lot of hippie nerds. I've got a very strong feeling that you have to outpsyche your audience. Like Commander Cody, where's his head at? He and I are friends but we're competitors and we're conscious of that. Everybody's conscious of that. Even the most laid-back nerds are conscious of that unless they've just given up on the whole ball game. Cody takes the opposite of my view of the Armadillo. His idea is good-time rock & roll, which is fine. We're closer to the Rolling Stones, which is mean, which isn't for everybody.

"But I think Cody made an error. He recorded an album at the Armadillo, and Franklin did his armadillo trip on the album, and Cody played a lot of good-time rock & roll there. I don't really view hippies as people, but no matter what you say about them, they're people in the sense that they don't like something that is too similar to what they are. In other words, as soon as the Austin hippies realize Cody's band tunes onstage, and he doesn't really have that star appeal, everybody will be more impressed with Waylon Jennings or somebody who takes more pride in his stage manner.

"Elvis Presley for example. He may fool around backstage, but when he's out front singing 'Hound Dog' that man believes there's nobody in the world that can touch him. You know Jerry Lee Lewis does. On the other hand, it may be that the people who really believed it were Judy Garland and Jimi Hendrix and Janis Joplin. Jerry Lee's at least sharp enough not to get torn up by the fact that what he's singing happens to be true, that he's weaving his own handbasket to hell. When you get big, you become a joke. I started as a joke, and that's a pretty good way to start."

We retired inside for another beer, then occupied the Friedmans' living room. Kinky was starting to feel badly; his numerous allergies were bothering him. He sniffed and said he usually sang through one nostril. He looked out the window and said, "None of this fools me. This area is about as sterile as any area in Austin. Nerds live up and down this street. If you sat down in an undershirt and played a banjo in the front yard, you'd get arrested. They're all Republican culls. But I don't think the Armadillo scene is any cooler. Yet I've always told people I love Texas. I love Texas, I really do. But I can't say anything good about it when I'm geographically here. I have to go elsewhere to appreciate it. Right now I'm digging New York.

"I've got to be honest with you," he said. "I don't know where this Murphey thing got started. I've never seen the man perform; he's been friendly the two times I've met him. I'm trying to remember why I don't like him . . . "

I said a lot of people didn't like Murphey.

"Him, or me?"

Well, both.

"Probably," Friedman grunted. "The Austin nerds don't like me because I got a lot of publicity for a bogus personality. Why, I'd kill any one of them with a fork. I didn't have to hang around Kenneth Threadgill's for ten years to be cool. I lived in this city for seventeen years. I went to high school here, I did the whole trip. I didn't suddenly become a guru with long hair. And I'll say this. We did the whole hype without any money.

"Of course I live here," he said, looking out the window again. "You don't get a lot of butt when you live at home. I've always lived out here, never met many girls in Austin, never been a part of the musical scene here. I had to come in from the top. Wasn't easy. It would've been a lot easier had I known these people and jammed with them."

Kinky walked us out to the car, stood on the curb a minute, and said, "Isn't Murphey playing at Castle Creek tonight?"

"I think so."

"I might go see him after I get through with the Temple Teens. Do you think I'd like him?"

"You might not like him but I think you'd like his music."

"Hm," he said. "I might do that. Let's see, you said you lived in New Braunfels?"

"Yeah, I'm the sportswriter for the weekly paper down there."

He looked at me. "Is that right? Well listen, we're moving out to the ranch by Kerrville. Why don't you come on up sometime?"

As we headed back toward the less advantaged Austin suburbs, I thought I might do that. Friedman had rounded the bend toward cynicism, but in spite of himself, he was more open than most of the musicians I'd met. I thought about his album. Its best cut made more sense to me now.

Faded jaded fallin' cowboy star
Pawn shops itchin' for your old guitar
Where you goin', God only knows
The sequins have all fallen from your clothes
Once you heard the Opry crowd applaud
Now you're hangin' out at Fourth and Broad
On the rain-whipped sidewalk remembering the time
When coffee with a friend was still a dime
Everything's been sold American
The early times is finished
The want ads are all read
Everyone's been sold American
Been dreamin' dreams in a roll away bed

My photographer was troubled. She was an old friend from Wichita Falls who in three years had worked and hustled herself into a career in a town where Nikkon cameras seemed to outnumber handguns. She had a way of piercing the reserve of her subjects, often by resorting to her feminity. But Friedman had rebuffed her. He was either too shy to reach, or he didn't like her. She chewed on her lip, then brightened. At least he had asked us back. A couple of days later she ran into Willie Nelson's daughter Lana, who had been seeing Friedman. My photographer mentioned the invitation, and Lana said, ''Yeah, he told me. Right after that he took off to Chicago.''

irish texas

For lack of anything better to do, in the spring of 1972 I found myself at a free rock concert west of Austin on a steep slope called Hill on the Moon. The site offered an impressive view of Austin, but the ground was covered with rocks that were too small to sit on and too many to move. The free beer ran out early, and the springtime warmth impressed upon many the fact that water was a more vital human need than music. The listeners' chops were soon sticky and colored from melting popsicles, and their sensibilities battered by the free music. One band of teenagers imagined they were Santana, another imagined they were Peter Townsend and the Who, who would have been appalled by the comparison. Some of the concert-goers seemed to enjoy it though. One man seized by some substance or another walked up to one of the large speakers, leaned his forehead against it, and just stood there smiling.

After the derivative Who finally called it quits, a man with electric frizzy hair and a New York accent walked onstage, identified himself as John Quarto, sat down in a chair, and started reciting Ginsberg-era poetry in a tremolo voice. An Austin rock concert was not to be confused with a poetry reading. Many of the listeners snickered in embarrassment, others bristled with hostility. "Next!" one young man said loudly. "Let's have some *music*. And some wine."

An older man with short hair and a pipe walked up to the stage and said, "Go on, man, I'm listening."

Quarto glanced at the man, said, "Thank you brother," and went on with his poetry.

The sweating poet endured to the end then departed in favor of a group of musicians wearing jeans and cowboy boots who plugged in their instruments and without any introduction started giving the crowd much better music than it deserved. It was rock & roll all right. The lead guitars embarked on periodic bluesey ventures and there was just enough percussion and bass to set the crowd in motion. Yet it was an unusual kind of rock & roll. The lead guitarist occassionally sat down to a pedal steel, and the apparent leader of the band, a scratchy tenor with gleaming blond hair and a dark red beard, occasionally unstrapped his guitar and started playing a methodical, stabbing piano. It was like somebody had turned a Baptist church into a country-western honky-tonk invaded by hippies. And the longer they played, the more evident it became that this was a music in which the instruments took a back seat to the lyrics.

> *As the rain ruins my alibi*
> *I'm down to telling you*
> *my red-eyed mind*
> *It's not that sun-bright path*
> *that calls me from my home*
> *It's just that fine*
> *backslider's wine*

I was on my feet drifting closer to the stage by then, and listening to the song, I looked around at these Texas Christian children lost in the wilds of Austin. They were on their feet too. The red-bearded singer left the piano, restrapped his guitar and said, "I'd like to do another song off my new album. I wrote it with the help of the poet that was just out here." The piece evolved from an acoustic guitar lead to Hollywood redskin music to stop-and-go rock, but lyrically it was a rallying cry of moral outrage:

> *People, people, don't you know*
> *the Indians ain't got no place to go*
> *They took old Geronimo by storm*
> *They ripped the feathers from his uniform*
> *Jesus told me and I believe it's true*
> *the red men are in the sunset too*
> *They stole their land and they won't give it back*
> *then they sent Geronimo a Cadillac*

242

"Who are you?" somebody shouted.

The red-bearded singer grinned. "My name's Michael Murphey."

After leaving North Texas State, Murphey had gone to Los Angeles, married a British girl, fathered a son, and signed on as a nine-to-five songwriter for Screen Gems. He hurried across town in the evenings to play backup bass in obscure country bars, but he was a cog in the wheels of a corporation. He cranked out over 400 songs during his stay in California, one of which George Hamilton IV took as high as number fourteen on the country charts, and his *Calico Silver* collection of songs about a Colorado silver-mining ghost town briefly revived the flagging career of Kenny Rogers and the First Edition. He had a home in the mountains east of town but the Los Angeles music business got to be too much for him, so he packed his family back to Texas. But he was scarcely down and out when he arrived in Austin. He had a few press clippings commending him as one of the most gifted young lyricists in the country, an A&M recording contract, and a forthcoming album produced by Bob Johnston, who had also handled the likes of Bob Dylan, Johnny Cash, Leonard Cohen and the Band.

I was a fanatic about Michael Murphey's music by the end of the Hill on the Moon concert, but one golden-haired, red-bearded country-rocker wasn't enough to prolong my stay in Austin. For two years I had been suspended between egocentic professors who kept me waiting in their outer offices and friends who smoked dope in the afternoons and schemed ways to get rich without working. I had grown stale on Austin, and I wasn't sure I ever wanted to live there again. Accordingly, I cut my hair and wondered what Australia might have in store for me. My finances being what they were, I shortened my sights to Denver, but Texas seemed intent upon punishing me for leaving. To raise money I drove nails in an East Texas mobile-home factory for a month with a foreman shouting over my shoulder, then when the time for my departure came I passed through Wichita Falls with the temperature 113 in the shade, and paused in the Panhandle town of Dumas long enough to make the mistake of asking the ice-plant attendant whether water dripping from a black rubber hose was potable. "I been drinking it fifty-three years," he allowed, "and it never hurt me none." A trio of boys threw a firecracker under my car in Texline, and when I finally reached Denver, I learned that the lady who invited me there was in Dallas with an old resurgent lover.

Shortly after I arrived, moreover, I began to hear a beckoning voice from home. An FM disc jockey announced one day that he was about to play the title cut off the best album currently on the market, and that cut was "Geronimo's Cadillac." "Listen," I commanded my friends, then said afterward, "Isn't that a great song?"

"Yeah," one of them said, "but that voice . . . ."

Denver was beautiful that summer, but I should have taken the precaution of commandeering Colorado license tags for my car. A comely physician's wife paused at my elbow during a cocktail party conversation and said after a moment, "Oh god, another Texan," and the signs of Rocky Mountain xenophobia were abundant everywhere. Don't Californicate Colorado, their bumper stickers read, Texans Go Back Where You Came From. Indignant, I did just that after a few weeks, and in defiance, I paid my West Texas working-cowboy uncle a visit on the way through. He looked at me like I was Atilla the Hun when I stepped out of the car, bounced me across a couple of pastures in his pickup, commanded my aunt to fix us some "cow," then made the mistake of turning on the television. There in living color, soaking wet from some English rain, was the dimpled face of Melanie Safka, followed by some lingering, suggestive crowd shots and Elton John hamming it up with the Beach Boys. My uncle watched in mute wonder for a minute, said, "What the hell's this world coming to," and went to sleep in his recliner. Nobody was safe from rock & roll.

For the next few months I wrote about shoplifters and high school football players for a small-town newspaper in East Texas, and Austin began to look better and better all the time. My only real contacts with the city during those weeks were the *Geronimo's Cadillac* album I had found in Dallas and impatiently awaited letters from sympathetic friends. The title cut of the album had made a very small splash on the national singles-charts and the album made its impression mostly in the Southwest, but it was still a notable achievement. "Geronimo's Cadillac" and "Backsliders Wine" were the standout cuts, but they were matched in tone and instrumentation by other cuts similarly rooted in the tradition of country music: lyrics swimming with overturned U-Hauls in Las Cruces, trains headed toward San Antone, grapevines growing silver green along the Natchez Trace, Wanda Lees and bordertown *señoritas* and Rosalees. It had all the trappings of country music, but the country steel was offset by a rock & roll keyboard, and the lead guitarist had a mind of his own, unlike many in Nashville. There was also a decided gospel tint to the album — a hymnal-worthy Ray Lewis song called "The Lights of the City" and a

244

Murphey song called "Harbor for My Soul" that evoked images of a tent revival in westside Fort Worth. But Murphey's most impressive lyrical achievements were the soft, acoustic songs that stood out least: a boy from the country who communicated with nature, the faith of Noah in a benevolent Rainbow Man, a latter-day Michelangelo waking up to his work in the city limits of Dallas. Because of the demands of rhyme and metrical simplicity, few popular song lyrics stood the test of printed poetry, but some of Murphey's lines did:

Rusty dawn again
Squeaking on its hinges there's a sunrise made of tin
Rainbows on your floor belonging on your wall
And what is worse you're not sure if you belong at all
The concentrated mind
Lags a bit behind
And lingers at the door
She won't be there anymore
And as you realize you've forgotten the date
You see an unfinished portrait done back in '58
Sort of makes you wonder if it isn't getting late

The only problem with the album was, again, Murphey's voice. Although pitched an octave higher, it was as rough as Jerry Jeff Walker's. It sounded like it belonged to an Irish laborer building one of the great railroads West. It wavered and cracked in the higher ranges of the louder songs, and in the quiet ones it was sweet as corn syrup, which softened the impact of his lyrics. But if he could write that well, he would probably make it anyway. Bob Dylan wasn't much of a threat to Frank Sinatra either.

I returned to South Texas in early 1973, working in nearby New Braunfels but spending most of my leisure time in Austin, and as my interest in Austin music turned into a magazine assignment and later a book, I had to take more than a stereophonic interest in Murphey. I learned that he had gone to Europe while recording his album and taken a long, thoughtful look, particularly at his forebears' Ireland. I also learned that the reason his voice sounded so bad on his album was that it was healing. He had lost even his speaking voice for several months; he jotted down lyrics on notepads and whistled new tunes to a friend with a guitar, but he silently walked the streets with an ulcer in his stomach, his career in jeopardy just as he was getting started. Murphey

245

was held in awe by some of his fellow Austin songwriters. He had performed his task in the Screen Gems factory so long that if someone gave him a topic he could churn out a corresponding song almost immediately, and to avoid sitting down one morning to find that he had nothing to write about but rays of light bounding off the piano keys, he had devised a system. When an appealing turn of phrase caught his attention, he wrote it out, filed it, and tabulated it to the very syllable. If people understood his system, he said proudly, they could construct a poetic, syntactically perfect sentence that made no sense at all, just by pulling the right tabs. Someday, he said, he wanted to write a book about songwriting.

Though that sounded like a rather mechanistic way of approaching the task of writing, Murphey was consistently able to blend his file of phrases, experience and philosophy into lyrics that abstractly touched the experience of many men, though he often enlisted the help of more instrumentally oriented arrangers when he set them to music. He recorded at Ray Stevens' 24-track studios in Nashville, and when he went to Music City he was accompanied by his Austin sidemen and arrived with as many as two dozen of his songs. He could do that because his producer was Johnston, who was very selective about the artists he worked with and had tremendous clout in recording-company offices. Johnston made a point of understanding what Murphey hoped to accomplish with each release, helped him weed out the bad cuts and thematically arrange the good ones, and the result of those sessions were meticulously produced packages like *Geronimo's Cadillac* and the second album, released in 1973, called *Cosmic Cowboy Souvenir*.

Murphey's voice was much stronger and steadier on the second album, and the instrumentation tended less toward honky-tonk country. The second side of the album was uneven in quality though graced by "Drunken Lady," but Side 1 was the best sustained work of music any of the Austin performers had yet recorded. The four songs derived from personal experience — uncomfortable gigs in outlying clubs far from Austin, the sobering time Murphey lost his voice, a trip with Gary Nunn to the South Canadian River in Northern Oklahoma. But the lyrics were a spiritual trip to imagined places beyond. Home, after all, was only a state of mind.

The title cut, "Cosmic Cowboy," had come to Murphey's mind while unhappily playing the Bitter End in New York. It began on a carnival note, an ironic view of children riding the range on the wooden steeds of a merry-go-round, and it continued to amplify the cowboy theme, blending touches from "Home on the Range" and "Bury Me Not on the Lone Prairie" into a highly romanticized contention that Texas was still a better place to be than New York or Hollywood, particularly for musicians. The next cut went so far as to liken Austin to a vision of heaven:

Now out in the alleys of heaven
There's a funky-feeling angel strumming chords
While the preachers sit and get stoned in their Buicks
Jesus Christ drives by in his Ford
And the clouds are like the feathers of sparrows
A thousand different colors of gray
It's the hustle of the paradise barrooms
And the glory of hanging out in space

In the last stanza of the song Murphey explained symbolically how the alleys of Austin and heaven were the same. The rains fell on the roofs of Austin, washed down the gutters and moved with the rivers out to sea, evaporated into the heavens then fell once more in the form of purified rain. Earth was heaven, Murphey was saying, here and now, if man would allow it to be. That earthly view of nature as God carried over into the next song, "South Canadian River," though this time Murphey's lyrics played second fiddle to Nunn's piano arrangement, which strayed so far from country music that it sounded like something off the Beatles' *Abbey Road*. The piano returned to the methodical, fundamentalist ways of old on the last cut, and the lyrics were a less esoteric statement of Murphey's spiritual philosophy:

It was a blessing in disguise
The truth is always a surprise
It's good to lose the things you love
Just to see what it's like
It only serves to reconfirm
You can't have love on your own terms
Thank you for opening my eyes
It was a blessing in disguise

My magazine collaborator contacted Murphey after the second album came out, and he consented to meet us in the *Texas Monthly* offices for an interview. I made the trip from New Braunfels, twiddled my thumbs and chatted with the editors for about an hour, then drove back disgruntled, already having second thoughts about this business of rock journalism. Murphey called my collaborator the next day profuse with apologies. Heavy rains had flooded his house, and he had forgotten the interview. Could we meet him in a restaurant called the Oyster Bar Friday evening?

The Oyster Bar was an airy place with a tropical atmosphere in the building once occupied by Rod Kennedy's Speed Museum. Jerry Jeff was on the bill a couple of doors down at Castle Creek, and Fromholz was in the restaurant with some of his friends, but for more than an hour there was no Murphey. Finally he came in wearing short sleeves, a beachcomber straw hat, and a bearded grin. "Sorry I'm late," he said. "I bet you guys were freaking out."

We moved to a larger table in another room, and Murphey said he had been at the university bookstore that afternoon, playing his guitar, chatting with record-consumers, and promoting his album. "They called me up and asked me to do this thing and at first I thought, no, I won't do it, but then I thought why not? It's kind of an ego trip not to do it, you know, a lot of artists think they're above it. But the albums are for sale. Why not admit it? I think that's a very legitimate kind of thing. What are you gonna do, pretend they're not for sale? If you try to do good work, you should try a little harder to sell it. It's when you're not sure it's good that you back off, I think.

"I didn't think I'd dig it, but it was really fun. We sat in the store with no microphone and no P.A. and no jive, and just played anything we wanted to play and talked to the people. They asked us questions about the album and we signed a couple of autographs, not too many. It's good to directly meet the person who buys your records. It's interesting."

My collaborator asked how he assessed his audience. Murphey said Austin was a special case. In Austin he sold a lot of records to AM listeners and older, straight people, but elsewhere they were mostly freaks who listened to FM radio. We talked about some of the technical aspects of recording, and Murphey said he would gladly record in Austin if Odyssey solved all the problems inherent in installing a 24-track studio. My collaborator asked Murphey what he thought about Nashville.

"Nashville is one of the most boring towns I've ever seen. There's nothing to do there at night except make records. Nothing else. It's really dull."

How did the country music centered in Austin differ from that of Nashville?

"I think it's not just Texas; it's the Southwest. Texas, New Mexico, Arizona, Colorado, Oklahoma, maybe even San Diego. I think that area really does constitute a different kind of music. For one thing, it's founded very heavily in the tradition of the West, you know, cowboys and Indians and all the things that go with that, but not on a shallow level. I think it's getting to be on a deeper level all the time. For example, Fromholz lives in Santa Fe some and Colorado some, but he plays down here a lot, so his music is as reflective of that environment as much as Texas. He wrote 'Texas Trilogy' and all those things when he was living in Colorado. But he's from Texas, so it all becomes a big cross-influence.

"How is it distinctive from other music? Well, there's a blues influence and a country influence at the same time, whereas in the South it's primarily blues. In Appalachia it's very Anglican, based on Irish and Scottish music. But in the Southwest and Pacific Northwest you have music that's very much founded in the tradition of the West, though it has the other influences because people from the East and South migrated there.

"It's a very unique sound, and it becomes more distinctive as it gets out West, because when you get out there you get into the ballad tradition as well. Story-telling is a very heavy-duty trip in the Southwest. I think most of the people who grow up here are used to having relatives who tell a lot of stories, and they're steeped in that tradition. Also, in this area there's a back-to-the-land feeling that's not present as much in New England or England, because there's no land to go back to. When I went to London I found that the people there are relating less and less to American music, because so much American music is starting to talk about man's relationship to the earth — getting back to the land and identifying more with nature. It's not country music as much as it is the experience of living in the country. You might call it *Whole Earth Catalogue* music, and English people do not identify with that at all.

"A lot of people in other places have a hard time identifying with what musicians are talking about down here, because people down here are on a traditional trip right now in music, and they're going back to their roots to find meaning. They're leaving the ashes of L.A. and going back home. The Nitty Gritty Dirt Band moves to a 5000-acre ranch in Colorado, and Willie Nelson leaves Nashville and comes to Austin. That has a huge influence on their music. But the Europeans have no concept of that, because the European's idea of making it is to get out of the country and move to the city.''

My collaborator asked Murphey if he spent much time in the country as a boy. Every summer, he said, first on his grandparents' farm and then as a camp counselor. I asked how he reacted to growing up in Dallas.

"Like most kids, until I was about sixteen years old I swallowed the trip hook, line and sinker. The Anglo-Saxon Protestant thing — digging football, trying to make good grades, balling in the back seat and going to church on Sunday. That's what people did. But I swallowed it a little bit more than others. Instead of rebelling when I was a kid I went the other way. I became radically conservative, both in religion and politics. I was actually ordained to preach in the Baptist Church and did preach for a while. I was gonna become a minister, that was my goal in life, although I was playing a lot of music too. Church music primarily.''

The piano?

"No, the guitar. I taught myself to play the piano later, but all the piano I know is based on the licks I heard in church when I was a kid.''

My collaborator said the gospel influence was obvious in his music.

"I think it's good music, and I think the one valid thing about that religious trip is the vibes behind it. The bad part is mixing it in with politics and logical thought. If you strip it down and recognize it as pure emotion, far out, but when you start trying to lay social and logical thought on top of it, then it starts to get weird.''

When did his religious trip begin to fall apart?

"I made good grades in school and I did a lot of reading, and when I started thinking about becoming a minister I really got into it. I studied classical Greek and Latin in college, and I was translating the Bible in Greek. That's when it began to fall apart. As anyone can tell you, education is the death of any conservative religious trip, usually. That's why so many conservative religions have their own institutions. The Baptists have to have them, and Oral Roberts really has to have them. He's got to keep out certain bodies of knowledge, or else he's in trouble. He can't expose these people to Karl Marx or Ashley

Montagu. He wants them reading approved sociologies or philosophies.

"But it was reading those books. By becoming more educated I began to wake up and realize there were certain things that didn't fit together, didn't make sense. I don't think I've ever lost my basic respect for Jesus's teachings. I still have tremendous respect for them and even believe in a lot of them, but I don't accept the theology that was hung on later. I mean that Baptist trip really twists what Jesus had to say around, and it was twisting my head around. I was trying as hard as I could to follow some kind of Christian trip but the harder I tried, the more I seemed to be steering away from churches and all those things. Every time I read the Bible — especially in Greek — I realized that what was being said was an extremely revolutionary, even communistic kind of philosophy. When you start saying if you see somebody in trouble give him the shirt off your back — freeze yourself rather than allow him to freeze — now what Southern Baptist is gonna do that? I never knew one that would. All the deacons used to go outside and smoke cigarettes while the sermon was on and discuss all their big used-car deals. Then they'd come in during the invitation, watch a couple of people get saved, and go home. That was all there was to it.

"But what really turned me around, more than anything else, was coming across a couple of good books by Albert Schweitzer. He's had a tremendous influence on my songwriting, and I'd say almost every song I've ever written has an underlying theme of what he was trying to get across, which was a philosophy called Reverence for Life: the idea that everything that's alive is sacred and equal. A blade of grass is equal to a human being and an amoeba is equal to John Kennedy and Richard Nixon.

I said that wasn't an uncommon philosophical sentiment. Murphey flicked his eyes in my direction and went on, "It's not uncommon but it's unusual. What Schweitzer tried to show was that the errors of all civilizations pretty much point to a lack of reverence for life. He personally felt that since his upbringing was as a Westerner he would derive his philosophy from Jesus's teachings, but he never tried to imply that Jesus was the only trip. He very much believed that the only way you could work things out was on a person-to-person basis.

"He wrote an incredible book called *The Quest for the Historical Jesus* in which he covered the history of the way people interpreted Jesus's life, and at the end he pretty much said that there are so few

251

facts to substantiate anything Jesus said or did, that about all we can do, if we want to accept his teachings, is to accept him as a stranger. I mean Jesus walked up to cats on the shore and said follow me, and he did that because he had something groovy to say, not because he was trying to lay down something about being God. He was trying to organize the Jewish people and show them that they were being thwarted by an extremely gummed up system of law. He was talking about a relationship between people.

"I accept that, man, I believe very much in what Schweitzer was saying. So much religion has been life-denying and life-negating, like the things of this world are what we must reject. Schweitzer said that the opposite is the case, that whether you believe in God or whether you believe in some great theistic blob or even if you reject God altogether, you still come down to the fact that the biological unit of the cell is here, whether God put it here or evolution put it here, *it is here*, and if we don't base our morality on the fact that it is the most valuable thing there is, and build our system on that, then we don't have a social system or civilization; we just have chaos."

Murphey was talking so fast and furious it was hard to get a word in edgewise. "Do you see any connection between the *Whole Earth* movement and the Jesus trippers?" I asked quickly.

"That Jesus trip has been going on for years," he said. "The fact that long-hairs are doing it now is just a reflection of the fashion that has crept into it. There were people like that long before anybody heard of the Beatles. I don't attach much importance to it, except I think a few very capitalistic people like Billy Graham have gotten ahold of it and tried to establish themselves as titular heads of it by pulling off big advertising campaigns.

"But I'm not really on a religious trip. I don't even like the word religion. I do think that it's important for people to think about the spiritual side of their lives, but only in the sense that it gives them some kind of viewpoint on where they're going. You can derive that from almost any religion, as long as that basic reverence for life is there. It's when you get into that trip of denying the world that you get yourself in a big bind. You can't deny the world, man.

"But there are still a tremendous amount of life-denying people, and a lot of them live in the U.S. I mean there are plenty of life-denying generals in the U.S. Army, who are sacrificing life for what they consider some high goal, and it turns out to be jive. And you can't blame it on materialism either. Like Alan Watts said, people think

252

Americans are materialistic, but there's no way they could really be materialistic because they're so impractical. If they were really into the material world and understood the way it functions, they wouldn't screw it up the way they do. The greatest materialists who ever lived were the Indians, because they understood how the material world worked. We don't understand it. We sacrifice our lives for all kinds of bullshit ideals that people stick down our throats.''

Well, my collaborator said. Were those just the problems of the rest of us, or did he have his own struggles?

"Sure," Murphey said, "there's a tremendous struggle going on inside me. My biggest problem in life is trying to overcome being an American, trying to identify myself as an individual and citizen of the world, of the cosmos, not the U.S.A. I love American music, but hey, we're on earth, we're all in this together, and the more you travel around the more you discover that America, at this point in its history, is an extremely negative influence on the world. I'm not even sure that flower power and all that is positive either. You go over to Europe and you see Americans bumming around the highways who don't have any jobs, they're taking advantage of a poorer economy, they're selling dope at best — so what is the impression Europeans have of these so-called hippies with supposedly high ideals? They just think they're a lot of time-wasting bums over there ripping them off. Right now there are American beggars on the streets of Amsterdam.

"So that's my struggle. You take so many things for granted, you assume so many things until you go overseas. Even from a freak's point of view it blasts you. It's different. You can't assume everything's gonna be groovy because you're kinda hip and you've got a guitar and you can make a little money writing songs, you know, smoke dope whenever you feel like it. That doesn't make you valuable. It just means you're an American kid. That's the biggest struggle I go through all the time. How far below the surface of the way I appear and act does my thinking really go? Who am I really, what do I really think? What's my true philosophy of life? As a man where do I stand, not as a symbol or a character?''

My collaborator asked where his music career fit into all that.

"Well, I don't totally reject the idea of being a businessman and an artist at the same time. I think it's possible to be both. I think artists tend to be notoriously poor businessmen, the reason being that they swallow the myth that in order to be artistic or creative one must be poor or starving. I swallowed it for years and still deal with it.

Everytime I make money I feel guilty. Everytime I sell an album I think, am I being a capitalistic pig? You pick up those myths and accept them without thinking."

Murphey talked about a painter who invested heavily in stocks and bonds, and the composer Charles Ives and the poet Wallace Stevens, both of whom were successful businessmen, then added, "Not that I'm saying that's necessarily the way to do it, or that you can't do it if you're starving. I'm just saying that human creativity and sensibility have such an incredible range that it can be done any number of ways, and to accept one little trip as being *the* trip is very narrow.

"I think it's very important for anyone who's going to get into songwriting to gain an awareness of business procedures, because if he doesn't he's gonna get cheated time after time after time. It's happened to me so long that I've had to gain some cleverness about business, because if I didn't my family would be broke, and I'd be in shambles and I'd never get my work out. I mean we're in the middle of one of the worst scandals we've ever had in the music business — drug payola and all that — and the guys who are about to get indicted are the ones the artists on the street have to deal with. They've been getting away with all that for the last twenty years. Now they're being caught, but in the meantime all the artists trying to get off the ground have been dealing with these guys, and if they didn't know the ropes about legalities most of them got ripped off or cheated. I was one of the ones who got ripped off for five years in L.A. I ran into plenty of those guys. I'm not bitter about it, but I paid my dues."

Who ripped him off? Screen Gems?

"No, they were an honest company, but I ran into some people that pulled off weird publishing deals on me and never paid me. Hell, if you write a song and put all your energy and effort into it, what are you gonna do, turn right around and sell it to the next idiot? You can't distinguish the idiots from the thieves and the nice guys without reading the contracts and understanding what they're saying. It's absolutely necessary to gain some business sense, because if you don't your work may suffer. You've got to sell your work to disseminate it, and I think it's very legitimate. All painters have done it, all writers have done it, all musicians have done it. It's part of the trip, man, just as much as that wagon of gypsies rolling down the road with guitars in the back and cups in their hands. It's part of the trip."

Like Faulker writing screenplays in Hollywood then retreating to Oxford to write his novels, my collaborator suggested.

Michael Murphey was the embodiment of Austin music. Though rock-oriented, his music was rooted in the forms young Texans had grown up with.

Accompanied by his new wife Caroline, Murphey was at once a leader and disclaimer of the Austin "scene". Messianic acclaim surrounded his arrival, and he paid onstage homage to Willie Nelson, but he came to Austin in search of privacy, a new lease on life after seven years in the music-industry cockfights of L.A.

Through an unorthodox concert production featuring his brother Mark,
demonstrations of his multi-instrument
capabilities, the addition of rhythm &
blues brass, Murphey tried to vary the
impressions his listeners took home
with them. His career was falling prey
to a fad of his own making.

Murphey was an artist attuned to business procedures, a scientific songwriter who doubted the worth of his craft, a budding star who questioned the rock ritual but used it to his advantage, a study in contradictions. His reserve was at times impenetrable, but his music appealed even to the latent sensibilities of the mentally retarded.

"Sure. You've just got to keep it in perspective. I'm not too fooled by what I'm doing. I know that writing pop music as a whole is a somewhat shallow occupation. It's something I don't want to do all my life."

Was he saying even the best pop music was shallow?

"Well, I think that any music can have a good effect on the listener. In that sense it's all the same. But in the sense of technical development, there's no doubt that one of my songs is more shallow than one of Stravinsky's symphonies. If I limit myself to writing 'Boy from the Country' for the rest of my life that means I'm never going to have a chance to grow and learn something else, and someday I want to write other things. You've got to expand."

Murphey paused and I tried to ask him what else he wanted to write, but he went on quickly, "By its nature, pop music has to be somewhat limited and narrow and shallow, and no matter how much beauty and intelligence you try to inject into it, the limitations of the pop market keep you from doing as much as you'd want sometimes."

My collaborator suggested Murphey was a rarity. He had never met any other pop songwriters who aspired to move on to other forms.

"Yeah, well once again it depends upon the sensibility of the individual person. What I'm trying to get at is that the pop field is given more credit and importance than it deserves. I think it has its place. It can be a very beautiful thing, I've enjoyed being a songwriter. Gershwin was a very good songwriter, but Gershwin also did other things. I haven't reached that point yet. I'm still just a songwriter, but I'd also like to be like him. Ultimately, you look at these great people and say will I ever create something that's *really* meaningful? Maybe your songs did mean something to some. If so, that's fine, but still, you have to aspire to something higher. Otherwise, you'll be a pop songwriter the rest of your life, and you'll always be trying to come up with one more top-forty hit."

He'd been talking primarily about writing, I said. What about performing? What went through his mind when somebody demanded that he sing "Geronimo's Cadillac"?

"Well, you have to try to look at both sides of it. I mean I put out the record. I did it, it's my responsibility. If a drunk comes up and says, 'Hey, play that song', I've got to live with the fact that I'm the one who made him want to hear it. So I can't put him down like some kind of idiot, or else I'd be saying I'm an idiot myself. I always appreciate it when someone likes something I've done, and I always try to play what people like to hear, within the range of what I've done. If somebody asks me to play something that's not my work I won't do it."

Why had he come to Austin?

"For a very simple reason. It's not too big yet. It's not so large that it just engulfs you, like L.A. or New York. And it's a place where you can be fairly familiar with what's going on. You know who the pickers are, but you can also relate to your neighbors who aren't musicians. It's a small-town kind of feeling. But I'm very much afraid that's going to slip away.

"I don't want to down-rap your article or anything, but I don't encourage the idea that there's any music scene in Austin. There are a lot of good musicians in this town, but I don't think anyone should ever come to Austin because there's a scene here. Because any time you start relating to a scene, you're in trouble. Scenes have destroyed an awful lot of places. I came here because it was a good, relaxed place to live, but you have to have your own scene together before you can make any kind of move.

"What I really think is happening is that the music business is decentralizing, and people are reaching out and finding places they like as towns, not musical happenings. I'm not pushing any big trip here. I do think there is a certain sense of community and togetherness among the musicians, if you want to call that a scene, because Austin is small. They know each other and want to help each other and there are a lot of cross-influences, but I've noticed even that is beginning to break down some. I know one thing. I'd hate to see people with guitars on their backs start showing up by the thousands, because they're gonna starve."

Murphey was shouting into a gale-force wind and he knew it. An Austin music scene was already a reality to some degree, and by moving to Austin and publicizing the move in his music, he had helped bring it about. But Murphey was breezy as a minor typhoon himself that night. The tapes wound on and on as he talked about the poets he admired, the metrics of songwriting, the underpaid and insecure Austin sidemen, the virtues of public television and need for public radio, the cocaine aristocracy of the New York recording industry, the rock ritual itself. "It's not worth one overdose, and it's not worth one person getting hurt. If that's what rock & roll is, then let's not have it anymore." A couple of kids who had hitched a ride into town with

Murphey finally gave up on him and went on alone, and I relinquished the interview to my collaborator, who seemed to be enjoying it. Finally I lost all track of what was being said. By that time we had been joined by a lady who interested me more than Murphey.

Murphey had certainly proved the most talkative musician we had run across, but I harbored doubts that he would have much to say if I met him on the street the next day. There was a deep inner reserve in the man. We had simply suggested lines of thinking, and he had expounded upon them. There was no real interplay of ideas, much less personalities. I suspected that his answers would have been much the same had he been sitting alone in a recording booth, answering print-out questions fed him by a computer. Of course, we were strangers, and he was sacrificing a weekend evening in our behalf, and we had requested an interview, not a bear hug. And the tapes proved as self-revelatory to me as a more famous set of tapes probably proved to Richard Nixon. I was an atrocious interviewer, too quick to agree, too eager to match my wits against those of the man I was interviewing. It must have been maddening for him to start to answer one question then get interrupted by another before he could finish. Still, something about Murphey troubled me. He addressed our questions like an academic, dissembling them into their intellectual parts, tying them into a neat bundle, dropping the bundle into the satchels of students who didn't interest him in the least. As far as I was concerned Murphey had many of the right answers, but he was too intense for my taste, too cerebral, too cocksure. Even when he was unsure he was sure of the reasons.

After my collaborator and I finished the article I ran across an essay Murphey had written for a Dallas-area magazine called *Buddy,* a low-budgeted but well-written monthly inspired by the legacy of Buddy Holly. In that short essay Murphey revealed more of himself in a few paragraphs than we had plumbed conversationally in three and a half hours.

"You walk down a street," Murphey wrote, "It's hard to feel alive, because you see signs of decay all around, and L. A. makes you a part of a decaying civilization and you react and withdraw or you go with it.

"Just trying to make someone hear your music is like trying to convince a very professional Satan he should get a part-time job working with the underprivileged. Mercedes-Benz people keep floating by wearing 400 pounds of uncomfortable clothes. You stagger out of a publisher's office after a soul-wrenching encounter between art and money, and you can't even breathe a sigh of relief. You can't even get home without a battle.

"Recording studios are like doctors' waiting rooms where everyone is waiting for 'Doctor Music' to arrive but he never keeps his appointment.

"You're growing up. You love a woman and you love your children. You love your music and you want to love making it. You want some spiritual direction that's not artifical or hip. You know there's a monster outside that's dying, and you're about to get wiped out by the final lash of its tail. So you simply pack it up and look for a place to start living again."

Murphey went on about looking for that place and finding one that wasn't ideal but vastly improved, about the other musicians in that place with similar orientations, about the audiences that responded to his music, about the nationwide decentralization of the music business. Then he added: "As you go about trying to find happiness in your music, living your daily life, you suddenly find the phone ringing a lot. At first it doesn't bother you. Then it gets to be every fifteen minutes. You go out to interviews. Publishers start showing up. People start talking about 'scenes' and a lot more start hanging on to the talk . . . Rushing around begins to seep back in again. People start talking big. People start competing. And then one day it hits you. It's all beginning to come back again. You're getting caught in the same web of 'telephones and managers, and where you have to be at noon'. "

I could sympathize with that. I was willing to leave Murphey alone, and I still valued his music. A Murphey concert could still be a gratifying experience in the right situation. One night I drove to Seguin, a German farming community northeast of San Antonio, to watch his homecoming performance at a tiny college called Texas Lutheran. It was a small crowd in a small, dimly lit gymnasium. Murphey and his band stood on a makeshift stage underneath a basketball goal. But it was an attentive, listening audience, the kind Murphey liked. When he had that kind of audience he talked as much as he sang, the message-behind-every-song performance tactic that few rock singers could get away with. Most were too stoned to talk in the first place, years of teenaged adulation had convinced them they were as close to the people as Mahatma Gandhi, and their wisdoms belched out in a gush of left-wing banalities. But Murphey no longer smoked marijuana, and as a youth he had studied his preachers well. He could get away with an occasional performance sermon.

He laid the groundwork by relating his experience to that of his audience: "I take it some of you people are Lutherans," he said with a smile. "I can dig that. I used to be a Baptist. You know Baptists—they're the Ku Klux Klan guys in the business suits. I did some reading and found out Southern Baptists split with the Northerners over the issue of slavery. As we all know, any good religion needs slavery." He talked about his mother: "When I was a kid she used to tell me, 'Mike, don't go to UCLA. Don't go to California. You'll get in some weird cult out there.' So like she said I went to California and got in this weird cult: country-western music."

Murphey's concert followed his customary form. There was a preliminary rock number or two, a relaxation toward country music, finally the slower songs he wanted them to listen to, a display of his multi-instrument capabilities. Murphey had been moved by his visit to his ancestors' homeland of Ireland, and he studied that country's native folk music, mastered a little Irish jig, and taught himself to play the concertina. Lowering his microphone to the level of the little instrument he explained, "My first interest is country-western, but I'm interested in folk music too — jigs and reels in particular. I understand there's such a thing as German Texans." Applause. "Well, I'm an Irish Texan. I finally got over to Ireland and England a few months ago, and I really believe that when a person hears the music of his people, something in him responds to it, even if he's never lived in the old land. You don't mind if I play this do you? I don't play it too often; the audience is usually waiting for the Grateful Dead, and not too up for the concertina."

Moving on to the piano, he said, "This song came out of something that happened while I was playing a club in Colorado. It was a place where rich Texans go to ski — a kind of Babylon in the snow. We were up there, hippies playing country music, when these cowboys came in. Just to prove they were cowboys, they beat up this thirteen-year-old boy, nearly beat him to death, and left him lying in the snow."

"Rednecks," somebody yelled astutely.

"But then when we were driving out we saw the cowboys lying in the snow —"

Cheers erupted in the gymnasium.

"No, wait," Murphey said angrily. "That's not the point at all. These hippies in another club down the street had found out about the kid so they went out and got two-by-fours and nearly beat the cowboys to death. It just seems to me there's got to be a better way, and I wrote this song thinking about both the cowboys and the hippies."

Murphey finished his set with an amalgam of "Geronimo's Cadillac" and "Cosmic Cowboy," and when they yelled him back onstage he stooped to play with a babe in its mother's arms, shook a few hands, took a seat at the piano, and said, "I want you to keep singing with me. Too many times you go to a concert and you're just an observer. I want you to be part of the act, and I want to be part of the audience. That way we can both get off."

Murphey's encore was a gospel cut off his first album, the Ray Lewis song rich with allusions to the teachings of the apostle John, heavenly shores, and lights of a heavenly city. Murphey got the crowd on their feet singing with him, then subtly stopped playing the piano, and the momentum of the chorus carried them on through. It was familiar music. I was back at 23rd and Grace.

Murphey was more overbearing in Austin bar gigs, for those crowds were often too busy honky-tonking to listen. Of that entire notable side of music he had recorded on the second album, the only lines they seemed to remember were:

> *I just wanta be a Cosmic Cowboy*
> *I just wanta ride and rope and hoot*
> *I just wanta be a Cosmic Cowboy*
> *A supernatural country-rockin' galoot*

Those were undoubtedly the most unfortunate lines Murphey had written. He said he had written the song tongue-in-cheek, never intending that it be taken seriously — at least at home — but increasingly his Austin appearances were populated by hooting hippies who fancied themselves goat-roping cosmic cowboys. Murphey's music was falling prey to a fad of his own making, and he knew better than anyone that could be fatal to his career. His concertina recitals became a consistent feature of his performances, and he enlisted the help of string quartets and jazz pianists to vary the impressions his listeners took home with them. His onstage political rhetoric grew harsh, and his place in the supposedly tightly-knit music community became somewhat suspect. He shed one sideman after another, and some of his recorded counterparts called him two-faced, though they were themselves two-faced enough to say it behind his back. The charge was confirmed by one backstage observer who overheard him lament the response of a Texas Opry House crowd to "all that honky-tonk" of Willie Nelson, then watched him greet the Austin guru as he came offstage: "Willie, I love you."

After the departure of Livingston and Nunn, Murphey's music began to edge more and more toward rock & roll, and he became more demanding of his audiences. When the times demanded he could be just as ugly as they were. One night at Castle Creek Steve Fromholz, his pride visibly wounded, found himself playing second act for his old comrade from North Texas, delivering a few rushed songs then standing aside to say, "And now, here's Michael Murphey." Murphey was no longer a club musician. The cigarette smoke nauseated him, and he resented the drinkers who preferred their talk to his music. When he came out that night and began to play a soft, intricate guitar piece one of the drinkers at a stageside table went right on talking. Knuckles whitening as he gripped the neck of his guitar, Murphey stopped playing and glared dramatically. The talker was too lost in the conversation to take the hint, and Murphey snapped, "I will not play unless there's absolute quiet. That's just the way I am."

Murphey might have just been in a sour mood that night. Perhaps he was courageous to voice the sentiment that goes through every musician's mind from time to time. But after he had commandeered silence at the table, he couldn't resist a couple of boots in the offender's ribs. Murphey loudly granted the man permission to resume his conversation when he stepped offstage for a break, and later, when a sideman had to repair a broken guitar string, he said acidly, "You can talk now." The problem with that kind of attitude was that it alienated non-musicians who might ordinarily have been drawn to his music. The next night, when Murphey performed in resplendent white, a Castle Creek patron remarked afterward, "Jesus, I thought I was in the garden of Gethsemane." Murphey was a man destined to go through life feeling he was misunderstood.

During that time, Murphey was experiencing traumas that would have left anyone irritable. After a couple of years of rocky roads his marriage had finally overturned, and so had his A&M recording contract. He had gone through a phase of rhythm & blues songwriting, the rock drummer who had played on *Geronimo's Cadillac* was again available, a thumping bass player who had worked with Aretha Franklin was also willing to help out, and the third album seemed a good time to break out of the country-rock rut. A&M didn't see it that way. They rejected the album, and after a few tortuous hours in the A&M office, Murphey found Bob Johnston's power had its limits. A&M was proud of Murphey's previous albums, though they had never sold too well, and they insisted they just wanted their old recording artist back. Murphey contended the principle at stake was freedom of artistic expression.

Johnston demanded that A&M either release the album or release Murphey from his contract. A&M exercised the latter option, and Murphey jumped to Epic. According to Larry Watkins, Johnston told Murphey a commercially successful beginning was a must with the new label, and the two sifted through his material to find the most commercially appealing songs available. The result of that effort, a plain-vanilla package simply titled *Michael Murphey,* was not as evenly balanced as *Geronimo's Cadillac,* and scarcely as thematic as *Cosmic Cowboy Souvenir,* but it was possibly better than either.

The album contained all the previous elements of Murphey's music. There was an Anglican song set in the town of Rye, another Anglican-flavored tune tending in message toward gospel, a high-voiced statement of personal theology called "The Observer," and a country-rock song borrowed from his guitar player, Craig Hillis, that rebelled against the modern life of supermarket electric doors, birth control pills, constant doctor's care and premature ejaculation. The album also contained an old Murphey song that his friends had sworn he would never record. It was sheer country, taking off like George Jones' "The Race Is On," fit for the self-parodying voice of Buck Owens.

"Fort Worth I Love You" was a take-off on the country-music cliché of a murderer's jailbreak, but the only crimes attributed to the prisoner, on whose arm the song title was tattooed in red and blue, were shooting down a Georgia woman's reputation and robbing her of her pride. Fort Worth, the escape artist said, was a wonderful place to hide. It was a song that Murphey discounted as frivolous, but it had considerable sales potential.

Epic hoped to assault the country singles charts with that brief number, and the flip side would hopefully catch on in the pop charts. Lyrically suspended in "Holy Roller" between people who believed God was dead and those who snored every Sunday in church, Murphey ventured a humorous solution, gospel rock:

> *Whatever happened to the stompin' shoutin' ways?*
> *Gettin' down, rollin' round about the Judgement Day*
> *I can't stand it no more, why don't we get on the floor?*
> *Why don't we do some Holy Rollin'?*

Though the lyrics of the song were no abrupt depature from Murphey's previous form, the arrangement was. There was more bass, more organ; Hillis played more like Freddie King than Chet Atkins, and Murphey was accompanied by a female chorus that sounded practically Mo-Town. It wasn't country-rock. It was closer to blues-rock, that fair-skinned derivative of black rhythm & blues. If there was a consistent theme in the new album, it was a defiant reaction to the way A&M had treated Michael Martin Murphey. The organ-based instrumentation extended to another song called "Ace in the Hole" in which Murphey described the problems confronting a band leader who tried to root his rock music in the black tradition of Jellyroll Morton, and again, even more bitterly, in the album's lead cut:

> *Hey boy, would you like to wind up out on the street?*
> *Tappin' out those songs you write with your feet?*
> *Well let me tell you mister, my best songs came from there*
> *The street is a hard mistress; at least it treats you fair*
> *Hey, nobody's going to tell me how to make my music*
> *No matter how simple it's got to be free*
> *Don't try to tell me how to make my music*
> *It's got to come out sounding, there's no damn way around it*
> *It's going to come out sounding like you and me*

Murphey plumbed one song from his Screen Gems collection for the album, and though it was a product of his country-rock songwriting phase, it seemed aimed at his 1974 Austin audience. "Say So Much" expressed a weariness with songwriting in general, a disenchantment with people who considered rock songwriters something more than themselves and wanted him to be their personal rock & roll idealogue. *"To live and breathe some point of view,"* Murphey sang, *"that's just the same as being dead."*

The album served note of a severance. Murphey's music would never be the same again; he was moving to Colorado and stepping away from Austin music. He was going to marry a girl from Dallas who taught retarded children, and they wanted to build a solar-powered home in the Rockies and administer a home for disadvantaged children there. He told a radio interviewer that he would still be around Austin, that he was moving primarily because he could no longer stand the summer heat, but he expressed to a newspaper reporter fears that the Austin music community was on the brink of big-time ruin, and he regretted any part he had played in bringing that about.

Murphey was trying to make it on a national scale, and there were indications he might. Most underground FM listeners outside of the state were familiar with "Geronimo's Cadillac," even though they didn't always associate the song with Michael Murphey. And while *Cosmic Cowboy Souvenir* was by no means a massive seller, it had made a quick appearance in the *Billboard* Top 200, which record people knew was nothing to scoff at. It greatly enhanced Murphey's reputation. He had a date pending on Don Kirschner's *In Concert* television series, and as record men also knew, just one of those three-song gigs had sent many performers over the top. Murphey's songwriting was too notable to go unnoticed for long, Willie Nelson and Carole King and Kris Kristofferson had first written songs for better-known performers, then because of the excellence of those songs, leapfrogged past them. At the very least, it was easy to image Murphey attracting a modest but fanatical following like that of, say, Shawn Phillips or Boz Scaggs, both of whom had Texas ties.

For the time being, however, Murphey's largest following was still in Austin. He had premiered *Cosmic Cowboy Souvenir* at Armadillo World Headquarters, and he did the same with the Epic release. Murphey told us he considered the Armadillo an exception to the beer-splashing, glass-breaking rule of the large music hall. He liked the exuberance of an Armadillo crowd because it was mostly positive energy. But even the Armadillo was changing. The state of Texas had belatedly granted its eighteen-year-olds the right to purchase intoxicants, and for those of us who altered our draft cards and driver's licenses at the age of nineteen and fell in love with the Armadillo a decade later, that begrudged liberalism had a negative effect. The teenagers who flocked to the Armadillo on weekends came not so much for the music, it seemed, but for a drunken good time. One rock & roll act was as good as another, as long as there was plenty of beer. When Murphey kissed his pretty wife-to-be that night and walked onstage in a Cisco Kid outfit, he gave the crowd some of the best rock & roll I had heard, but when he tried to settle them down for one of his softer numbers, he ran into trouble.

"Rock & roll!" somebody yelled as he tried to explain his song.

"Eat it!" another inexplicably shouted.

"Look," Murphey pleaded, "I know you can't boogie too well to some of these songs, but I'd like for you to be patient and listen."

Murphey was in a much better mood than he had been at Castle Creek, possibly because word had gotten around that Frances Farenthold was going to make an appearance. Running in a scandal-charged atmosphere in 1972, Sissy had mounted a brilliant campaign for the Democratic gubernatorial nomination, finishing second but striking fear into the hearts of the conservative vested interests and derailing the political career of Lieutenant Governor Ben Barnes, a man Lyndon Johnson had predicted would be president one day. Later that summer she had finished second behind Tom Eagleton in the balloting for the Democractic vice-presidential nomination at the Democractic National Convention, and those performances had established her as a leader of the liberal wing of the Texas Democratic Party. But now, in 1974, she was making a suicidal second run for the governor's seat, trying to dislodge an entrenched incumbent who had drubbed her handily two years earlier and done nothing particularly praiseworthy or condemning since. Dolph Briscoe was a dull, rich rancher in the governor's mansion, difficult to attack. But Sissy was still a magic name among young, politically alienated Texans, and a surprise appearance at Armadillo World Headquarters would scaracely hurt her in several Austin precincts.

When she was quietly ushered into the backstage area between sets, I was surprised by her femininity. I had expected a rawboned, Texas-talking hellcat, but instead she was an attractive woman in a pretty dress. In my brief career as a journalist I had learned that I was better at eavesdropping than interviewing, and I leaned against the wall close to where she sat chatting with Eddie Wilson and Mike Tolleson. Standing beside me was one of Murphey's drummers, and as I tried to catch what she was saying he tapped me on the shoulder and said, "Do you want some of this?" I saw nothing wrong with an occasional between-set toke, and I accepted the drummer's generosity, but that was the first time in years I had felt guilty about smoking marijuana. It seemed a breach in diplomacy, a lapse in protocol, to break even an inane law within reach of a woman who had been nominated for the vice-presidency, who symbolized the hopes and frustrations of so many Texans. Of course, we weren't standing on the steps of the state capitol. We were backstage at Armadillo World Headquarters, the home ground of Texas country-rock. Musicians lived in a world all their own.

When Sissy went out unannounced ahead of Murphey, there was a shocked silence of recognition, and then bedlam. The spotlights were too bright for her, and she cupped her hand over her eyes and uttered a single sentence: "This year we will have victory, but tonight . . . we have Michael Murphey." They would scarcely have victory; she would carry only two counties. And while the statement may have been politically astute, it struck me as the worst thing she could have said for Murphey who was a talented man trying to retain a grip on reality in the midst of rock & roll worship.

The book was edging toward a conclusion by then, and I had most of the material I needed on Murphey, but my photographer was stumped. She had contact sheet after contact sheet of him in performance, but she couldn't break down his barrier to get anything more. Larry Watkins wasn't much help, for he stepped very lightly when he dealt with Murphey, and was reluctant to intervene in her behalf. Since I had established some kind of relationship with Murphey, I told her I would request another interview and she could establish her own contact then. When I called Murphey there was not much recognition on the other end of the line, just an expectant silence. He said he would meet me again at the Oyster Bar, said goodbye, and hung up.

Two hours and a couple of shrimp dinners came and went that Friday, but no Murphey. I shrugged it off and drove back to New Braunfels, but my photographer, harassed by her deadline and insulted, was fuming. Watkins tended to regard her as a pretty girl first and a professional photographer second, and she accordingly applied the bitchy screws to him. Larry finally advised us a couple of Sundays later that he had left word for Murphey to meet us at his lakeside house that afternoon, and we made the twenty-mile drive to find Murphey had taken his fiancee to the airport and would return later that afternoon. Embarrassed, Watkins said we could either go back to town or wait. My photographer was determined to stick it out.

As the afternoon wore on toward evening, Craig Hillis's wife tried to make us feel at home while an Austin couple taped Murphey's unreleased album. On first impression, I found myself more in sympathy with A&M. It wasn't rhythm & blues. It verged on Frank Zappa, faltering in gait, confused and directionless. Murphey had been reading his poetry though. In one Coney Island song he adroitly borrowed a couple of touches from Lawrence Ferlinghetti. The couple talked about Murphey's music. Hillis's wife talked about Murphey's travel preparations and photograph collection. Watkins talked about Murphey's new album. Even in his absence, Murphey was the center of attention.

Hillis drifted in as it got too dark for any photography, and so did Murphey's dinner guests, Eddie and Jeannie Wilson. Off-duty, Wilson could be one of the most entertaining men I'd ever met. My mood lifted appreciably after the Wilsons arrived, but still, I was an uninvited guest in Murphey's home, intruding on a dinner party with friends. I couldn't have been more uncomfortable had I been sitting bare-assed on a prickly pear.

Several hours after we had arrived, Murphey came in through the kitchen, hands stuffed in his overalls pockets, and said hello to everybody. The decibel level of the conversation decreased remarkably. Watkins conferred with Murphey briefly, then after his client went into his bedroom, Larry summoned me from my chair and said quietly, "It can't be too long. He's got to pack." I felt like I had been granted an audience with the Pope.

My photographer sat in the corner talking for a few minutes before she realized we had gone, then asked where we were and barged through the door as Watkins and other underlings watched in horror. Murphey lay on his bed looking at me, glancing up in surprise when my photographer burst through the door. I introduced them, she sat down in a chair and folded her arms across her chest, and Murphey adjusted to yet another unwarranted intrusion. I manufactured a couple of questions to pass the time, but it was forced conversation, dominated by the metallic neutrality of Murphey's eyes. The dogs had run the prey to ground but, still, he held them off. The conversation breathed life only when he mentioned his collection of old Indian photographs, and explained the technical problems of turn-of-the-century photographers. My photographer corrected him on a couple of points, and he eyed her with something that approached interest. She knew more about that part of the world than he did.

Murphey was formidably aloof, the most distant man I had ever met. He was jealous of his privacy to the point of common discourtesy, and he knew better than anyone what a sham the rock music rite had become. In his *Buddy* essay he wrote of his audience, "You know they should be thinking about their *own* lives not yours, or the existence of some 'scene'." But he was surrounded by people who sacrificed large parts of their own identities in his behalf, and disclaimers to the contrary, he cherished the power inherent in his position. It wasn't every man of twenty-eight who could direct a thousand hippies to sit quietly and listen to Mozart, and while the crowd roared approval conclude a song with the improvised line: *"And Nixon's the only dope I'd like to shoot!"*

I respected Murphey for his graceful turns of phrase. Our backgrounds were strikingly similar and so were our personal philosophies. But I didn't know Michael Murphey, and I no longer wanted to know him. He had shown me the angry intelligence, the flickering studied gaze, but whatever was going on in that creative mind was a mystery to me. I didn't dislike him, but I was ready to part company with him. It was the nature of the business, I supposed. He was hooked, if only on a regional basis and rather against his will, on the horns of stardom, and I was just one of the many parasites swarming around him. If we had ever met on common ground, we might not have shaken hands as friends, but we probably would have voiced common resentments. But there was no common ground between star and flack. Only a clash of overburdened egos.

I was finally realizing that this business was not for me. If I was going to retain any appreciation for commercial music, I was going to have to burn all my Armadillo backstage passes, pinch the groupies' asses farewell, and get back out in the crowd where I belonged. As time went by I found myself defending Murphey to friends wearied by his demanding ways, and more significantly, I caught myself whistling his tunes as I went about my work. For more than any of the other performers,his music had touched me. I remembered the afternoon I brought boredom to the Hill on the Moon and exchanged it for excitement, the Armadillo night I became one of those backsliding winos under the influence of good company and the *Cosmic Cowboy* premier, the solitary evening I weathered a romantic disappointment listening to "Blessing in Disguise." I knew that was supposed to be an adolescent response, identifying one's personal experience with the lyrics of a pop song, but somewhere in that thicket lurked a theory of art.

Most of all, I remembered the Christmas-season afternoon in Alan Price's meadow west of Austin, when Rusty Wier, Bobby Bridger, Jerry Jeff Walker and Murphey played a benefit for an organization called Free the Slow. Only a couple of hundred people spread their blankets on the yellowed grass, but that was probably all the crowd the beneficiaries of the concert could have handled. There were the usual trappings of an outdoor concert — couples snuggling for warmth and erotic pleasure on the hillside, a girl in Barnum & Bailey facial paint juggling tennis balls, too many dogs to keep track of, a couple of hippies on horseback. But mingling with the crowd were institutionalized people of varied ages and ailments who would be children as long as they lived. Polite society called them retarded. The runny noses and anguished grins were a source of discomfort for Wier. Bridger was uneasy because his quiet music was sandwiched between the country-rockers, and the crowd seemed to drift away from him. Walker was oblivious to his surroundings as usual. But sunshaded and warmed by a Mexican serape, Murphey fairly beamed. Whatever else one could say about the man, he wanted his music to accomplish some good in the world, and that afternoon it seemed to. I sat on a hillside rock drinking a borrowed beer, watching a young mongoloid man in a sportcoat dance a frenzied twist to one of Murphey's rock numbers. Then Murphey began a song that I considered his best. The lyrics were personal, rooted in his own anxieties and restlessness, but in its urban psychological bruises and yearnings for an ideal home, the song seemed to catch the spirit of a Texas generation. It began with a cantering guitar lead, Herb Steiner's steel riding overhead like a whistling bell:

> *I'm tired of drinking your muddy water, baby,*
> *and sleeping in your hollow log*
> *I'm gonna take up with a stranger*
> *and get myself a faster moving dog*
> *Goodbye you empty closets*

and my true love of seven years
I'm on a southwestern pilgrimage
  to be a frontier sonneteer
Goodbye you auctioneers
  and you guillotine racketeers
I'm looking for a holy man
  out here on the old frontier
I'm gonna take along a lady
  who ain't never seen a mountain before
I'm on a southwestern pilgrimage
  where the middle class can't hunt me down no more

As Murphey stepped away from the microphone and Steiner and Hillis took over, a gaunt institutionalized man with an aged jacket and a stubble of beard climbed the hill toward me, peering out from a mental clock stopped sometime in the fifties. "Wh-wh-what's your name?" he said.

I told him and he squatted down beside me.

"H-h-h-how many dogs you got?"

"One. I'm babysitting another right now."

He nodded in apparent satisfaction. "Wh-where you from?"

"Wichita Falls, originally."

"I know where that place is at," he said with sudden clarity. As Murphey stepped back to the microphone the man grinned, slapped his knee and cupped a hand behind his ear.

I should have been a gypsy all along
  and I know that now
But I got slowed up
  I let a city woman drag me down
And the contracts and the circus acts
  they make it so I can't relax no more
But my stomach never hurts me much
  when I'm sleeping on the floor
That old buzzard's flying all around
  my same old Texas sky
And I take that as a sign
  that it's time to either lay me down or fly
So it's out of my house

> *and it's into my trucking clothes*
> *I'm on a southwestern pilgrimage*
> *where the wheel stops nobody knows*

I remained ambivalent about the man, but I approved of his music. So did the man-child beside me.

willie the lion

If Michael Murphey was born to play his guitar under clear skies in a meadow for retarded kids, Willie Nelson was born to assemble his band on a flat-bed truck in the service ramp of a Ford dealership and play for used-car salesmen. That was the difference between Michael Murphey and Willie Nelson, the difference between Nelson and others. The rest of the recorded Austinites were folk and blues and rock musicians who had drifted into country music by chance, convenience, or necessity, but Nelson had been country from the outset. The prevalent strain of Austin music was a bastard mix of styles and traditions deemed country for lack of a better label, and while there was less suburban-bred, college-educated condescension toward Grand Ole Opry country in Austin than in Los Angeles, there was some of it. But Nelson was a man who had grown to maturity in a rural environment. He had never gone to college, and he had probably never given it much thought. He had been scrapping for his nickels and dimes and saying yes sir to the rich folks almost as long as he could remember, and though he was now a rich man himself, he was still a musical representative of the hardhats and waitresses, carhops and door-to-door salesmen courted in the polls by George Wallace. Yet he grew his hair long and raised a beard and ran around with Leon Russell. Nelson had bridged the gap between freaks and rednecks in his own mind, and that made him the most appealing performer in town.

A searchlight played in the clouds over Austin one October evening, heralding the arrival of the '74 Fords. In case anyone was interested. After years of more and better highways, bigger and faster cars, and cut-throat gasoline wars, Texans were finally finding out about waiting in long lines and tanks that cost ten dollars to fill. Knowing that Texas still sat on one of the richest oil reservoirs in the world, a few small-town newspaper editors were reflecting that now was the time to secede from the Union. In times such as those, a puttering Suburu was a better buy than a gadgety Torino, and new Ford dealers needed all the help they could get. Knowing their new models were unlikely to generate must interest on their own, somebody at the McMorris dealership in downtown Austin decided to call up an old friend and say: Willie, would you like to do me a favor?

Nelson got a lot of those calls in Austin, and his drummer Paul English, who doubled as a sort of local business manager, received many more. English and his wife were so harangued by requests for Nelson performances for a while that he finally got an answering service and kept his own number a closely guarded secret. He was getting twenty calls a day and it got the point where he'd pick up his phone to dial and a voice would say, "Hello, Paul?" Nelson didn't accede to all those requests, but he had a reputation for finding it hard to say no to anybody, and he played more than his share of those gigs that benefited some cause or organization's pocketbook more than his. Though it was widely disregarded (to many a star and wheeler-dealer's eventual chagrin,) an old axiom in the music business suggested that one be nice to old friends while one was on top, for one day soon one was liable to find one's chin on their doorstep. Besides, Willie Nelson's daddy was a Ford mechanic for twenty-six years.

Nelson agreed to play in honor of the Ford Motor Company debutantes, and word of that immediately sent traffic rushing in the direction of McMorris. There wasn't even enough room on the truckbed for all his band members and the acoustics of the automobile service department were designed for blaring horns, not country-western music. But those were the happiest prospective customers McMorris had entertained in a while — businessmen in shirtsleeves who enthused on the fringes of the crowd, forty-five-year-old mothers who slung elbows and hips in order to deliver their requests first, possessed young women who pirouetted in apparent ecstacy and clasped their hands in front of their bosoms as if in prayer, gazes fixed on the pot-bellied form of Willie Nelson.

One man, however, was ill at ease. He wore a lavender shirt, a white tie and white loafers, and was pressed against the wall, an alarmed look on his face, beads of perspiration on his abundant forehead. Obviously a victim of acute claustrophobia, he had the look of a man who was about to be stoned to death with crumpled beer cans. A taller man in a black sportscoat stepped out of the show-room entrance, handed the perspiring man a slip of paper, and directed him toward the stage. The subordinate eased along the wall, avoiding the crowd's touch as he took the very longest way around, then plunged into the crowd and handed the slip of paper to Nelson. Willie read it, grinned, and said that number was coming right up, but the lavender-shirted man was already trying to make his escape. Before he reached safety an elbow collided with his ribs, and he jumped and looked around, fist instinctively clenched. A towering long-haired man smiled benignly. Red-faced, the man stalked back to his assigned position along the wall, wishing midnight would hurry up before McMorris Ford got wrecked or stolen.

A friend and I were accompanied that night by a young woman whose first love was classical music, though lately she had been turning an ear toward Doc Watson and *Sweetheart of the Rodeo*. It was the first time she had seen Willie Nelson. We stood at the edge of the crowd, valuing our toes, but then Willie's grinning gaze fell on her. "Hm," she said, standing on her tiptoes and moving a few steps closer. For the time being at least, I had lost her.

The Willie Nelson phenomenon began April 30, 1933, in Abbott, Texas, a bypassed community in the cotton-farming country near Waco. Broken homes and wasted marriages and displaced children were subjects that would surface often in Nelson's song-writing, for he learned his lessons first-hand. His parents went their separate ways when he was a small child, leaving him to be raised by his grandparents. His grandfather was a blacksmith, but music was also a part of Nelson's inheritance. Both grandparents had mail-order music degrees. He watched them study and practice at night in the dim light of a kerosene lantern, and before his grandfather died in 1939, he taught Willie to play a few chords on a guitar. Nelson never had another music lesson, but at the age of ten he landed his first gig playing rhythm guitar for a Bohemian polka band in West, six miles away. His grandmother reproved him, "Willie, I thought you promised me you'd never go on the road." Nelson's first regular band assignment sounded like a song by June Carter: Willie played bass/ his daddy played fiddle/ sister Bobbie played piano/ the football coach played trombone. One night they played for the gate and went home with eighteen cents apiece.

Nelson worked at one job or another from the time he was twelve, trimming trees and laboring on the railroad after high school, and he didn't leave Abbott until 1950, when he joined the Air Force. Discharged, he married a Cherokee Indian girl and they had their first daughter, Lana. Living in Waco, they barely got by as Willie peddled vacuum cleaners, encyclopedias and even Bibles out of a broken-down car he had to park on a steep grade if he hoped to get it started again, teaming in the latter assignment with a man who later gained command of all the radio stations in Albuquerque, New Mexico. Still playing and singing when he could, Nelson wanted his work to bear a little more relevance to his music, and he talked his way into a disc jockey's job at a small station near San Antonio. While living in Abbott he had hung around the radio station in nearby Hillsboro just long enough to note the equipment was manufactured by RCA,and when the Pleasanton station manager asked him if he had ever done that kind of work before, Willie said sure, but he was used to working with RCA equipment. The manager put him on the air with ten minutes of news and a string of commercials, one of which he'd never forget: "Pleasanton Pharmacy, whose pharmaceutical department will accurately and precisely fill your doctor's prescriptions." The station manager hired the tongue-tied young announcer for forty dollars a week.

In the mid-fifties Nelson hosted a music and talk show on a country-western station in Fort Worth, and he played nights and weekends in a strip of bars on the Jacksboro Highway that resembled a latter-day Dodge City. Most of the customers and half the musicians carried a gun or at least a respectable blade, and his favorite club was one where the management had courteously strung chicken-wire in front of the stage to protect the musicians from beer bottles tossed occasionally from the crowd. Still a disc jockey, he moved on to Oregon and then returned to a station in Pasadena, near Houston. He was writing songs by then, scribbling them out in paragraph form on napkins and bus tickets whenever inspiration visited, and he even had a record deal with a fly-by-night company, but living in Texas was a distinct disadvantage. He sold "Family Bible" for fifty dollars, sold "Night Life" for a hundred and fifty, and it required three investors to come up with that much. Willie's producer didn't like the latter song so he recorded it on the sly under the name Hugh Nelson.

Inevitably, Nelson made the country pilgrimage to Nashville, and he was one of the lucky few. He was jamming with what bands he could when Hank Cochran heard his songs and signed him to Pamper Publishing, which was owned in part by Ray Price. Nelson knew Johnny Bush,who was Ray Price's drummer, and Price asked Willie if he knew how to play the bass. Nelson told an understandable lie and taught himself to play the bass in a hurry, and after that things took off for him. Faron Young recorded "Hello Walls." Price recorded "Night Life," followed by Rusty Draper. Patsy Cline recorded "Crazy." Clyde Gray recorded "Family Bible." Fred Foster recorded "I Never Cared for You." Willie recorded "The Party's Over." In that short span, Nelson's lifetime income was assured. In addition to the Nashville artists drawn to his succinct, down-hearted lyrics, his music ranged into music fields as foreign as Perry Como, Little Anthony and the Imperials, Lawrence Welk, Stevie Wonder, Harry James, B.B. King and Eydie Gorme. Eventually more than seventy artists recorded "Night Life," and when Nelson heard Aretha Franklin's brilliant version, he told friends he'd never sing that song again.

The monetary effect of all that would require a calculator. In addition to the cut a songwriter got every time one of his lyrics sold on a record by another performer, he was paid every time one of those songs received air play. A songwriter who contributed an unknown second side to a hit single even got an equal share of the take. Most country-music fans were familiar with Ray Price's recording of "Danny Boy," but few except Willie Nelson's banker remembered the flip side was "Let My Mind Wander." Intimates said Nelson's songwriting income alone amounted to about $150,000 a year.

Of course, even a wealthy man could go broke in the music business. If a songwriter had hit Nashville in the early seventies with that much force, he would have been an immediate recorded superstar even if he sang with no teeth and a cleft palate.But Nelson arrived a decade early, for those were the days when only the singers were important. Nobody cared who wrote the song except the men behind the scenes, and artists who needed hit material. Nelson wanted to go on his own, but his band leader advised him not even to try. Willie responded by stealing Price's band: drummer Johnny Bush, fiddler Wade Ray, steel player Jimmy Day, who had performed on the *Louisiana Hayride* and even accompanied Hank Williams. Nelson made the mistake, he reflected later, of "buying the band a station wagon and credit card." The band went on the road in the station wagon with a trailer hitched to the rear, but the trip west ended in misfortune. Trying to get back to Texas from California, Nelson and Bush threw their suitcases on an open boxcar then huffed and puffed and watched sadly as the train outran them.

Nelson's first marriage had ended in divorce after ten years and three children, and he had run off with the wife of the disc-jockey association president who would later emcee Willie's induction into the Nashville Songwriters Hall of Fame. With his new wife he retreated to Fort Worth for a couple of years, took a brief look at Los Angeles, then returned to Nashville. Those were the frustrating mid-years of his career. He continued to sell his songs and recorded eighteen albums — two with Liberty and the rest with RCA — but neither company did much to promote his singing reputation. He showed up on television with Porter Wagoner and Glen Campbell, and he once wired a $500 loan to his friend Roger Miller, who had driven to Hollywood in a smoking Nash Rambler. The next thing he knew Miller was a hot man on the charts with "Chug-a-Lug." Like Pee Wee Reese risking his country-boy neck for Jackie Robinson on the first Brooklyn Dodger swing through the South, Nelson ushered Charley Pride through that same hard-core racist territory at a time when black churches were being bombed and freedom-marching blacks were confronting police dogs in Selma, but Willie lived to see the day when Pride would sometimes forget to speak to him.

Finally, after five years, Nelson was ready to put another band together, and he wanted to move Bush up to guitar. Playing in Houston with a drummer borrowed from Skeeter Davis, he ran into an old friend from the rough-and-tumble days of Fort Worth. Paul English had owned a leather shop in Fort Worth, which allowed him enough time to play trumpet in the country bars, but in the intervening years he had become a drummer, and when he ran into Willie again he was playing the country-club circuit in Houston. "It was the kind of thing where you rode an elevator up thirteen floors then walked down to the twelfth so you could enter through the back door," English said. "I didn't mind it though. I was making a hundred fifty dollars a week, and I liked the people in the kitchen better anyway." English told Nelson he could beat Skeeter Davis's drummer any day, and Willie said, "Well, hell, I'll just hire you then." Though castigated in official Nashville circles for his association with the rock & rolls Byrds, Bush eventually went out successfully on his own, and English became to Nelson what Travis Holland was to Steve Fromholz. English was blind in one eye, his speech was slurred because of an old adenoid operaton, and with a black goatee and a cape wrapped around his scarecrow frame, he looked like the devil himself, but he was the most loyal of Nelson's sidekicks. Willie and his band made some prestigeous performances on major bills during those years, but it was a rough way to travel: thirty or forty straight one-nighters, jumping four or five hundred miles a night — once they played in New York, Arkansas, North Carolina and Texas, in that order, in three days.

Nelson had other reasons to be disenchanted with Nashville. Pamper Publishing had become a multilevel conglomerate but the majority stockholders, Ray Price and Hal Smith, were no longer on speaking terms. Frank Sinatra had recorded an album of Nelson's songs but strongly hinted he wanted to buy Pamper before he released the album. He knew how many records he sold, and how big a cut the publishers got. But Price wasn't willing to sell to anyone he didn't know or trust, and Hank Cochran approached Nelson and said, Willie, why don't we buy Ray's half of Pamper? Because of his annual BMI income Nelson had more banking credit than a lot of Texas oilmen, so he floated the loan for $500,000 and the agreement was signed in Price's den. Never a man to stay very much on top of his business affairs, Nelson noticed that he was getting a lot of angry letters to pay this or that bill, so he told his partners he wanted out. Cochran and Smith assumed the loan, and Willie broke even on the deal, but his old partners later sold the Pamper conglomerate for 2½ million dollars. The Frank Sinatra album never came out.

By 1969 Nelson had divorced again and married a pretty platinum blonde from Houston named Connie. They owned both a home in Nashville and a farm in Ridgetop, about thirty miles from Nashville. But in six months Connie wrecked the car twice, and the house in Nashville burned down. When he heard about the fire Nelson rushed home, wrestled from the grasp of observers who tried to stop him, and rushed inside to retrieve his battered guitar and stash of dope. Nelson and his family, Paul English and his family, and bass player Bea Spears retired to a dude ranch deserted for the winter in the Texas Hill Country near Bandera and waited for the house to be rebuilt. Disturbed only by golfers on an adjoining course who knocked on his door occasionally in search of new balls or a nineteenth-hole beer, Nelson wrote a lot during those weeks, and as usual much of his writing was of a personal nature:

> *It's been rough and rocky traveling*
> *But I'm finally standing upright on the ground*
> *After taking several readings*
> *I'm surprised to find my mind's still fairly sound*
> *I thought Nashville was the roughest*
> *But I know I've said the same about them all*
> *We received our education*
> *In the cities of the nation*
> *Me and Paul*

Though Nelson returned to his farm in Ridgetop, he was already severing his ties with official Nashville. Chet Atkins, who was top guitar player in town and also one of the city's biggest businessmen, was the Nashville head of RCA, and he was already worried that Waylon Jennings and Willie Nelson might be the ruin of Nashville. It wasn't their fondness for marijuana or long hair, for Nashville wasn't half as hidebound and sanctimonious as its old leaders tried to make it appear. It wasn't their experimentation with country music. Rather, they were going outside the proper channels to get what they wanted. Jennings went over Atkins' head to the New York executives of RCA, one of whom had a large photo of Nelson in his office. "Hoss," Waylon said, "you already made a mistake with that one." The official said he knew it, and gave Jennings the kind of deal he wanted.

Nelson had balked when RCA requested that he renew his contract ahead of schedule. If he didn't, that old ploy went, the albums he'd already recorded just might not get released. Neil Rashen, a hustling New York manager with a hard-nosed reputation, heard about Nelson's hassles and volunteered to try to get him off the RCA hook, providing Willie granted him his managerial business afterward. Nelson agreed, and the matter was dropped into the hands of Rashen's experienced lawyers and the executives of RCA. Willie's RCA contract guaranteed him $10,000 a year, and knowing Nelson was not

284

going to sign under any circumstances, RCA agreed to let him go, providing he returned $1,400 he had been overpaid. Free to barter at last, Nelson took his business to New York, where Atlantic offered him $25,000 for his signature. Another company offered him twice that amount, but English pleaded with Nelson not to sign with that label because word was getting around that he was a maverick and a move might be afoot to shut him out altogether. Paranoia perhaps, but the two men had been in the music business a long time, and Atlantic looked particularly trustworthy because they had never before signed a country artist.

Nelson agreed to work with seasoned New York producer Jerry Wexler, and Atlantic made a New York studio available to Willie and his band, Doug Sahm and his band, and anybody else they invited. The musicians churned out thrity-three recordings, some upbeat and many slightly crazed, many serious to a fault, according to some of the musicians. Write something light, they said, but Willie didn't have a light song in mind until he sat down on the commode one day and picked up an envelope that read "Another Individual Service Provided by Holiday Inn." Instructions on how to use the sanitary napkin disposal were printed in four languages on one side, so he turned the envelope to the side that read "Preferred by Particular Women," and scribbled:

> *Shotgun Willie sits around in his underwear*
> *Bitin' on a bullet, pullin' out all of his hair*
> *Shotgun Willie's got all of his family there*

Shotgun Willie was like a dog released from its kennel for the first time in weeks, sprinting off in all directions because of the pent-up energy, and it marked a new stage in Nelson's career. When he had recorded with RCA, he had laid down a basic track and the engineers and producers took over from there. He never knew how many orchestras were going to surface on record behind him. But he had a good measure of control over his music with Atlantic, and working with Wexler, they switched the arrangements from Ray Price to Ray Charles. The result was a revitalized music, the closest a recording had come to capturing the magic of his life performance. In material the album ranged from Bob Willis' classic "Stay All Night" to Johnny Bush's "Whiskey River" to Leon Russell's "Look Like the Devil," but the tone was set by the humorous title cut and another one of Willie's battered songs of the road:

> *We were headed home to Austin*
> *Caught pneumonia on the road*
> *Takin' it home to Connie and the kids*
> *A wheel ran off and jumped the railroad*
> *Then ran through a grocery store*
> *If you wanta buy a bus I'm takin' bids*
> *And the devil shivered in his sleepin' bag*
> *He said travelin' on the road is such a drag . . .*

Connie Nelson put down an apartment deposit in Houston when her husband jumped to Atlantic, but he took one look at the sea of concrete and decided he'd rather move to Austin, where his sister Bobbie was already living. About the time of the *Shotgun Willie* release, Nelson surfaced on the Armadillo stage with his band: Bobbie at piano, English on the drums, Bea Spears on bass, and Jimmy Day on steel. Spears, a gaunt young man who had been with Nelson a long time, quickly gained a reputation as the best bass player in Austin, but Day, widely considered one of the two or three best steel players in the country, looked like he was on his last legs by the time he got to town. He mesmerized the Armadillo crowd that night with his version of "Greenfields," but he was soon in the Soap Creek Saloon in the impoverished company of Greezy Wheels, a sometimes highly regarded country-rock band that had unfortunately lost its leader to the state department of corrections on a marijuana rap, and Day played so poorly when he joined Commander Cody that his new band fellows were convinced he was trying to sabotage their music. As time went by, Nelson gained a new guitarist, Jody Payne, who had once been married to Sammi Smith and was still her lead player when she came to Texas toying with the idea of joining Willie as permanent second act. He also took on a rock-oriented harmonica player, Mickey Raipheld, who always seemed to be jamming when he played with Nelson. Raipheld told friends that was because he never knew where Willie's music was headed next.

Raipheld was a charter member of the so-called Interchangeable Band of Austin sidemen, but that was as close as the younger community of Austin musicians got to active involvement in Willie

Nelson's music. They all seemed to admire him, but he stood apart from them. For one thing, he ran with a different crowd. The backstage gang which materialized at a Michael Murphey concert was comprised primarily of hippies who were very stoned and very rock-oriented, though they wore cowboy hats and boots and drank Lone Star beer because all that was in style. The people backstage at a Nelson concert were older. Many of the women were too flabby to run around with their bellies bare, some of the men were missing a tooth or two, most all of them drank like they were trying to forget something. Though Bea Spears could have played with any rock & roll act, Payne had trained himself over the years to cool it with his guitar when Sammi was out front singing, Paul English would have been lost in a fast-moving rock number, and though Nelson was a good guitar player, his style was essentially country, simple and understated, tending more toward flamenco than flaming rock when he really worked out. And to some people, Willie's lyrics were even suspect. Michael Price of *Rallying Point*, who admittedly was prejudiced because he thought he had been wronged by Nelson in a business dealing, said, "Compare one of Willie's song with one of Murphey's. Willie doesn't say shit."

From the viewpoint of a magazine publisher whose first issue had called for a new constitutional convention in Washington and the ouster of Richard Nixon from office, Price was quite often right. There was very little ideology in many of Willie's lyrics. Then again, he was working within the country tradition. Country lyricists had never set out to win many people over. They simply aimed their remarks at a reasonably well-defined demographic audience of working-class whites, trying to make that audience respond: why, that's the way I feel, that's the way I felt yesterday. Merle Haggard told a *Time* magazine reporter that country songwriting was just journalism. Of course there was honest journalism and dishonest journalism, but Haggard was right that there was little advocacy in country music. Most country lyricists just observed and listened and reported what they'd seen and heard, even if they got it second-hand on the NBC News: kids rioting in the streets, the dissolution of the American family, the persecution of an Army lieutenant just because he followed his orders and killed a few gooks. It was a poetry rooted in working-class conservatism, hardly a revolutionary literary form.

But Nelson was better at it than most because he had been one of those people until he was nearly thirty years old. He knew how tight-lipped and unlettered those people were, and he didn't flower his lyrics with poetic flights of fancy. Instead they were short and to the point, versed often in southern working-class dialect, and they worked better, perhaps, than the lyrics of any other country songwriter in the country. When the jukebox needle settled down on the grooves of one of Willie's sad songs, the maligned and politically manipulated class of wage-earners didn't necessarily weep into their beers, but they watched the bubbles rising from the bottom of the glass, and they read Willie's words into their own lives.

The second reason his music worked so well was his voice. Most recorded country singers sounded like they were always imitating somebody else. Couple that nasal exaggeration of drawls and you-alls with the vapid message of most country songs, and the result was an unwitting self-mockery. But despite all the cornball nonsense, a genuine, believable country voice occasionally slipped out from under the Nashville crushed carpet. Jimmy Rodgers had that distinctive country voice, Hank Williams had it, Ernest Tubb had it, Hank Snow had it, Johnny Cash had it, Merle Haggard had it, Waylon Jennings had it, and so did Willie Nelson. Willie could do more with a monotone baritone than anybody in Austin had ever heard. When he was in the hands of the saccharine arrangers in the mid-sixties, he had had his own moments of vocal dishonesty, but as he aged he learned to free his voice to wander over the syllables, bending them up, down, sliding into the next note. He sang like something inside him was in agony; he was unlikely to sink much further but was unable to climb any higher. Billy Joe Shaver wrote a song about Nelson that likened him to a Texas norther, and that was the emotional effect of Willie's voice. It wasn't the turbulent, barreling rush of air at the leading edge of those cold fronts, but the biting, chilling winds that came afterward, shuddering against the window panes at night.

Though *Shotgun Willie* had taken a couple of rock & roll detours, Nelson's next Atlantic release returned to the country straight and narrow. Willie had already recorded one concept album, *Yesterday's Wine*, that his country faithful considered the most impressive thing he'd written — a journey from his mother's womb through life to his casket, where the narrator watched the mourners for signs of hypocrisy. But *Phases and Stages* promised to make a larger

288

impression, for Atlantic intended to promote it lavishly. Nelson had already recorded half the album for RCA. The title cut "Phases and Stages," appeared as a single in 1972 though it went unnoticed because the throwaway second cut, "Mountain Dew," climbed unexpectedly into the top twenty. Nelson and his band recorded a version of the album they liked in Nashville, but the album was re-recorded in Muscle Shoals, Alabama utilizing studio sidemen because Wexler now had a stake in Willie, and wanted his cut as producer. *"Phases and stages,"* the new album began, *"circles and cycles/scenes that we've all seen before/let me tell you some more."* It returned to the time-tested country theme of divorce, proposing to tell both sides of the story, and the woman on Side 1 was scarcely liberated:

> *Washin' the dishes, scrubbin' the floors*
> *Carin' for someone who don't care anymore*
> *Learnin' to hate all the things*
> *that she once loved to do*
> *Like washin' his shirts and never complainin'*
> *except for red stains on the collar*
> *Ironin' and cryin', cryin' and ironin'*
> *Carin' for someone who don't care anymore*
> *Someday she'll just walk away . . .*

Nelson carried the scenario through the woman's decision to leave in the middle of the night, her sexually defensive note instructing him to pretend she never happened. Then there were the younger sister's observations as the woman slept through the days then finally started going out to the corner beer joint, her jeans fitting tighter than they did before. Finally the woman regained her voice and confessed that she was falling in love again, but it was the saddest song yet, full of reluctance and misgiving. The piano and violin trailed off to a nonconclusion, evoking an image of the woman sitting alone in a loveseat, afternoon sunlight filtering through a living room curtain.

The second side began with the husband ordering bloody marys on a plane from L.A. to Houston, joined him again that night as he sat on his bed his head swirling drunk with complaints that love was nowhere to be found. The next morning he awoke with 'he saddest song on the album, a realization that the rest of his life started from there. Then

Nelson touched on the more bewildered and bitter sentiments that followed the first shock:

> *It's not supposed to be that way*
> *You're supposed to know that I love you*
> *But it don't matter anyway*
> *If I can't be there to control you*

Hoo, lord, what would Germaine Greer have done with those journalistic lines? As uncomprehending of womanhood as ever, Willie's character returned to his hard-drinking, hell-raising ways of old on the album's last cut:

> *Well I'm wild and I'm mean*
> *I'm creatin' a scene, I'm goin' crazy*
> *Well I'm good and I'm bad*
> *And I'm happy and I'm sad*
> *And I'm lazy*
> *I'm quiet and I'm loud*
> *And I'm gatherin' a crowd*
> *And I like gravy*
> *I'm about half off the wall*
> *But I learned it all in the Navy*

A sexist perhaps. According to *Rallying Point*'s Michael Price, an unreconstructed racist. Known as Cocaine Willie by the Fort Worth police department, a man with enough DWI's to suspend his license indefinitely, though a magistrate made an exception so Willie could continue to make his usual $100,000 a year. A man sued by the Texas Attorney General because he failed to pay all his entertainment taxes. But in Austin Nelson could do no wrong. He was just as natural as dirt, and when he walked through a crowd he knew everybody who spoke to him. When he was introduced to someone, his brow creased in slight discomfort but then his grin lit up, and he stuck out his hand like a boy raised to be friendly. As a young man he had probably sold a lot of Bibles just on the strength of that personal look and handshake. In addition, Nelson acted like Austin was the center of the universe. He played fashionable Max's Kansas City in New York, knowing all along that it was a record-company hype that assured him favorable

290

Though he no longer looked the Nashville part, Willie Nelson was a country musician from start to finish, and remnants of his old audience consented faithfully to his changing appearance. Among them were golfing buddy Darrell Royal and Texas state legislators Peyton McKnight (below, far left) and Jumbo Ben Atwell.

Suspicious when he dealt with music businessmen, Nelson led the rebellion against the Nashville establishment and became an inspiration for a new breed of country performers. Below, from left: Nelson chauffeur Billy Cooper, "Delta Dawn" songwriter Alex Harvey, Waylon Jennings, Nelson, Lee Clayton, Ray Wylie Hubbard.

Leon Russell infiltrated Nashville with Nelson's assistance, conceivably the man who could usher Willie into the national spotlight. But Nelson's most faithful sidekick was still drummer Paul English (below left), and though his Texas audience was large, ranging in age from grandmothers to grade-schoolers, he was still a regional phenomenon.

Nelson weathered some hard times in Nashville, but he settled down on a forty-acre estate west of Austin. He spent most of his time with his four-year-old daughter Paula Carlene and his wife Connie (upper right). A neighbor was Lana Nelson, a daughter from his first marriage.

treatment in *Playboy* or *Village Voice*, but he got a bigger kick out of playing an out-of-the-way beer joint in Round Rock called Big G's, where the crowd drank and sang along for three dollars a head. When he was inducted into the Nashville Songwriters Hall of Fame he showed up at that white-tie affair in boots, faded jeans, a frayed denim jacket and a sweat-stained straw hat, and after he played his songs and was asked for a statement, he said, "I forgot the lyrics." In Austin, on the other hand, he would occasionally compromise. When Nelson was voted entertainer of the year by the local Headliners Club, Connie rented him a black tuxedo just in case, and Darrell Royal called him three times on the day he was to receive the reward, exceedingly anxious about what he was going to wear that night. At the last minute he decided to wear the formal attire because he was going to be standing beside Danny Thomas and didn't want to make him feel uncomfortable, but he told his band members to wear anything they wanted. Dressed stiffly in his black tux, Willie staggered in shock when the curtain went up behind him and his men grinned at him in formal white suits. Willie cracked afterward, "I haven't seen Paul dressed up like that since the last time he went to trial."

His number-one booster in Austin was Darrell Royal, who had a few boosters around the state himself. DKR, were three initials dropped into Texas conversations with all the veneration and awe once reserved for LBJ and FDR, and never achieved by JFK. From the day in 1957 that Royal stepped on the Texas campus spouting Oklahoma aphorisms, he was the best coach there ever was. His teams had turned Southwest Conference football into a predictable bore, and though his image had been tarnished by recurrent charges of racism and a book by a former player that portrayed him as a corporate executive who cared only about winning, Royal was graceful even in self-defense, and he probably could have run for governor and won if he'd wanted to. But he was more interested in taking his teams to the Cotton Bowl and hanging out with country musicians, and though his latest All-American fullback had just torn the ligaments in his knee, Royal was anxious to talk about his role in Austin music.

(An audience with Royal was enough to freeze the water in a Texas boys knees. For years I nurtured an obsessive adolescent daydream: on a gray November afternoon in Fort Worth, I would take a handoff in Armon Carter Stadium, jakeleg past a couple of TCU Horned Frogs, streak eighty yards for the touchdown that assured another Longhorn trip to the Cotton Bowl, hand the ball politely to the referee, then race into the fatherly embrace of DKR while the University of Texas crowd shot its rocks collectively. Years after I had taken to rooting for Rice, I found I still could not separate the man from his persona. The instinctive response was still to address the man as "Coach.")

"After I got to Austin," Royal said, "I went to country shows at the municipal auditorium whenever I could, but I was just another spectator out in the crowd. In the course of things, though, we won a few football games, and people started noticing I was in the crowd, and the promoters started asking me to come backstage. So that's how I became personally acquainted with the performers.

"It just kinda happened. I remember I used to get telegrams from Buck Owens after Texas-Oklahoma games, and I didn't know which Owens that was until he came in one time, and they took a picture of us together that appeared in *Billboard* magazine.

"I met Willie Nelson the same way. The team was staying out at the Holiday Inn one night before a game, and Willie was there too, and he left a message at the desk and came up and talked. He gave me a record that I took home and listened to, and I got to know him after that. I knew the stories behind his songs and what he was trying to say in them, and I became a kicked-in-the-head Willie Nelson fan."

Nelson was welcome in other establishment corners. Every organization, worthy cause, and politician in town wanted him on their side, for a Willie Nelson appearance assured a crowd. When a number of politicans staged a street-dance to cover their campaign expenses, Willie opted instead for a similar celebration a few blocks away designed to raise money for an Austin symphony orchestra. That was an event that probably would have struck some New Yorkers as extremely funny: a troupe of square-dancers who shuffled about in the street while professors buried their beards in watermelon, matrons in long gowns who praised symphonic music and Willie Nelson between gulps of beer, and a younger woman in charge of the chocolate-cake sales, who instructed her customers, "We don't have any forks. You'll have to use your fingers." On the other hand, the Austin symphonic movement benefited from the dance by about two thousand dollars at a dollar per customer.

Though Nelson was a prized performer in respectable Austin society, he was still valued most by the younger, more disrespectable mobs who followed him about. History was etched in the lines of his aging face, and he was their link to their Texas past. Larry McMurtry populated his Texas novels with characters like Willie Nelson. His fictional young people were forever tossed about by the upheaval of changing times, but their steadying influence was always an old-timer who was set in the old ways but remembered what it was like to be young. In McMurtry's book and movie *The Last Picture Show*, the last thing his character Sam the Lion did was give his young friends enough money to go whoring in Mexico, mourning the fact that he was too old to go along. Though Willie Nelson was by no means an old man, he played a similar role in the Austin community. He had known the Depression and World War II, but he was sympathetic toward the views of those who hadn't. If McMurtry ever wrote a novel about country musicians, he would need to consult Willie Nelson. Willie had seen it all.

Within the confines of his profession Nelson's most remarkable achievement was slipping Leon Russell over on his old friends in Nashville. Russell was born at variously reported times in Lawton, Oklahoma, started playing piano at the age of three, grew up in Tulsa, migrated to Hollywood about the time John Kennedy was elected president, and according to *Rolling Stone*, "assembled a list of studio credits that tests the pop music trivia freak: Jackie DeShannon, Righteous Brothers, Crystals, Bobby Sox, Gary Lewis and the Playboys, Harper's Bizarre, Glen Campbell, Jerry Lee Lewis, the Byrds, Bobby Darin, Ronnie Hawkins and the Hawks [later the Band], Herb Alpert, Frank Sinatra, Bob Lind, Dorsey Burnett, Brian Hyland, Damita Jo, the Ronettes, and Paul Revere and the Raiders." Russell caught on with Delaney and Bonnie Bramlett, stole the show in *Mad Dogs and Englishmen*, founded Shelter Records along with British promotor Denny Cordell, and became the prevailing American rock superstar after everybody else overdosed. Russell knew about Armadillo World Headquarters before most people in Los Angeles — he helped Freddie King record his live album there in 1971 — but when he appeared across the street in the Municipal Auditorium that same year, he was still very much the rock messiah.

His rock show was not so original as it was perfectly orchestrated — a saxophone player and rhythm & blues singer, a cowboy-hatted harp player with a good country-rock voice, a black girl thrusting and jiving beside his piano as Anglo males rushed forward like lemmings bound for the sea. Musicians who knew Russell insisted he was one of the nicest, shyest people one would ever meet, even if he was a tad crazy, but there was something repugnant about that act. A troop of nazis followed Russell around, shoving groupies, hangers-on and working photographers alike out of his way, and he enjoyed his little games with the crowd. After he played his introductory solo pieces at the piano, he said with a measure of contempt, "Now it's time for the rock & roll portion of this program. Are you ready?" In the midst of a rock number of almost unbearably intensity, he signaled a sideman with the petite gesture of a symphonic conductor reproving his cellist. When he neared the end of a number he raised his hand high to signal the conclusion, then played his final note with his little finger. Maybe it was showmanship, but it verged on power tripping.

What nobody suspected during those rock & roll days was that a decade earlier a sideman named Leon Russell had played on Willie Nelson's second Liberty album. Leon had tried to make it in Nashville, and had been rejected. Of course Nashville sidemen didn't necessarily have close personal relationships with the singers they worked with, and many years and Willie Nelson albums had come and gone since that time. Nelson rediscovered Russell when he heard his daughter's *Mad Dogs and Englishmen* album, and he went to see one of those rock concerts in Houston. Impressed enough that he wanted to meet Russell, Nelson got his old friend in Albuquerque to find him a gig that would cover travel expenses, and he went backstage to shake Russell's hand after the concert. Russell told him that his favorite song was "Family Bible." The most unlikely alliance in American music was joined.

When Russell went country he even changed his name. The *Hank Wilson's Back* album caught a lot of people by surprise. Country purists like Austin columnist Townsend Miller sniffed that it was the worst thing they'd ever heard, seasoned rock observers wondered what kind of hype Leon was up to now. On the other hand, Paul English insisted that Leon's motives were pure; he had always wanted to be a country musician. But whether he wanted that or not, Russell would always just be another rock & roller playing around with country unless he won acceptance in Nashville. He had recorded several country standards on the *Hank Wilson* album, which was something of a tribute to the reigning Nashville heads of state, and when Willie ushered Leon into Nashville in the spring of 1974, it was like Henry Kissinger running interference for Richard Nixon in Peking. The studio musicians in Nashville had always respected the old greybeard, but it was a major, formal concession for Ernest Tubb, Roy Acuff, Bill Monroe, Earl Scruggs and Jeane Pruett to show up to play and party on film with Leon Russell. Nelson even took Russell to the home of Chet Atkins. They must have laughed a lot when they went back to their hotel rooms.

Back in Austin, when Nelson made his debut at the Country Dinner Playhouse, a young man waiting in line gripped a young publisher's arm and said, "Don't look now, I'm not sure it's him, but I think I just saw Leon Russell."

"Really?" the publisher said, wincing from the fingernail impressions in his arm, then Russell walked by again and the young man said, "It is, it's him, did you see that?" Leon sat at a table with Connie Nelson during the performance, staring straight ahead like a sphinx, and he made no acknowledgment when Nelson announced his presence and the crowd pitched into a frenzy. Word got around to the people waiting for the second performance that Russell was inside, however, and during that second set Willie's people had to surround the table to keep the people away from him. Toward the end of the set, he leaped from his chair, stepped onstage, sang a couple of duets with Willie, then sang several numbers of his own, making sure the crowd noticed the frayed cuffs of his bell-bottom jeans and his shiny white loafers. Leon Russell had gone country. Though the audience was more transfixed by Russell, it was still Nelson's crowd. He played far past the legal closing hour, encore after encore, then when he tried to quit a young woman jumped onstage and attacked him with affection. Moving fast to save him, Steve Kirk's subordinates hauled her away kicking and yelling. In stark contrast, Willie and Leon went out to eat afterward at an all-night roadside cafe, and they were just another hungry tableful of customers. They were outside the arena, and nobody recognized them, so they were just people.

Russell's apparent conversion to country music could mean a great deal to Willie Nelson's career. People in Nashville weren't likely to push Nelson as a country superstar, but Russell was a trend-setter. If he stayed with country and didn't prove a fickle friend, Willie just might ride to national recognition and acceptance on his coattail. Think of that: Willie Nelson smiling all across this great land, the subject of a *Playboy* interview, maybe even a *Cosmopolitan* centerfold, doing a world of good. Still, I wondered if the cultural synthesis he had forged was strictly an Austin phenomenon. His most avid Austin followers were hippies who happened to have rediscovered boots and cowboy hats. What would happen if the movement were tested out where the real rednecks lived?

> *Now John T. Floores was workin' for the Ku Klux Klan*
> *Six foot five, John T. was a hell of a man*
> *He made a lot of money sellin' sheets on the family plan*

John T. Floores lived in the country northwest of San Antonio, and he owned a so-called general store in a spot on the map called Helotes. Judging from the clutter of sings out front, he had a wealth of things to offer — sausage, real estate, insurance. But inside it was just another dance hall in the country. Pennants hung from the ceiling, along with a few advertisements, one of which offered a ''run-down beat-up shack'' for sale. Beer was available at the bar, but no liquor. It was a reminder of the past.

John T. was also a friend of Willie's from the old days. One Saturday night a month Nelson tried to get down to Helotes, raking off a lion's share of the gate but packing John T.'s joint with enough thirsty people to strain the resources of Pearl beer. I had been hearing about those Helotes gigs for several months before I finally drove over one night in November of 1973. The joint was so crowded I could barely get in, and then I couldn't find the people I was supposed to meet. I lingered in the back room, browsing through John T.'s free magazine rack, which was also a cause for hindsight. LBJ played with his grandson on the May 1972 cover of *Life*, Roger Staubach and Bob Griese scrambled on the cover of a January 1972 issue of *Time*, and Spiro Agnew proclaimed ''If I Run I Can Win'' in an April 1973 issue of *U.S. News & World Report*. It was the kind of crowd in Floores's store that I had hoped to find. Freaks from Austin, cedar-choppers from the sticks. As I stood by the vending machines looking for my friends a young woman walked by, nipples flipping under her thin blouse, and my gaze followed her through the entrance into the ladies' room, confronted there by a stout woman with wildly ratted black hair and heavily penciled eyebrows who glared so hard it almost knocked me off balance.

One of my company happened by with a beer in her hand and led me through the crowd of people sitting on the dance floor. I found the lady who had lured me to Helotes accepting swigs from the whiskey bottle of a booted, hatted young fellow who looked like he was about halfway between Austin and the sticks. He bent over and whispered something in her ear, and she turned around and said, "Do you want to go outside and smoke a joint?" The young man gave me a cold look and after that kept his whiskey to himself.

Colder and cheaper beer was out in her car, she said, and since nobody was making music at the moment, we walked outside past Asleep at the Wheel's bus, looking down the road at a Mexican *cantina*, which was equally packed and from the appearance of things — a fight in progress on the parking lot — equally exciting. We got a couple of beers out of the cooler but found that we had no opener. Searching for an icepick or axe handle, soon we stood like beggars on the roadside, asking if anyone had an opener. A young man happened by and said, "Come up here. I'll open the damn things for you."

He opened the door of an Oldsmobile, snapped the lids off our bottles with the safety belt buckle, and handed them back to us. From the look on his face, the word in his mind was: helpless.

"Thank you," I said. "Is this your car?"

"Hell no."

"Well, how'd you know you could do that?"

"I don't know a thing about it. I can just get a beer open when I need to."

Nelson had started his set by the time we got back inside and reclaimed our seats on the floor. It was the same hypnotizing music, and Willie was joined at one point by Sammi Smith, sexy as all get-out in a tight gray sweater, but there was uneasiness abroad in the land. Occupying the tables were the people who had been buying Willie Nelson's records all along; the ones who worked hard all week, went dancing on Saturday night, showed off their labels of expensive bourbon, and got down to it. Their problem in Helotes was that the dance floor was occupied by Nelson followers from Austin, whose concert procedure was to press as close as they could to the stage, sit down and stare up into his loving eyes. One table of whiskey-drinkers seemed particularly resentful. Their apparent leader was a burly fellow who looked like the Marlboro man except his moustache was waxed, his head was shaven, and he wore one large earring. All in all, he was the most frightening man I'd ever seen, and he had no redeeming sense of humor. He leaned over to confer with a younger, less formidable man who swallowed hard, nodded resentfully, and made his way into the crowd, where he fastened a bobbypin to the locks of a young Austinite, then searched for the footing to deliver the first solid blow. The Austinite pulled the pin out of his hair, looked around at his antagonist, managed a sickly grin, and turned back to Willie Nelson.

"Get them hippies off the dance floor!" the customer with the earring yelled. "We wanta *daince!*"

That old-time feeling was coming back. The tension in the neck muscles, the paranoid wondering whose unbarbered head the Jack Daniels bottle would collide against first. If Michael Murphey took me back to 23rd and Grace, Willie Nelson had taken me back to the MB corral. After a couple of impassioned requests by the management, Nelson tried to affect a compromise. Maybe some of the hippies could make room for some of the cowboys . . .

Listening to the grumbling from both sides, Willie washed his hands of the whole affair. "Y'all work it out," he said. "I'd like to do a new song now. It's called 'Sometimes It's Heaven, Sometimes It's Hell.' Sometimes I don't even know."

After a year of waiting and warding off women who wanted to tag along, I was finally going to talk to Willie Nelson. My photographer and I drove out Highway 290 past the cut-off to Jerry Jeff's house, followed the road a few more miles, then turned off a paved cowpath that wound through thick woods, past a few farmhouses, down to a low-water crossing. My photographer pulled up to a cattleguard, I opened the gate, and we drove up a gravel road toward a large, split-level ranch-style home. Nelson was outside in a T-shirt and bluejeans, inspecting a couple of horses for signs of affliction while two men stood nearby. I had seen them backstage at Willie's concert at the Texas Opry House the night before, but I didn't know them.

Willie waved hello as we got out of the car and invited us to come along while he robbed the nests of his chickens. He said his place used to be headquarters of a big ranch, and showed us a storage shed once reserved for wetback laborers. He said he owned only forty-four acres of the surrounding land.

A couple of hundred yards down the slope from his house was a clear, shallow stream called Barton Creek. Connie came out and said she was going to the store. She wanted Willie to take their daughter Carlene fishing.

Nelson disappeared into the house for a minute and came out with a fishing pole. "I couldn't find any hooks," he told his daughter, "I guess you'll have to fish without them."

He took a gardening trowel down to the water's edge and turned over a couple of shovelfuls of dirt while Caroline threw her line in the water. He introduced us to his friends, Jay Milner and Lee Clayton. Milner was a man about Willie's age, cowboy-hatted that day but a former New York journalist and later the editor of an underground paper called *The Iconoclast* that scandalized the Dallas establishment. Clayton was closer to my age, squinting and quiet and thoughtful. He was also shy. When my photographer said she had seen him before at Castle Creek, he said, "Yeah, I remember your camera." Blushing, he said, "That didn't sound right, did it? What I meant was that I remembered a lady photographer."

Clayton, I would later learn, was a Texan who had made his Austin debut on the preliminary bill of the ill-fated '72 Dripping Springs Reunion. He had been living a nomadic existence for a couple of years, but like Nelson, he had migrated to Nashville and written an impressive song, "Ladies Love Outlaws," that was recorded by Waylon Jennings. He had recorded one album of his own, and also like Willie, had tried to form his own band and gone broke. Clayton was considered one of the most promising songwriters around by the Nelson-Jennings-Shaver crowd, but I didn't know any of that at the time. All I knew was that he had the air of an insider when he came in the Texas Opry backstage area the night before and told Gary Nunn he had gotten his hair cut recently. Not wanting to be ignorant in the presence of a celebrity, I tried to coax some information out of Milner while Clayton and Nelson were helping Caroline with her fishing pole. "Lee got his hair cut since he was here last, didn't he?"

"Yeah, ever since he hit town he's been telling people who he was. Last night at Castle Creek he went up to Doug Sahm and said, 'Hi, I'm Lee Clayton. I got my hair cut.' "

I learned no more about Clayton that day and I never could find his album, but I liked him immediately. As we were walking up a slope toward the house, he knocked me off a copperhead I had stepped on. Willie killed the snake, and resolving to stop walking around barefoot at night, he ushered us to chairs in a little room with a wide variety of potted plants and unobstructed views toward the grounds.

Nelson was more willing to talk about his past than any of the other performers I had met. He discussed his parents and grandparents, the first gig in West for eight dollars and the family band with the trombone-playing football coach. Then he remembered reporting to Lackland Air Force Base in San Antonio: "The first day I was there a sergeant got up in my face and started shouting, so I just knocked the shit out of him. That's what we were used to doing. They didn't do much to me, I guess they wanted to give me a second chance. I finally decided hitting him wasn't the answer. But I began to get tired of the military way of doing things, and an old hay-baling injury of my early youth finally got to me, so I regretfully ended my career in the United States Air Force."

"When did you decide you wanted to make music for a living?"

"As soon as I found out I could. When I first made that eight dollars in West. Later on I'd been picking cotton and baling hay for fifteen cents a day. It wasn't a difficult decision."

He discussed his early music career in Texas then said, "I went to Nashville in a '41 Buick that I was behind two payments on. It made it to Nashville and just settled to earth, never moved again."

My photographer asked if he had been encouraged to come to Nashville.

"No, I just went in cold, on my own."

"Isn't it hard to make it like that in Nashville?" she asked.

"Damn near impossible," Nelson replied, glancing over to Clayton for confirmation, continuing that Nashville songwriters and musicians were so jealous of their money and stature that they became as much of a problem as the recording and publishing companies.

"It's like a circle," Clayton said, "the ones on the inside, the ones on the outside. Unless somebody on the inside notices you, you're never gonna break in."

Nelson recounted his early days in Nashville, and I asked him about the Charley Pride episode. He said a friend called him and recommended, "Man, I think you ought to book this nigger on the tour. He sings his ass off.

"I said you gotta be crazy. We can't take no niggers into Dallas and Shreveport. They'd hang us. But I heard a couple of his records on the car radio and he didn't sound colored at all. I called Crash back, and said listen, if you can still get that nigger . . .

"When we got to Dallas I made out the program to where I'd follow him. Pride walked out and said, 'I guess you're probably wondering what a man with a permanent tan like myself is doing singing country music, but I like it and I hope you enjoy hearing it as much as I enjoy singing it.' He Uncle Tommed them into a standing ovation. They were yelling for Charley Pride all through my set. The next night I said bullshit, I'm not following him, so I went on before, and Hank Williams Jr. went on after. They couldn't boo Hank Williams."

"Tell him about the time you kissed him onstage," Milner said.

"That was in Shreveport or Baton Rouge, I think. We didn't know what was going to happen there, so I really laid it on about him and when he walked out I kissed him, kissed him on the mouth. Of course we had to move on fast to something else, but by the time they got over the shock he was already playing, and he had them hooked."

Clayton laughed and said, "Yeah, but later on they were looking for the guy who kissed that nigger."

Clayton exclaimed suddenly and pointed outside. Nelson had three or four peacocks on the place, and the male was showing his colors, stomping and calling, his feathers shimmering. The female moved away, apparently disinterested.

"That means he's horny," Nelson said. "I think I'm going to start wearing him for a hat when I perform."

"Dr. John would pick that right up," Clayton said.

"Yeah, and give him a pill that'd make him flare up every night."

Clayton was most taken by the spectacle. He seemed to drift away; one could almost hear the songwriting wheels turning. "That tells you how far man has gotten away from nature," he said. "On our side the woman's the one that primps up." He asked Willie if the birds had a regular mating season.

"Well, I know he's always in season. He does this every day."

Coaxed into a reflective mood, Milner discussed the changes ten years had affected in Austin. He said when he first came to town politics was on everybody's mind, for the liberals appeared on the verge of taking over state government. Now the politicans were back in the same old rut, and nobody seemed to pay much attention. I said the politicians were courting the musicians just like everybody else.

Nelson said, "Yeah, but I've noticed some of the politicians are having trouble lining up the musicians now."

"You're not doing much of that, are you?" my photographer said.

"No, I decided to stay out of politics this year."

Clayton nodded. "It didn't help Sammy Davis Jr. much."

"How did you like living in Nashville?" I asked Nelson.

"I liked Tennessee very well. I've still got a farm down there. But I eventually just quit going to town. They have their own way of doing things there.

"I was just in Nashville. A lot of new blood's coming in, younger people. They're doing everything they can to change their image. Because places like Austin are growing, their image is starting to hurt them, and when that happens it'll hurt their pocketbooks, so they'll change then. It's a hard town, there's no doubt about it. They don't give a shit if you pack up and leave, in fact they'd just as soon you did."

"Are there a lot of places to play in Nashville?"

"No," Clayton said, "it's mostly a place for songwriters."

"Sitting around and talking to writers in Nashville is the most depressing thing in the world," Willie said. "There are just so many of them — and it gets to the point where it's niggers and dogs and writers, stay off the grass.

"The thing about Nashville is that those session musicians are so good that it sounds like manufactured music. There's no feeling to it at all. And you can't help that when you're playing nine hours a day every day. But they're making so much money they can't afford to change. The musicians know they could do better. But they make more and more money and they make good records, all right, but the trouble with them is that they're too perfect. And just because a man's a good studio musician doesn't mean he'll be a good night-club musician, and vice versa. Also, when you get in a studio in front of the mike and a red light comes on, you tense up."

Clayton said, "Some of the best music in Nashville is the first couple of run-throughs that never got on tape."

"Also," Nelson went on, "a lot of them have their own publishing companies, so they want to record their own stuff. That way they'll make more money. So pretty soon music becomes a business."

"Which is the reason you start making music in the first place," Clayton said. "To get away from business."

"Does that mean the reverse is true in Austin?" I said. "That the imperfections of Austin music are its virtue?"

Nelson blinked and leaned forward. "I didn't get the last part of that . . ."

306

"You said Nashville music is too polished. Is Austin music unpolished?"

Milner guffawed. "That's not what you said the first time around."

Nelson grinned and looked over at Clayton. "No, I'd rather think that we're somewhere between perfect and half-perfect. The mistakes, we call that soul. I'm always building on mistakes, trying to turn them into hot licks, and that's not always easy to do."

Milner observed that Nelson played differently in different situations, and he often played tricks on the crowd. The night before he had played "Bloody Mary Morning," a virtual rock number, then gone straight into an agonizingly slow song, "I Still Can't Believe You're Gone." "That popped their necks," Milner said. "That's dangerous."

"Well, you have to catch them with their feet in the air," Willie said. "Like kissing a nigger onstage."

Clayton laughed again at the effect that act must have had on the audience. "You've given us a new expression, Willie. Kiss a nigger."

"Maybe a new song," Nelson said. "Kiss a Nigger Good Mornin'."

Milner told a story of a musician who came to Austin and witnessed one of Nelson's performances then went away expressing belief that Willie could do anything he wanted with those people. On the other hand, my photographer said, the Texas Opry crowd the night before had worked itself into such a frenzy that they were trying to swarm onstage and assume control.

"I always thought that would be a hell of a way to go," Clayton said. "Being ripped apart by a crowd."

"What about Austin?" I said. "Can the music here get off nationally?"

"I think it already has," Nelson said. "Jerry Jeff and Michael Murphey are getting a lot of national attention. There's got to be a big rush — I can already see the songwriters coming, songs by the trunkload."

Could Austin be another Nashville?

"Easily. As soon as the money gets down here. As soon as the recording studios get set up."

"In order for that to happen, won't the money and technicians have to be imported?"

He nodded. "Everbody's waiting for me to do it, but I'm not ready to get that far into it yet. I would like to record here, however. But we'd have to get a good engineer and a couple of good Nashville musicians."

My photographer asked if there were enough good musicians in Austin to man those studios.

He nodded again. "It wouldn't have the Nashville polish, unless you brought in a couple of hot-shots who could do it just like that, and mix them with the others, who are slower. The musicians in Austin could learn a lot from Nashville musicians. They're good here, but what they lack is the ability to work in one unit. It would take some time, but pretty soon you'd know who the top three guitar players in Austin are."

"Wouldn't that be perpetuating the same thing?"

"Sure. The first thing you know you've got the clique going again, and the top three won't want to let the fourth one in."

"And you've got another circle," Clayton said. "When it really gets good, that's when it'll start going bad."

Wasn't that an alarming prospect?

"Well," Nelson said slowly, "there's nothing to stop us from setting up in Luckenbach, if we want to. The organizers are gonna come in, but I think we can frustrate them. Just by making a point of never getting caught with any of the money people."

"Will you move if it gets too bad?" my photographer asked.

Willie's daughter was playing the piano in another room. He gazed out at his peacocks, the manicured slope down toward Barton Creek, the woods beyond.

"No, I don't know what could ever make me move."

PART III

It's the fault of whoever's name is stamped on the ticket.

Michael Murphey

the day
of the locust

A highway patrolman stood in the middle of the road, directed the traffic onto a whitened strip of pavement that veered off to the right. No cause for alarm; there were too many people to frisk. Though maintained by the county, the detour was one of those roads that made the state of Texas so proud. Graded about the time of Job and paved shortly after the electric cooperatives rendered kerosene lanterns obsolete and rural folks exchanged their outdoor crappers for septic tanks, it served the needs of the farmers and ranchers and a few reclusive dope-dealers, ushering their produce to market. You could get to anywhere in Texas by car. Or so we thought ...

It was the Fourth of July, with a honky-tonk twist — the first of Willie Nelson's Picnics. My magazine collaborator and I were getting too creaky in the joints to subject ourselves to many more outdoor music festivals, and as we motored out Highway 290 toward Dripping Springs, we had adjusted our sunshades and checked our waterbag for leaks and wondered what lay in store for us. A year earlier the 1972 Dripping Springs Reunion had flopped financially, but it was the first large-scale mix of the opposing Austin cultures. Aspiring, dope-smoking gate-crashers were taken aback by the sight of uniformed security guards toting shotguns, and a Veteran of Foreign Wars trinket vendor was equally taken aback by a young man who flipped his Frisbee in the air and remarked, ''If we'd quit having wars we wouldn't have any veterans.''

The uneasiness had extended onstage. Tex Ritter sang awhile then emceed awhile too long, cracking lame Black Panther jokes and trying to bar Tom T. Hall from the microphone though the crowd was bellowing for an encore. Roy Acuff declared that *he* was the by-god king of country music, then crowed in triumph when an emcee announced that Merle Haggard was in a state of collapse and wouldn't make his scheduled appearance. ''If that had happened to me or one of the boys in my band,'' Acuff claimed, ''we'd a *been* here.''

The final contrast, however, was reserved for last. Loretta Lynn came out in Easter-Sunday curls and petticoats and bowled the crowd over. Several encores later, the crowd had worked itself into a shouting stomping frenzy, and the last performer on the bill, Kris Kristofferson, didn't care for that kind of mood. He wanted a listening audience but people in the darkness kept yelling at him, demanding a song from his new companion Rita Coolidge, who was singing harmony at his side. ''Jack off,'' Kristofferson finally growled in response. With irreverent disregard for Kristofferson's temperamental outburst, the crowd continued to ignore his efforts to gain their respectful attention. He sang a few rough numbers then stalked offstage, cries for encore be damned.

This year my collaborator and I had been promised, the uniformed security guards would be replaced by a few friendly hippies hired to make sure traffic flowed in the right direction. This year according to rumor, Roy Acuff and Loretta Lynn would be replaced by Leon Russell and Bob Dylan. Best of all, this time earnest commoners had turned into card-carrying party regulars. My collaborator and I had proudly pinned press passes to our shirts, and just the night before, we had measured our East Coast competitors and found them wanting. We had chatted amiably with John Prine, and today we would meet Rita Coolidge. Pant. As we drove out we had allowed the more frenzied traffic to pass and discussed the implicatons of what we were seeing. Judging from the vehicle count, Willie Nelson had guessed right; Texans were primed for the honky-tonk of their lives. Maybe what people were saying was true. Maybe this time it would be a country Woodstock, the inspiration of an artistic, social, even philosophical movement. As we neared the town of Dripping Springs, my collaborator had looked out the window at a helicopter battering the air overhead and said, ''Willie the Fourth.'' We both laughed.

But then, just after we passed the highway patrolman, the stream of traffic logjammed. A mile of cars in front of us, none of them moving. It was to be expected, we supposed, and it wasn't far to the festival site. A predictable delay. We drummed our fingers on the dashboard and watched a couple of buzzards wheel over the sun-bleached landscape, then I looked down and noticed my temperature gauge needle was edging over toward the danger zone.

"Stop it now," I warned, but the needle defied me. I shut down the air conditioner and we rolled down the windows, but the indicator continued to torment me. As the needle edged into the danger zone, I pulled the Toyota into the ditch and parked it. "To hell with this," I said. "Let's walk. If we take out over that hill it's only a couple of miles."

As I remembered the terrain from our press-party trip the night before, the festival site was within relatively easy walking distance, though the road took a roundabout way of getting there. The heat was still bearable if you got a little breeze, the Hill Country was in faded summer bloom, and our feet were fairly well equipped for hiking. Why not make this a real outing in the woods?

Trouble of it was, the two or three hills I remembered turned into four or five. I walked fast, reverting to my old Camp Pendleton route-step to cover the distance more efficiently, but my collaborator kept getting entangled in brambles, looking around nervously at our tail — a horse and Holstein and Hereford yearling. Like Herb Steiner, he was a Texan by way of Brooklyn and California, and the sight of all that hooved tonnage unnerved him. "Hey. Um, are those things all right? I mean . . ."

"Aw, don't worry about them," I scoffed. "They just think we're taking them to feed."

Then we saw the Angus bull.

Stepping quickly along, we climbed another hill past a house and my collaborator wondered aloud if we might get shot for trespassing.

"Nah. If they didn't want us on their land they should've fenced it."

I heard someone shout, and I peered through the trees to our right. A young man sat on the fender of a car, drinking beer. Uncapping my waterbag, I wet my lips and thought a minute. Surely we hadn't been slashing through hostile brush all this time within shouting distance of the road. The terrain was playing tricks on me. As I remembered the road, it should have curved off in the other direction a long time ago.

313

Oh well. What I needed was a compass. I still thought I knew the general direction to the festival site, and I led my collaborator away from the road at a more drastic angle. We stalked up one particularly steep hill, then looked down.

It was moderately steep precipice, though it was difficult to gauge precisely because of the six-foot jungle of weeds, brush, and brambles. We summoned our energy for the effort, then I looked down at my shirt. "God damn it," I said. "I've lost my press pass."

By some minor miracle, I only had to retrace my steps a few yards to retrieve the blessed credential, and we plunged over the cliff into the thorny jungle, keeping track of each other with our thrashing and cursing, expecting to feel rattlesnake fangs sink into our calves at any minute. Finally we crashed out into a clearing, removed the shredded leaves from our teeth, and saw a group of children throwing a ball around a couple of hundred yards away. A camp counselor in sneakers, khaki bermudas and T-shirt walked toward us and said, "Hidy fellas. Can I help you?"

"No, we're just trying to find the rock concert. Do you know where it is?"

"No, not really," he said. "Several miles, I believe."

Several miles? How many were several? "Well, how far away are we from the road?"

"It depends," he said. "If you walk along the creek there, maybe a mile. But if you cross it you'll run into the road in no time."

I looked at the stream, and saw no bridges. "How deep is it?"

"Oh, you'll get wet, but you won't drown."

My collaborator and I took off our boots and rolled up our jeans and forded the creek, then walked in defeat back toward the road. I couldn't understand it. I hadn't hallucinated our drive to the festival site the night before, and I was better at estimating distance and direction than this. "Some pathfinder," my collaborator grumbled.

When we got to the road we saw that the pavement had played out into gravel, and cars, people and dogs were clothed in a chalky coat of white caliche dust. We hitched the first ride available, and jostled along uncomfortably, more stop than go, sweltering during the long waits. We could move faster — or at least cooler — walking than that, so we got out and trudged onward until the traffic started moving again, then hitched another ride. Minutes wore into hours as we battled exhaust fumes and drivers that wouldn't stop and that white, suffocating dust. Finally hitchhiking banter was a thing of the past. "Get in," someone would glumly say, and we would collapse on their tailgate, gasping for oxygen. A haunting suspicion began to creep into my mind. What if there were two roads to the festival site, and the highway patrolman had directed us down the wrong one? We could be ten miles away from Willie's Picnic, and we were moving at a walking pace. There was also no way to turn back. The motorists had long ago taken over the oncoming lane, and their cars overheated side by side. Foolhardy souls walked along the roadside carrying large coolers of beer, finally gave up and salvaged what they could, gave the rest away. One girl sat with her chin in her hands in a bar-ditch beside her footsore dog. The cries of infants were heard from time to time. Willie Nelson's Picnic had turned into a one-way traffic jam in the wilderness.

Finally, my day began to pick up. We had hitched a ride in a Ford van for the second time and I sat nervously in the back. The driver's son had taken an instant dislike to me for some reason. Every once in a while he eyed me meanly and hefted a toy truck in his hand, apparently weighing the consequences of bouncing it off my skull. But then the Ford lurched to a halt, and my collaborator and I were joined in the back by a sorority of hippie girls from Dallas. "Water," one of them said, demanding my waterbag. I surrendered it and watched rather jealously as it was passed around. I doubt Jesus himself would have allowed the harlot to drink from his well had he known she was going to drink it dry. Wedged against the wall next to me, however, was a comely red-haired girl with something of a smile in her eyes. She said her Corvair had given up the ghost, apparently for good, several miles back. Our bodies were thrown into frequent contact as the van lurched and braked, and as cool a customer as they come, soon she let her pale little thigh rest comfortably against mine. It was wordless communication, but I do believe it had meaning. What picnic, I thought as something began to stir inside my jeans, but then the driver of the van shouted hooray.

Standing in the roadway, hair gray and matted from the dirt, was a shirtless young man directing all customers without tickets down the road to the right. Advance buyers could proceed straight ahead. The Texas Highway Patrol (or maybe it was Willie) had indeed done us in. I remembered this intersection. Several men had been discouraging campers here the night before, and the road I remembered veered off to the left. The girls began to gather their belongings, and one of them opened the van door. The red-haired girl looked at me. I looked at her. She moved her thigh away and made signs of following the others. "Wait," I said dispassionately, foam frothing at my lips. "Don't run off. You've got your ticket, don't you. Don't you?" She shook her head and tugged her cut-off jeans back down to decency. "Look for me," she said as she clanged the van door shut.

The van driver decided to park disastrously early, and my collaborator and I soon found ourselves on the roadside again, only this time the traffic was moving fast. The dust billowed over us and driver after driver passed us by, and only after we could no longer run our fingers through our hair did we hitch a final ride. As we neared the gate we encountered more dusty people standing by the roadside. I felt like a passenger in one of Rommel's tanks. The desert natives extended their arms to us and shouted in some unknown tongue:

"Don't try to get in without a ticket!"

"Don't try it; they'll make you go back!"

"I just happen to have a couple of extras!"

"Two for the price of one!"

Finally our driver pulled over and began his long arduous search for a parking place, and my collaborator and I stretched our stiff legs and walked toward the entrance gate. No one was there to take tickets.

Nobody to take the customers' tickets?

No one to stamp our hands and fall to their knees at the sight of our press passes and anoint our heads with oil?

What is this?

If anybody was high priest of the Austin movement the big-time, it was Willie Nelson, the grinning, gentle rebel who made the music industry come to him on his own terms yet remained the almost universally admired nice guy and artist. He had become a symbolic figure, the one man whose approach to life and music made sense of Austin's curious mix of freaks and rednecks, trepidation and ambition, naivete and striving professionalism. Though it was still a highly localized phenomenon, Nelson had become a cultural hero, and he knew it. He also had a couple of kids to educate.

Nelson had turned over a lot of money in his life, but that was his whole problem. People kept getting rich at his expense, and he didn't delude himself into thinking that. He watched it happen. Logic should have told him he wouldn't make a very good businessman. He stayed up and drank all night and played music for his friends, then staggered into the office every few days to see what was going on. He expected people to treat him as nicely as he treated them, but he was dealing with people as shrewd and tight-fisted and conniving as some mean old Texas writer. The music-business people took him for a ride every time they could hook a boot in his stirrups. What was interesting, though, was that unlike many of his old Nashville friends who looked past the promoters and franchise entrepreneurs to the staid relative safety of Wall Street, Nelson stayed in the ring with the music businessmen. He tried to be careful, but he sank his money into music-business ventures time and time again, and almost always he came out wondering where the profits went. The best he could do, it seemed, was break even.

Surveying his Texas domain, however, and noting that the site of the '72 Dripping Springs Reunion was still available, he thought he might stage a little one-day festival featuring Austin performers and some of his friends from Nashville, and maybe sneak out of that canyon with ten or fifteen thousand. The only thing that had gone wrong the year before was the lack of promotion. The weather and crowd interest were fine the first time around, and that was a year before Austin music really boomed. Now everybody in the state was excited about long-hair country music. In addition, anything with Willie Nelson on its masthead was bound to go over big. All he needed to do was borrow $25,000, kick in a couple of thousand of his own, keep a tight rein on the business end of it, and hire nobody to work for him except Texas people he could trust. The only problem was the weather. Scheduling an outdoor festival was a precarious venture in Texas. If you scheduled it too early in the spring you ran the risk of a numbing late cold front, and if you scheduled it too late you ran the risk of mass heat exhaustion. By the time Nelson got rolling on the project, though, it was too late to schedule it in midspring. It would have to be midsummer. All right. Why not make it on a holiday, thereby strengthening the prospects of a large crowd? Texans were used to getting sunburned on the Fourth of July anyway. Hell yes. There might even be a movie.

Enter Michael Price, publisher of *Rallying Point*. Price's interpretation as a character in Austin music depended upon whom one talked to. Some insisted he was just another carpetbagging hustler who happened to have grown up in Texas and learned the native dialect.

Others accepted him as a moderately fiery radical who ate mescaline in his mid-thirties and wanted to move back to Texas like so many others. Whatever the truth of Michael Price, he adopted Willie Nelson during one of his visits to New York and determined to make a national figure of him. Riding with Willie one night in the Texas countryside, he noticed that a weak-watted rural station played a Nelson song every few minutes, with increasing regularity until they played an entire side of *Shotgun Willie*. "What the shit is this, Willie?" Price said. "Do you own that station?"

Nelson grinned and said, "Let me listen a minute. I think it might be better than that." The disc jockey eventually announced the call letters of the station and Willie said, "Yeah, that's the one. I used to push a broom for that old man and now he loves me."

Price's idea of a movie included an initial segment like that. The camera would be in the car with Willie as he talked and drove through Texas and his music played on the car radio, then there would be a sudden cut to a mock World's Fair at Luckenbach, which promised to draw about 20,000 highly diverse but similarly crazed Texans. The final cut would be the Willie Nelson Picnic, cameras moving about and focusing alternately on performers and crowd in the manner of *Woodstock*. It might make one hell of a movie. It also might mean the national acceptance of Austin music.

Price had a friend in New York named Francois DeMonil who had a lot of money and wanted to make films, and he had a friend in Houston who was already a film veteran by his late twenties and could assemble a professional crew on command. DeMonil's parents were French, but they were also some of the richest wildcatters in Houston. DeMonil could raise the money if he thought it wise, and he fronted $15,000 and agreed to film the movie, providing Nelson could get releases from the big-name performers. Hell, that was no problem. These people were Willie's friends. Up the hill and over the top, boys. On to fame and fortune.

Possibly because of Nelson's good name, but probably because the canyon near Dripping Springs was owned by a rancher named Burt Hurlbut who was bound and determined to do anything he wanted with his land, the Hays County commissioners were no obstacle to the festival. There were some strings attached to Hurlbut, of course. He wanted $2500 for the lease of his land and $350 for personal inconvenience, control over the concessions, and some work done to

318

Willie's Dripping Springs picnickers came from both camps of the Texas country audience, though the freaks adapted to the discomfort with greater ease.

Preparations for the festival were hectic and disorganized, but a variously costumed crowd of 40,000 proved that Nelson had guessed right: Texans were primed for the honky-tonk of their lives.

restore the facilities. Roads needed to be regraded, the Port-O-San privies were in bad shape, and new lights needed to be strung. And of course, contracts for that labor would need to go to local electricians and plumbers and graders who had lost heavily at the Dripping Springs Reunion.

Nelson was getting himself into hot water by inviting everybody he knew of any worth and talent to make an appearance, and his old inability to say no was increasing his pot to a boil. Some acts that should have been in the audience talked themselves onstage. The primary case in point was an act called the Threadgills, a wholesome group of teenagers whose father fancied himself one of the better Texas songwriters around. Drawing on the name of his famous third cousin, Kenneth Threadgill, the father was trying to turn his throng into an Austin version of the Partridge Family. The Threadgills signed on, but nobody remembered to invite Kenneth Threadgill, and when the time came for the cut-off, that was just too bad.

Worse than that, nothing was getting done on the business end. Nelson's trusted but inexperienced gang of friends had no real idea what they were doing, and finally, on June 23, Willie went to the most trustworthy music businessmen he knew of — Eddie Wilson and his herd of Armadillos. Wilson came aboard for $5,000 for his establishment, $5,000 for his site manager, a modest $500 for himself, $500 for his lawyer, $1,000 for his accountant, and whatever clerical and incidental expenses the project might entail. Wilson and his gang worked like wild men from the outset, and for a few days everything began to look better. A promotion campaign was launched quickly, and radio spots began to be heard all over the state.

But then the movie began to unravel. The *mañana* attitude Eddie Wilson talked about began to get to the film crew. DeMonil's strawboss spent idle hours waiting for Wilson's site manager to arrive, blaming it on the Armadillos' fondness for marijuana, and Price and DeMonil were growing increasingly nervous. Price went into the project with the understanding that Nelson was his own manager, but he soon found that Willie had hired a man to say no for him, Neil Rashen, who said no to just about everything Price proposed. More nervous than Price was DeMonil. He had $15,000 on the line, and he wanted those performers' releases. Nelson's attitude was typically based on trust. Go ahead and film it, he told DeMonil, and he would talk to the performers privately about the film. Let the performers see the finished product, and if they liked it, they would sign releases. Even the most obstinate artists needed that kind of exposure. If they wouldn't or couldn't obtain releases, edit them out. That's the way they did it at Woodstock.

Granted, the filmmakers argued, but *Woodstock* was a shot in the dark that saw light against long odds. DeMonil was talking about a $100,000 investment. He wasn't about to fork over that much on Willie's assurance he would *talk* to the men and women in the film. Finally, DeMonil started consulting the performers' agents and managers, something that Willie would have known never to do, and their unanimous answer was: absolutely not. A week before the festival the film came down, as the saying went in the movie business, throwing the Armadillo site manager into a panic because he was depending on DeMonil's strawboss to arrange for the construction of a roof over the stage. The filmmakers accused the Armadillos of employing DeMonil's $15,000 to finance the promotion drive. Willie Nelson said he had DeMonil's money in a safe the whole time. Ugly words were exchanged. Lawsuits were threatened.

Still, there was an outside chance a film might come about. Kit Carson, a Hollywood director who promoted a movie festival in Dallas every year, was reputed to have Kris Kristofferson ties and he knew Mike Tolleson. He had been poking around the area, sniffing out the possibilities of a film of his own, and he still might be able to do it. However, Michael Price barged into the Armadillo office and said, "Gentlemen, if one camera rolls out there I'm going to sue your asses off."

His audience responded that no contracts had been signed.

"Contracts!" Price responded. "I have your handshake and verbal agreement. Don't tell me how Texas business works."

DeMonil quickly got his money back, but the damage was done as far as Price was concered. "There went my magazine," he said as DeMonil departed with a bitter taste in his mouth. Though he had had his differences with the Armadillos, particularly Mike Tolleson, Price reserved his harshest remarks for Nelson. "Sure, I'd work with Willie again," he said. "That's the only way I could ever get him back. But if anybody ever has a chance to say anything to Willie Nelson, tell him he made a mistake."

As June turned into July more trouble signs dawned on the horizon. Performers' contracts went unsigned. Tom T. Hall never was officially invited but he made plans to show up anyway. Doug Sahm, who according to some was the source of the Bob Dylan rumor, couldn't be reached by his manager. Kristofferson was in New Mexico July 1 when he found out he was going to make an appearance at Dripping Springs. Charlie Rich called and said he might just sue his old friend Willie for using his name in the promotions. Even the simplest of details were hard to iron out. Everyone who showed up to pick up his or her press credentials at the Armadillo was invited to a special press party at the festival site the night of July 3. Lots of beer, barbecue, and meat for their stories. But plans were made for that very slowly. "Cabrito?" concessionaire Burt Hurlbut drawled. "Now how many people do you figure a scrawny little ole goat will feed? Four or five, you imagine? What's the price of beef these days?"

That night at the festival site people wandered around from campfire to campfire inquiring if this were the press party. John Prine, who spoke with a slight lisp, stood by one of the concession stands and looked at a cold burrito someone had handed him. "I got off the plane and somebody told me we were going to a barbecue. So we go bouncing off thirty miles into the country and I'm still expecting a barbecue . . ." He looked at the blackness around him. Waylon Jennings was there in his gunslinger black leather, slapping old friends on the back, but performers were otherwise scare. But the press was there: *Texas Observers*, Mad Dogs Incorporated, Townsend Miller and his bag of harmonicas, a young man with a British accent who said he had never covered country music before, hefty New Yorkers in Oldsmobiles who hailed slender Texans in Toyotas to a halt at the entrance gate.

"Whereya goin'?"

"To a press party."

"There's not any press party. There's *nothin'*."

Even those who stood around the favored fire were made to feel uneasy. Two long-hairs in cowboy hats drank the free Pearl and peppered their language with cocksuckers and worse, and an older, short-haired man took offense.

The long-hair who had spoken too loudly became extravagant with apologies, but his friend was militant. "No, now what's the deal here? I mean he said a simple word. A word. Who are you to tell him he —"

"Well, he's drinkin' my beer," the man said angrily, "and he's leanin' on my pickup truck. I'm tellin' him to shut his mouth."

What few people knew was that the performers were there all the time, hidden in the bowels of four and twenty motor homes scattered about the premises. Leon Russell was there to make his Hank Wilson debut, somewhat ludicrous in appearance with all that hair and an undersize cowboy straw hat, and Willie and Leon and Kris and Waylon and all the others stayed up all night, performing the best music of the festival before an audience of friends.

The next day Nelson went onstage at six in the morning backed by a blinking, greybearded drummer named Leon, and the festival was underway. It was pleasant for a while. Steve Fromholz, who had just recorded his Michael Nesmith album and didn't know the roof was about to cave in again, played his early set then hung around the backstage, talking about his forthcoming release. John Prine played his set and left. Hank Wilson drank a lot, emceed a little, declined all interviews, and led a swarming horde of groupies around the backstage area. *"Leon,"* a journalist yelled. Leon bounced off both doorsills and disappeared into the Winnebago. Nelson, who had impulsively shaved his beard and cut his hair following a particularly hot golf round with Darrell Royal, walked around greeting old friends and making new ones. Sammi Smith requested directions to her dressing room. Billy Joe Shaver and family got caught in the traffic jam, but after a couple miles' run with guitar in hand he bounded onstage just in time to play his set. Kenneth Threadgill, who had motored out in his Winnebago with younger friends, got Jennings and Kristofferson together in hopes of breaking his recording stalemate. Eddie Wilson found Threadgill and asked him if he was willing to perform.

"I didn't bring my band," Threadgill said. "I'm just a guest out here."

"Yeah, but Willie really wants you to play," Wilson said.

Everybody was there. In fact, everybody in the world was there. In most music concerts of any size, a journalistic pecking order was inevitably established. First priority went to *Rolling Stone*, with deference toward *Crawdaddy, Creem, Zoo World*, and *New York Times Magazine*, in about that order. After that, it became *Texas Monthly*, who's *Texas Monthly*? Or, *Texas Monthly*? Are they freaky enough? The Armadillos didn't work that way, however. They were generous with their press passes to a fault, dispensing them not only to photographers who came all the way from Japan, but to a couple of girls who had hitchhiked from New York to see Waylon Jennings and told the Armadillo interviewer they were the Long Island country station, WHN. Apparently a lot of professional photographers had traded in their Leicas for Instamatics. That backstage overload resulted in a clash between the music industry's most obnoxious elements — the flunkies and the hangers-on.

Flunkies were those lower-echelon employees who manned the barrier between paying customers' hell and performers' heaven. They were always underpaid, always instructed to use their good judgment but follow their orders, i.e., to keep the masses away from the celebrities. Hangers-on were those who longed to see those magic people close up, to watch them scratch their asses and pick their teeth, to smell their very farts. Of course, hanging on was an understandable passion. If one lurked around backstage areas long enough, he was bound to come across some dope of remarkable quality.

As the backstage crowd grew, tempers began to wear short. Waylon Jennings said he was not going to play because he simply did not have room. Mrs. Darrell Royal, known among friends as a down-to-earth woman who once invited a black tile-setter to her special box at a football game (thereby triggering a rush by regents' wives to meet the visiting African ambassador,) made the mistake of asking one of the harried Armadillos to fetch her a glass of iced tea.

"Those goddamn hillbillies," Eddie Wilson fumed.

Finally, it was decided, enough was enough. The backstage madness had to stop. Lacking an experienced foreman, the novice security guards were faced with a murderous task. Nobody else backstage, they ruled, press passes or no press passes. They formed a cordon, warding off the displeased people who were yelling at them. A cameraman named Happy Jack, who had signed on with the UPI crew which was going to deliver secondary footage to Nelson for his private use, had to go in and out frequently because of the nature of his job, and finally he screamed unhappily at one of the flunkies: "What the *hell* did you give me a press pass for if it's no good, you *son of a bitch*!" A security guard intercepted a young woman with a pass affixed to her skirt, yelled, "I've told you three times you can't come in here," and shoved her to the ground.

Listen, *Rolling Stone*'s Chet Flipo quietly chided Wilson, who barreled about with a walkie-talkie pressed against his ear. You can't do this. These people have a job to do. Somebody's going to burn you.

"All right," Wilson said. "To prove a point, I'll try to get you past them. I don't even know if *I* can get you in."

Finally, as the sun sank lower and the day cooled off, things began to look better. The set was finally cleared during Charlie Rich's set, and Paul English got married onstage as groomsman Waylon Jennings scowled out at the noisy crowd. Despite the inconvenience of the traffic jam, most of the people in the crowd seemed to be enjoying themselves. One girl, who had hitchhiked from El Paso — 593 miles — on the basis of that Dylan-Russell rumor, said she liked the music fine, though she was unfamiliar with most of the performers. She supposed they were local acts from San Antonio. Some took off their clothes to get uniformly sunburned. Each of the performers was greeted with an earthquake roar of sound. But the crowd stood in long lines in front of the portable privies, waited for ice that never arrived, purchased drugs from people they didn't know. Personnel from the Austin Free Clinic, who were only being paid free beer for their trouble, rushed around attending the more serious casualties — primarily those who ingested common toadstools peddled as psilocybin mushrooms. The less serious cases rested where they fell. One doctor, summoned to the side of a fallen man by a panicked journalist, inspected the patient's mouth, opened his eyes, then walked away from him. "Heat exhaustion?" the journalist asked. The doctor shook his head. "Wine prostration."

As dark fell on the festival, Kris Kristofferson, who was in a much better mood than he had been the year before, stood beside Rita Coolidge, who sat in a chair, pretty and affable but afraid of the crowd. (Her fears proved warranted. During her set one of the hangers-on was so overwhelmed by her charms that he leaped from behind an amplifier to hug her, only to grab an armful of a nimble security guard named Smokey.) As Kristofferson began to play, Happy Jack and the rest of the UPI crew began to complain. They had been promised they would be able to set their f-stops at four and leave them there, but the lighting was insufficient. A crewman for Showco, the Dallas production company which was providing the sound and lighting, yelled, "In one minute I'm going to knock your eyes out with two super troopers!" In one minute the the lighting improved all right, but it only took an instant for the overloaded circuit message to reach a transformer miles from the festival site, and Willie's Picnic plunged into total darkness.

Hangers-on began to skulk like hyenas back onstage. Somebody raised a call for flashlights and Coleman lanterns. A mysterious young man walked up to a dead mike, announced the lights would come back on at 3 a.m. When somebody finally produced a gasoline generator for the microphones, an emcee asked for patience, and a drunk deputy sheriff suggested that everybody get naked. As a large portion of the audience groped toward the parking lot somebody thought of plugging into a Winnebago, and the show, not so loud and much dimmer, got pathetically underway again. Tom T. Hall, who once likened himself to Hemingway on a nationally televised talk show, came out and said that it was just great that country people could let their hair down just like rockers — not that he had anything against rockers. He broke a string on his guitar, and following the lead of his Woodstock predecessors, threw his $300 instrument to the crowd. A fistfight ensued. One musician or another played until 2:30 the next morning, and dawn found a pile of garbage that would have filled Armadillo World Headquarters wall to wall, floor to ceiling. Nobody had thought to retain a refuse collector. It would cost $14,865.11 to find one at that late date.

The gross revenue of the festival amounted to $111,398.60. That was a fair-sized coin sack, but a Department of Public Safety helicopter observer estimated the crowd at 40,000. Even at reduced advance-ticket prices, if that were true the gross should have run to something like $420,000. The Armadillos blamed the disparity between the two figures on Nelson's "used-car salesmen." Willie's crowd blamed it on the Armadillos. Some people went so far as to call the others thieves. Actually, there weren't that many tickets unaccounted for, and the biggest problem was probably those unattended gates, those tickets that went unsold as the people flowed in. As days passed, the accusations died down but resentments smouldered, particularly on Nelson's side of the camp. The total performance bill was $14,302.52. Willie and Waylon and Charlie Rich and Tom T. got $2000 apiece, Kris and Rita and Sammi Smith got $1500 each, Billy Joe Shaver got $1000 and John Prine got $540.02. The Threadgills took home $263.50; the rest, Leon Russell included, played for free. Armadillo World Headquarter's collective income amounted to $13,719.90. The security guards divvied up $1950. The canvas roof over the stage cost $1350. The plumbers took home $1083. Four security horsemen rode off with $750. A misplaced radio cost $43.42. Nelson was able to repay his $25,000 loan, and his performer's fee covered his personal investment, but by the time he reached the end of the auditors' report, the balance amounted to nothing. Literally flat zero. Willie had broken even again.

At least that's the way the story pieced together. My collaborator and I didn't wait around for the bitter end. As the sun descended we reflected that this might have been a legitimate way to spend the Fourth of July had we been liberating North Africa or laying a transcontinental railroad, but our primary purpose had been pleasure. We had been joined during the day by Lucy, gentle veteran of Woodstock, and she was practically barefooted as we parted company with Willie Nelson. After we had walked a few hundred yards, my collaborator spied three people in a nine-passenger station wagon pulling out to leave, and he ran up to the car, begging a ride. The woman driving the car frantically rolled her window up and the station wagon sped away.

We crested the next hill and looked down the road at a shirtless long-hair who stuck out his thumb at an approaching pickup. The driver, a much older man wearing a western hat, accelerated and as he passed the young man he stuck his fist up out of the window, middle finger extended. I saw his glowering look as the pickup barged past, then the white choking cloud closed in again.

Eventually a red-faced man in a '59 Chevrolet stopped to give us a ride, and I got in beside his girlfriend while my collaborator and Lucy climbed in the back. The woman sat with her back arched stiffly, smiling companionably as the driver kneaded her thigh. His only control over the vehicle was a wrist looped loosely over the steering wheel.

"I wished I had some beer to offer y'all," he said. "Hey, come to think of it there is some hot Falstaff in the floorboard."

I stared out at some hippies splashing in the creek my collaborator and I had forded several hours earlier.

"Hey," the man said. "Didn't I see you havin' some trouble with those boys backstage?"

I muttered in affirmation and asked if he were a journalist too.

"Nah, I'm just one of those fellas that gets it in his head to go anywhere people tell him he can't. I got two of those boys lookin' the other way and walked right in. Wasn't much to see though.

"But there sure was some people that wanted in. One old girl got so excited when they turned her husband back that she just bit the blood outa one of those fellas' arms."

"Oh?" I said, brightening. "How did he react to that?"

"He acted like it pissed him off."

Finally we arrived at the Toyota, thanked the man, and headed back to Austin. We stopped at a store in Dripping Springs for soft drinks and as my collaborator and I waited outside for Lucy, two girls approached, requesting directions to Willie Nelson's Picnic.

"Don't go," I said. "It's terrible."

"But is Leon Russell there?"

I nodded sadly, knowing that was enough said, and gave them my press pass.

As we pulled back on the highway, eight o'clock shadows stretched far to the east, a few Stars and Stripes fluttered from flagpoles, and judging from the number of cars, there was a good crowd at the Wednesday-night service at the Dripping Springs Church of Christ. A semblance of sanity at least. My spirits began to rise as we gained speed and Austin came into view. Out of habit, I punched on the radio. Affirmatively, my collaborator punched it off.

"No," he said. "No more fucking music."

epilogue

If that sounded like I was being a little hard on my subject, let it stand. Like many Americans of my generation, I had fantasized my share of guarded moments over the turn my life would have taken had I been one of those lucky fellows with guitars slung like machine guns on their hips, mowing the audiences down. Look at those hungry women chewing the lacquer off their fingernails in anticipation of a tryst with a rock star. Think of seeing the counry in that fashion, a sailor with a sexpot in every port. Ponder, like Willis Ramsey, the ego salve oozing from a national television appearance. Think of never having to go to work at eight o'clock in the morning.

Unfortunately, my perspective had been altered. Active research for this book began at the Willie Nelson Armadillo concert in April 1973, and endured until May 1974, the enamel on my teeth considerably worse for wear. The picnic at Dripping Springs fell closer to the first date than the last, so maybe it was nitpicking to harp on that subject too much. But more than anything else I'd seen, the Dripping Springs festival documented the war waged every day between the musicians and music businessmen. For a while there, I was starting to feel like a jeep driver sporting a U.N. helmet in the Sinai Desert.

In the months since the festival, passions had subsided and animosities had turned into indifference and forgetfulness, if not forgiveness. Francois DeMonil called Willie Nelson when they were in the same town. Michael Price had kind words for the Armadillos. Willie Nelson and Eddie Wilson smoked pipes of peace. The name of the game in Austin was getting along, at least on the surface. When I

331

asked Wilson for his perspective on the Dripping Springs festival, he said he couldn't remember much of anything that happened a year ago. Dripping Springs, he said, had worked beautifully, considering the wildly diverse elements thrown into one working heap. Then he blurted, "I'm still not convinced long-hair hippies were throwing women on the ground out there." With that finally off his chest, he talked more amiably about the improvements the Armadillo was making, and the perfect site for an outdoor festival he had discovered. It was almost inside the Austin city limits, right under everybody's noses. Next time the Armadillo hooked a claw in a large festival, it would work.

Nelson proceeded doggedly with his festivals. The second one, near his hometown of Abbott on Labor Day 1973, stumbled through about as much unceremonious confusion as the first one, but the third, scheduled for three days over the Fourth of July weekend of 1974, promised fewer hassles, unless the crowd got out of hand. This one was being advertised nationally, and it was situated in the sixteen-acre infield of an auto speedway near College Station, the home of Texas A&M. Aggies were playing country music in their dorms when Teasips at the University of Texas thought Chubby Checker was all the rage, and they would welcome this invasion from Austin. This time the performer's contracts would be signed and in hand well before the show, and none of the big names would be used to promote the festival, for they could make bigger money elsewhere. If they came, it would be on a voluntary basis. Nelson had lured Tim O'Connor away from Castle Creek to weed out the backstage hangers-on from the working journalists. It was all to do over again. This time the rumored special guests were Bette Midler, Aretha Franklin, and Paul McCartney.

Willie aborted our interview at his house by offering me a plate of barbecue. As we ate he talked optimistically about the anniversary picnic at College Station, but he added, however, "A movie will never happen. That's where the businessmen get in on it."

I asked him if he was going to promote festivals indefinitely.

"Every time I do it I say this one will be the last," he said as he forked a piece of meat. "But I can't quit. If I did I'd put forty thieves out of work. I guess I'd like to do one a year. See how long we can keep it going."

He said he hoped to lose a little less money this time around, and my photographer blinked. Did he mean he actually *lost* money on that throng the year before?

"It wasn't intentional," Willie said. "I discovered that you can't be onstage playing and watch the cash register at the same time. We had forty or fifty thousand people at Dripping Springs, but here they come telling me, 'Damned if we didn't sell but 2500 tickets.' This year the gate's gonna be in the hands of professionals. We got us some bank tellers from Dallas."

I asked him if he would be willing to work with the Armadillos again.

"Shouldn't have to for a couple of years. They oughta be able to make it that long on what they made last year. Now if they ever get real down and out, I might help them out again."

Jay Milner, who was handling publicity for the College Station festival, recalled a man he had seen on the caliche road with two armloads of groceries the year before. His house was on the road to the Dripping Springs site, but he couldn't get within two miles with his car, so he was walking along biting dust like everybody else. Milner said the man mentioned something about killing Willie Nelson.

"Yeah, they love me in Dripping Springs," Willie said. "I've made myself pretty scarce around there. A few months after the festival we were coming through and the radiator overheated, so we had to stop. I pulled my hat down and slunk down in the seat hoping nobody would recognize me, but the kid checked under the hood and washed all the windows then came up beside me and said, 'Are y'all gonna do that again this year?' "

Willie grinned at our laughter than attacked his barbecue like a little boy. End it there, with Willie Nelson laughing at the folly of his business ventures. I couldn't help liking the man. He had known my next-door neighbor, and made music in the MB Corral.

Lee Cochran was dead of a heart attack and expressway engineers had long ago reduced my Keeler Street neighborhood to a rubble of uprooted trees and razed foundations, but the chain-link fence separating my yard from the Cochrans' was still intact. I doubted I would ever fully comprehend the nature of the musician's existence. However, I had hung around the flower bed long enough to hazard a few generalizations.

As trite as it might sound, the wellspring of musical ambition was the home. If encouragement and example weren't abundant in the early years of learning, it was extremely unlikely a boy would spend long hours indoors honing his voice or mastering some instrument when he could be out on the gaming fields chasing pigskins and pussy. Well-meaning parents who demanded that he absorb culture from a piano stool weren't enough either, as Eddie Wilson learned. The parents and sisters and cousins needed to be actively engaged in music themselves. If he was influenced by older people who amused themselves and their friends by making music, his appetite for musical accomplishment was whetted. He could see the man with the banjo or burly bass voice was enjoying himself. He could see the musician was the center of attention, no matter where he stood. And if those musicians who influenced him had moved their music from the parlor to the public bandstand, the urge to follow in those footsteps became almost irresistible.

Often as not the aspiring musician would scorn the junior high band hall and a cappela choir room, but even if he studied music as it was traditionally taught, he would gladly exchange his position in the snare-drum marching ranks for a Gene Krupa set in the den, and his violin would likely turn into a fiddle one day. He could join a teenaged rock group, and find that the girls in his class seemed to like him a little more. If he stuck with it long enough, the DeMolay dances would turn into midnight gigs in hard-nosed outlying bars, where at first he would be intimidated by the tinsel laughter and clattering billiard balls. But there he would come into contact with the real musicians — the veterans of a thousand nights on the road, the ones who treated their frustrations and disappointments like jokes played upon themselves, who situated their memories by way of the good and bad times they had seen. The young musician would learn from them that the best music was that which felt natural, and he would learn how to be a hedonist. That way of life transpired in back seats and motel rooms and somebody's sister's summer retreat, populated by street-reared men whose names didn't matter and wild women whose sheets were stained. The young musician would want that way of life to be his own. He would no longer be contented with college history classes or a job at the automotive parts house. He would want to sleep till midafternoon like the old-timers who got him drunk the night before.

Pass over all those years of despairing that he would never make it. They wouldn't matter half as much when he did, and they would become the meat for his own stories. When success finally did come, the change in his life would be dramatic. One day he would be just an ordinary young man with a complement of friends camped on the outskirts of his talent, and the next he would shake some stranger's hand and scrawl his signature on a recording contract. He would scan the list of stipulations in his contract with no real interest, for nothing would hold him back now. His life expectancy as a recording artist wouldn't be a long one. Unless he was exceptional he could count on more years than an artillery forward observer but fewer than a professional athlete. And for the rest of his career his friends would be offset by strangers who would tell him what he should or should not do.

That would hardly matter at first. He would wake up one morning with the realization he had an album out. His voice would be heard on the radio, his face would be recognized by many. And unlike artists in most other mediums, he could break down the barricades between himself and his audience. He would perform his art in public, and as he stood spotlighted he could look down the throats of his admirers. He would gauge his success not so much by critical review or the number of records sold, but by the looks on their faces. They would jump up and down to his beat.

He would soon find, however, that he could no longer get out of the spotlight. When people would see him in the all-night grocery testing his TV tubes, they wouldn't jostle past him as they would any other man with his share of boredom and heartburn. They would recognize the persona, the face on the album cover. That would be an ego prop for a while, but then there would be too many of those staring faces and they would all want a piece of his life. They would all want to be the friend of a celebrity. That way they could be partially famous themselves.

God, hanging out in bars would begin to get tiresome. There was something Puritan about American taverns, a darkness without intimacy, as if shame were a requirement for being there. The clubs would all look the same from the stage, a blur of shadowy forms and glowing cigarettes and clapping hands. Concerts wouldn't be much of an improvement. They would be too many miles apart. Some gigs would be better than others, but realization would dawn upon him: he was a musician, a man, but these people wanted a demigod, and this charade of unending enjoyment was more work than pleasure.

His audiences wouldn't understand that he had sung his songs too many times to retain much appreciation for them, and he couldn't allow them to see that. He was a jester in the court of the masses, and knowing how fickle that audience could be, he would sing the songs he needed to sing to stay on top. The pursuit of music would come full circle on him. He would like to retreat with his music to the parlor, but that would mean the death of his career. So he would go on with it. He wouldn't favor himself with illusions about his art. Making music was a craft, and the love of his life was a business.

Entrenched in positions of corporate power, meanwhile, would be those who talked in terms of industry. The musician would dwell in the offices of men who treated him to their mastery of hip slang and assured him they had only the best interests of his career at heart, but he would regard them as pickpockets with legal training. They would know the stipulations of his various contracts by heart, and he would have to honor those clauses if he wanted to continue making a living off their money. The musicians would be a product to them, and if the product showed signs of faulty design or wear, they would simply discard it. The musician would be a captive of a medium based not on art, but money; not on music, but greed. And he thought he was going to be free.

Horse shit, Eddie Wilson would have snorted. Country-western, soap-opera melodrama. If a musician paid so much as a year's dues he had a pretty good feel for what he was getting into, and what was all this crap about the evils of making money? The alternative to a capitalistic music business was an art supervised and financed by the state, subject to the rigors of its orthodoxy. Sure, there was bribery in New York and insensitivity in Los Angeles and blacklisting in Nashville, but there were also men in those cities motivated by an honest interest in the music. Anyway, the same set of rules didn't apply in Austin. Very few sunshaded, fast-talking hustlers called Austin home, and those who did were johnnies-come-lately, easily recognized. That music business wasn't a rip-off in Austin, and it wasn't all that sinister. The problem with musicians was that they were so insulated in their lifestyle, so uncomprehending of business-world reality, that they were bound to be plundered. They got so paranoid they couldn't trust anybody except other musicians, and not all of those. But they were in

336

good hands in Austin. Everybody was trying to make his daily bread and keep a good thing going. Without music businessmen the musicians would have been nothing. They'd have been playing on street corners for handouts.

Wilson's vision of a Texas Nashville was, for the moment, little more than a dream. The large new club, Texas Opry House, was prospering at the expense of the others. The first casualty of the competition was the Pub; fittingly, Steve Fromholz played the last bill. Odyssey Studio's *Rolling Stone* housewarming had been indefinitely postponed, and coastal producers like Nelson's Jerry Wexler wondered to *Stone* reporters whether the music scene in Austin was a mirage. Rusty Wier was the only recorded performer who had come up through the Austin ranks, and none of the unsigned performers had A&R men lined up outside their doors, contracts in hand. A recording studio needed to be profitably filled virtually twenty-four hours a day, taping an album per week, and the Austin community of musicians was still too small for that. For the time being, Austin was still a place where musicians could make a living playing the bars. The principal signs of music-business progress were in publishing.Nelson had moved the headquarters of his company from Nashville to Austin, the publishing arm of Leon Russell's Shelter had formed a partnership with Larry Watkins' counterpart at Moon Hill Management. Maybe Austin was destined to become a town for songwriters. It was the center, after all, of an extremely lyrical music.

Of the recorded Austinites, the newest, Wier, was the hottest. AM programers shied away from Murphey's "Holy Roller," for even primitive religion was not to be taken lightly on the air waves, and though his album sold steadily, it moved at a trickle. Murphey sold his Austin lakeside home to B. W. Stevenson, moved to Colorado and remarried. His most hopeful development was a new booking agent who hoped to put him on the road with the leaders of the Macon music community, the Allman Brothers and Marshall Tucker. Despite all the advance fanfare, Stevenson's *Calabasas* failed to clear the runway, and he was reported in search of a new recording company. Kinky Friedman's new album was reportedly more accomplished muscially but equally irreverent lyrically, and the danger loomed that he would again be denied the air play he needed. Walker seemed no closer to a major breakthough than he had ever been, Fromholz and Bridger were still without recording contracts, Ramsey still distrusted journalists, bided his time, and tinkered in his studio. That blocky little building on Baylor Street possibly held more in store for an Austin music industry than Wilson's Armadillo. Shelter Records had contributed the equipment to Ramsey, a curiously philanthropic thing for them to do, and when Russell casually asked Willie Nelson if he might like to use the recording equipment sometime, one wondered if the man from Tulsa was pondering a colony in Austin. Already he had a publishing inroad and a tentative recording foot in the door. Maybe Russell was the one who would bring it all about. If that was an alarming prospect for those who knew only the onstage Russell, it was a hopeful sign for aspiring musicians, for Russell was one musician with an uncanny business sense. He had approached the music business from all its many angles, and he knew how a music community ought to work. Of course, it might then become Leon Russell's movement. When NBC's *Midnight Special* crews mobilized for Nelson's College Station picnic, the man who interested them was Leon, not Willie, and they had never heard of Michael Murphey. The product of their Texas music research, aired in two parts, would acquaint the television audience with Russell's Oklahoma heritage, then employ Leon, not Willie, as host for a festival that featured Waylon Jennings, Bobby Bare, John Hartford, Rick Nelson and David Carradine. Though Bobby Bridger was the only recorded Austinite absent from Nelson's lineup, Willie and Murphey would be the only Austin performers who made the *Midnight Special*.

But there was no way to chart the future of Austin music, for it had broken all the rules so far. Even if financed and administred by outsiders, Wilson's idea of an Austin music industry probably deserved its chance. Nobody else was doing much to alter Austin's course. The Colorado River town lake was filled with polluted swill, inner-city land-owners and even governing boards of Christian Churches were destroying ornate Victorian mansions in favor of more and better parking lots, and on a radio interview, when Bobby Bridger questioned the need for a reflective-glass manifestation of a banking ego in the downtown area, he received abusive calls for a week. Even the University of Texas had ridden the wave of unthinking growth; an enrollment ceiling had come ten years too late to save the sophomores from computers and teaching assistants, the graduate students from academic rat-race.

In a field in northwest Austin in the fall of 1970, a young woman had shamed an aging boy with a fair country line into the admission that he had never learned to ride a horse, but now as I drove down the road with

338

the grill of a dump truck in my rear-view mirror, I noticed that field had been yielded to the white gravel scar of expressway construction, and I wondered where the horses had gone for pasture. As in most American communities, power in Austin resided in money, not politics, and the music businessmen could possibly generate enough revenue to exert positive influence on Austin's direction. A few musicians might get crushed along the way, but then again, perhaps an Austin music industry would be different. Eddie Wilson had more stake in Austin's future than I ever would. It was his hometown.

I suspect that my reluctance to endorse the idea of a Texas Nashville stemmed not so much from a reporter's skepticism, nor from any excessive compassion for the plight of musicians, but from an awareness that if songwriters ever swarmed the streets of Austin and gathered in the warmth of streetlights at night, one day soon I would no longer see something of myself in their faces. When I asked Steve Fromholz what he would be doing when he was forty, I wondered the same thing about myself. This was a young man's business, a young man's musical fancy, and those of us who had migrated to Austin and accepted the musicians as our spokesmen had come in search of something we were not likely to find: a prolonged youth. Two and a half decades of perspective from Texas had taught us that the world we inherited was a large, disordered mess, and Texas was neither worse nor better than other places. It had a great deal in common with other parts of the country, more than most Texans cared to admit, yet because distance was a part of our inheritance, there seemed more room to move around and breathe in down here. We were a nostalgic generation all right, but our favorite memories were not the *American Graffiti* coke dates and drag strips and sock hops after the Friday-night football games. Rather they were the outdoor times — the boyhood walk down the sandy road in front of Granny's farmhouse, the camping and canoe trip down a river, the naked plunge in a lake with a favorite lady.

Yet even that spatial sense of freedom was diminishing. In the winter of 1972, I ventured from Dallas toward Austin one drizzling Sunday, grateful for the company of two young women who had delivered a repossessed automobile from Boston to Big D, and were now counting the miles as we drove southward. One of the young women had grown up in Austin, but the other, a thin girl with an Italian name and an observation per minute, seemed to regard her trip to Texas with all the wide-eyed, exotic fascination of Marco Polo. She talked about the Revolution a lot, once shouldering an imaginary rifle to squeeze off a round at some unfortunate National Guardsman, and between Waxahachie and Waco she marveled, "My god, you have trees down here. The trunks are just shorter."

I drove in silence for a minute and she stretched and grinned. "Just think. Some day this will all be one big suburb."

"I don't think so," I said. "There's just too much of it."

She laughed politely. "That's the same old Texas chauvinism, nicely put."

It was the wisdom of an outsider, but it came back to haunt me. Ours was a generation slow coming to maturity, and our fascination with Austin music had been the last dying gasp of our adolescene. We had hoped to preserve the countrysides of our youth, but Texas was changing and it was going to continue to change, with or without our blessing. In that sense, the movement would fail. There was no staving off the passage of time. The young men with guitars in their hands had sung our songs for us, but only time would tell whether the lyrics carried much weight. Yet whatever the future held in store for us, we had benefited by those musical years in Austin. We had come back home.

acknowledgments

Once drafted, the list of persons who midwived this book surprises me, for during its delivery the sensation of being alone became at times almost unbearable. Though I am indebted to all, the list should begin with "my collaborator" Don Roth, who performed much of the research legwork and contributed many helpful suggestions along the way; "my photographer" Melinda Wickman, who tolerated my snoring bulk on her sofa and my pencil-thieving ways; my editor David Lindsey, who knew the difference between structural order and chaos; and my friends Jim Creel and John Moore, who lent moral support.

Of course, it could not have been possible without the cooperation and assistance of the musicians and music businessmen. The musicians were both exasperating and accommodating, wary and, I think, more open at times than they intended to be. For their encouragement and sympathy, Steve Fromholz and Bobby Bridger rate very high on my pop list, regardless of their *Billboard* ratings. The men and women on the business end of the art were equally helpful. I am particularly grateful for the contributions of Mike Tolleson and Ramsey Wiggins of Armadillo World Headquarters, Tim O'Connor of Castle Creek, Bronson Evans of Texas Opry House, and Larry Watkins, Tom White, Patti Ricker and Johnny Bob Pharr of Moon Hill Management.

Because I did not come to Austin until 1970, I was dependent upon the recollections and observations of others when I attempted to retrace the development of Austin's music community. Extremely helpful in this area were Stan Alexander, Sandy Lockett, Bob Brown, Rod Kennedy, writers Richard West and Bill Brammer, and Ellen Moore, who maintained a useful file on local music in the Austin-Travis

County Collection of the municipal library and contributed her intuitive interview with Kenneth Threadgill.

I am also indebted to my sister, Lana Fields, who helped me locate the skeletons in my Wichita Falls closet; Liz Urban, who provided last-minute typing relief with grace and humor; George Runge, who sensed my impending collapse and offered an employment leave-of-absence, and the editors of *Texas Monthly*, who accepted the rambling proposal for the rambling article that turned into a book.

Emotional credit must go, however, to Doctor Gonzo, the bastard Collie pup who provided companionship when the pages were blank and the right words wouldn't come. The good doctor knew a number of weekend homes and nights without food because he was picked from his litter by a writer who wasn't sure he could write, then with the end of his neglect in sight, he wandered fifty yards from his waterbowl and got flattened by the twentieth century. I used to think people who mourned dogs like they were human were dangerously sentimental, but like Mr. Bojangles I guess, the next morning I caught myself crying in the shower. I'd like to have another one just like him, but I suppose that must wait until I can afford to move my residence out of the automotive flight patterns.

It's strange that I should say that. For a better part of a century, Texans have been flocking to the cities in search of a better way of life, but now the tide seems to be turning. That reversal is the stuff of the songwriters' songs, and the reason for this book.